DATE DUE

DEC 23 1989		
JUL 1 9 2000		
SEP 2 1 1990		
APR 0 2 1998		
NOV 0 9 1998		

DEMCO 38-297

BETWEEN STRANGERS

Also by Lori B. Andrews

New Conceptions: A Consumer's Guide to the Newest Infertility Treatments Including In Vitro Fertilization, Artificial Insemination, and Surrogate Motherhood

Medical Genetics: A Legal Frontier

BETWEEN STRANGERS

SURROGATE MOTHERS,
EXPECTANT FATHERS,
& BRAVE NEW BABIES

LORI ANDREWS

1817

An Edward Burlingame Book

HARPER & ROW, PUBLISHERS, NEW YORK
CAMBRIDGE, PHILADELPHIA, SAN FRANCISCO
LONDON, MEXICO CITY, SÃO PAULO, SINGAPORE, SYDNEY

FIRST EDITION

Copyedited by Nick Allison

Designed by Karen Savary

Library of Congress Cataloging-in-Publication Data

Andrews, Lori B., 1952–
  Between strangers.

  "An Edward Burlingame book."
  1. Surrogate motherhood—United States—Case studies.
  2. Surrogate motherhood—Moral and ethical aspects.
  3. Surrogate mothers—Legal status, laws, etc.—United
States.   I. Title.
HQ759.5.A54   1989   306.8'743   88-45544
ISBN 0-06-016058-6

89 90 91 92 93 CT/HC 10 9 8 7 6 5 4 3 2 1

To Clements, my partner in parenting

CONTENTS

ACKNOWLEDGMENTS

WRITING A BOOK is like creating a child. You can't do it alone. Many people helped me see this book from conception to delivery. My agent, Amanda Urban, had confidence in a book that would explore surrogate motherhood as a realistic option, even as other of her writer clients were actively protesting to get surrogacy banned. My editors at Harper & Row, Edward Burlingame and Kathy Banks, were likewise open-minded and encouraging, prodding me with complex questions about mother love, parenting, and women's choices. My sister, Lesa Andrews, transcribed countless interview tapes, serving as a second opinion about the sincerity and motivations of the speakers. My dear friend Jim Stark took a sharp editorial pen to the manuscript, and rooted for me from the audience as I discussed surrogate motherhood with Phil Donahue and Dr. Ruth.

I am also indebted to the people who allowed me in their living rooms, their conference rooms, their courtrooms, or their hearing rooms in order to document the stories of their encounters with surrogate motherhood. And a special message of thanks must go to Clem, who within one week in May of 1988 helped me deliver both this book manuscript and our five-pound son.

AUTHOR'S NOTE

MY INTEREST IN surrogate motherhood began a decade ago. In September 1980, I gave my first speech on the subject at an international meeting of infertility specialists. Since then, I have crisscrossed the country many times to learn about and comment on the evolving phenomenon of stand-in moms. In 1981, I visited Carol Pavek as she was putting the finishing touches on her midwifery clinic and trying to decide whether to be a surrogate for pay. That same year, I discussed the concept with Bill Handel in his chaotic North Hollywood office, as he first started to get his surrogacy practice off the ground.

I was present at, and often an active participant in, many of the events discussed in this book. I served on the Project for Reproductive Laws in the 1990s, testified at two of the three New York hearings, and was a member of the Michigan Task Force on Reproductive Technologies vs. Best Interests of the Child (indeed, I was the member who slipped away to the Silver Spur).

To me, the most striking aspect of each event was how people with good hearts, good minds—and equal amounts of good will—nonetheless could have such radically different reactions to the issue of surrogate motherhood. From the intensity of their responses (and my own), something more was going on than just an intellectual debate about a new reproductive arrangement. People were willing to take immediate positions on the issue on the basis of very little information about how surrogacy worked or how a legal policy on surrogacy would affect other legal rights. I realized that understanding surrogate motherhood could help us to understand ourselves and our relationships to our families, and to contemplate the role, if any, that law should take in the regulation of reproduction and parenting.

PROLOGUE

THE MEETING AT THE MEDICAL SCHOOL started pleasantly enough. I was offered sherry in a small beveled plastic cup, mock Waterford. I settled into the chair at the head of the conference table and began my lecture, "Surrogate Motherhood: The Ethical Challenge for Physicians."

The small seminar room in which I spoke was part of the brain research facility, but the subject of the discussion involved more primitive emotions than the type of cognition that was being explored in other parts of the center. In surrogate motherhood, a woman is artificially inseminated with a man's sperm, carries the pregnancy, and then turns the child over to the father and his wife to rear. To some people, this is a marvelous act of generosity. To others, it is a cruel abandonment.

In a dispassionate tone, I began to describe what I had learned about the motivations and experiences of surrogate mothers. Following this I planned to review the existing laws, describe the ethical issues that arose in clinical practice, and speculate about the emotional taboos that surrounded surrogacy arrangements.

I hardly made it through the first page of my prepared text. Several doctors had shifted to the edges of their seats, as if to pounce on my words. The women in particular couldn't wait to interrupt.

"Surrogacy is the most demeaning activity for women," declared a psychiatric resident. "I don't see how you can call yourself a feminist and not protest against it.

"I deeply resent your tone," she continued, her voice rising. "I don't think you are taking seriously enough the dangers that surrogacy represents for women and children."

"It's horrible that women are turning to surrogate motherhood," added a medical student. "It's as if they feel the only way women are valued in this society is for their reproductive functions."

"Surrogate motherhood is a conspiracy between the medical and legal professions to control women's bodies, just as the laws against abortion were a conspiracy between male doctors and male lawyers," said the resident.

"It's disgusting, a form of slavery," added someone else.

"You're prejudging surrogate motherhood, using loaded language," responded a philosophy professor. "What Lori is suggesting is that we try to better understand the experiences of the people involved in surrogacy. I've met a surrogate mother, and she was quite convincing in describing the benefits of the experience for her."

"So?" said a medical student. "Prostitutes may like the money they make, but they're still degraded and exploited."

"And what about the children?" asked the resident. "They are going to be completely screwed up. Look at how damaged the children of divorced couples are."

"Any problems result from the fact of the divorce," countered a retired social worker. "With divorce, the child is usually separated from a parent who has had a lengthy relationship with him. The problems may not apply to surrogacy where the separation occurs at birth."

People from all sides of the table were anxious to have their say. Physicians silenced their pagers in order not to miss a word. Some began writing furiously and passing their comments to others.

"Surrogacy exploits women," said the resident. "Mary Beth Whitehead was married to a garbageman. She wanted the $10,000 to pay for her children's college education. The surrogacy center lawyer should have had a duty to tell her that she could have made more money in another way. He should have been required to tell her that wouldn't be enough to pay for college."

The woman in the next seat addressed her tentatively. "Garbagemen make a decent salary, and $10,000 saved away now would certainly pay for college at a state school," she said. "I'm not sure what I think of surrogacy. But it seems to me you're applying your own values to the situation."

The controversy continued, with points and counterpoints rising up and crashing like contractions during labor. After nearly a decade of speaking about surrogate motherhood, I was still amazed at the intense emotions and the angry conviction that the issue always evoked.

Surrogate motherhood takes us into uncharted social territory. What happens when a child is created not through an intimate act, but through a pact between strangers? How does the surrogate relate to this growing life within her? What are the biological father's feelings for the woman who is carrying his child? How does his wife stave off jealousy and prepare to mother the child born to another woman? What do the surrogate's own children think about their half-sibling being sent to another family? And, most important, what will the contracted-for child think of his or her unusual beginnings?

Beyond the complex personal dimensions, surrogate motherhood raises profound dilemmas for policymakers. Does the arrangement exploit surrogates, or does it further reproductive choice? Will the existence of surrogacy lead to a demeaning image of women as baby factories, or will it add support for a view that women are masters of their own destiny? Is the expanded family created by surrogacy destructive of traditional values, or does it add another rich dimension to the human experience?

The answers to such questions deserve, and require, a close examination of the actual participants in surrogacy arrangements. But some people refuse to look at the surrogacy experience. Slavery, they call it, turning away in distaste. Reproductive prostitution. Baby selling. They urge lawmakers to abolish surrogate motherhood, making criminals of those who create families in this manner and of the doctors and lawyers who help.

Fewer than a thousand children have come into the world through the wombs of paid surrogate mothers. But the practice casts a large shadow over the emotional, social, and legal components of parenting. History and science fiction have both taught us that the types of technologies that are available shape the nature of a society. As important as the technologies—and having much further-reaching implications—are the policies that a society devises and implements to deal with technologies. The decisions made in the surrogacy context about what is in the best interests of women and children will provide guideposts for other reproductive and parenting choices—such as access to abortion and the assignment of custody in traditional divorce cases.

Surrogate motherhood cannot be judged in isolation. It is caught up in a tangle of laws, emotions, and beliefs that touch us all. In many ways, the existence of surrogacy is the culmination of a series of individual and societal choices that have been made over the past two decades. The 1960s acceptance of sex without procreation has led to the 1980s practice of surrogacy, offering procreation without sex.

The gains in reproductive rights in the late 1960s and 1970s led both to the need for surrogate mother arrangements—and to legal precedents upon which to defend these contracts. In a series of cases, the U.S. Supreme Court held that decisions about whether or not to bear children and how to raise one's children were protected by the constitutional right to privacy. Access to contraception and abortion is constitutionally protected. The biological and social importance of being a parent is so great that people's individual choices about childbearing and child rearing must be respected, except when the parenting arrangement is truly harmful to children.

The birth control pill and legalized abortion allowed women to plan their pregnancies, providing them with the chance to become true participants in all walks of society. Nadine Taub, a Rutgers law professor and director of the Project on Reproductive Laws in the 1990s, points out that "the degree of control women are able to exercise over their reproductive lives directly affects their educational and job opportunities, income level, physical and emotional well-being, as well as the economic and social conditions the children they bear will experience."

As a result of the social changes due to reproductive control, more women are postponing childbearing while they pursue education and careers. But since peak fertility for women is age twenty-five, women in their middle to late thirties who decide to start a family sometimes learn that fertility has passed them by. At the same time, they're discovering that fewer babies are available for adoption, because reproductive control has also changed the alternatives for women who in the past would have carried babies to term and given them up. So they have sought out women whose own view of reproductive freedom encompasses helping create a child for another couple. The reproductive haves and have-nots come together in surrogate motherhood.

For the past two decades, women have fought for control over their reproductive functions. Control over the circumstances in which they conceive. Control over the circumstances in which they give birth. Yet surrogate motherhood raises a paradox about control. To some women, it represents the ultimate in a woman's control over her body. To others, it represents a lack of control, a pregnancy made to order for the biological father.

Although paid surrogate motherhood has existed for the past decade, it wasn't until the Baby M case that the issue captured public attention. When Mary Beth Whitehead decided to break the contract and keep the child that she had agreed to bear for Bill and Betsy Stern, the tug of love began that turned a private agreement into a public cause.

For over a year, the attentions of this country and the world were focused on the New Jersey trial and appeal to determine the fate of the Stern/Whitehead child, known to the court and media as Baby M. During the same time period, the Vatican issued a lengthy statement condemning surrogacy and all other nonconjugal reproductive arrangements as sinful. Legislative committees in over two dozen states debated whether surrogate motherhood should be allowed and, if so, under what regulation. Special interest groups—reproductive rights organizations, adoption agencies, feminists, medical societies, and right-to-life groups—met for often anguishing debates about how the court should decide the Baby M case and how the legislatures should react to the phenomenon of wombs for hire. And during that same time period, over a hundred other surrogates gave birth to children and quietly, outside the public eye, turned them over for adoption by the contracting couples.

What is it about the Baby M case—and surrogate motherhood itself—that caused front-page headlines for months? Why did it stimulate debates from the ivory towers of academia to the floors of Congress, from grocery checkout lines to psychiatric conventions? Surrogacy became a national preoccupation because it challenges our existing ideas about the family and causes us to rethink our closest relationships—our bonds to our parents and our children.

The past two decades have seen a drift away from a uniform, traditional view of what makes a good parent. Working mothers, househusbands, single-parent households, and blended families have all become rather comfortably accepted as part of the societal terrain. Seen in its simplest terms, surrogacy merely added a new color to the broad spectrum of parenthood, but for many of us it put into bold relief the question, What types of arrangements really are in the best interests of children?

The experiences of women are central to the societal debate on surrogate motherhood, crucial to our understanding of the complex relationships generated by this new form of family. Across the country, a wide range of women from different walks of life are invisibly tethered together by the issue of surrogacy. The proper societal approach to surrogacy can be developed only by understanding the experiences of these women. Some of them have been surrogates and can speak knowingly of the joy or harm the process brought them. Some are psychologists and sociologists who can describe how society's acceptance or rejection of surrogacy will influence how women are treated in other contexts. Still others are female lawmakers who can provide insights on how laws on surrogacy will affect legal rights and responsibilities in constitutional law, family law, employment law, and criminal law.

The stakes in the surrogacy debate are high. They are nothing less than the future of the family, the standards for parenting, and the societal image of women.

All the names in this book are real except for Andy and Nancy, Randy and Jerry, John and Elizabeth, Sandra and Hillel, and their children. I have respected these couples' anonymity so that they could choose the time and place to tell their children about their unique beginnings.

PART I

MAKING BABIES

MAY DAYS

A MAY BREEZE rustled the lace curtains at the Fertility Center of California, where Lorrie Jones waited impatiently for her name to be called. She had had to pressure her way in here with a call to her doctor, telling him that if he didn't do the insemination immediately, she'd be through ovulating and they would have to wait another month. He argued that she wasn't due to ovulate for a few more days, but who was inhabiting her body, him or her? Doctors—men—always expected your body to run like a computer: a smoothly functioning, completely predictable program. But women knew that various events influenced the delicate synchrony of their reproductive cycles. A cold, stress, lack of sleep. So many things hastened or slowed the release of an egg. But the signs of impending fertility were obvious. The night before, Lorrie had noticed the hint of pain in her ovaries and the change in consistency of her cervical mucus. Today was the day.

The insemination itself was a quick, painless procedure. Not exactly a romantic way to make a baby. Yet Lorrie felt this pregnancy would be far more special than her previous two. Those had been achieved without deliberation, by making love with her husband. But each had brought problems. The first had occurred when she had only been married for two months. She was barely adjusting to being a wife and being away from her family for the first time; the pregnancy made her unhappy and confused. The second pregnancy came also as an accident, at a time when she and Casey were at rock bottom emotionally and financially, and she vacillated over whether or not she would keep the baby at all. It was a tense situation, and for most of the pregnancy, giving up the child for adoption seemed to be the best solution. But when the blond head emerged from her body, she realized that she couldn't wrench this little soul from her family.

What a difference this time! Here was a pregnancy that was wanted not only by her, but by a couple who had tried unsuccessfully to have children for years. Lorrie pictured the closeness that the three of them would have during the pregnancy. Hillel would ask lovingly about how she was feeling. She and Sandra would have lunches together and shop for baby clothes in the afternoon. Her friends and relatives would respect her for her boldness and generosity, and for once she would really show her father, who was always telling her that she never completed anything. There were those half-finished piano lessons, the court reporter school she dropped out of. But this would be a turning point for her. Here was something she could complete. She would go through the inseminations, participate in the counseling sessions, follow through with the pregnancy, and then give the baby up to Sandra and Hillel. It would be like a graduation of sorts. She would enter the ranks of the five hundred women who had been surrogate mothers.

May of 1986 was also a new beginning for Bill Handel, the Beverly Hills attorney who was presiding over Lorrie's contractual pregnancy. Bill had been in the surrogacy business for five years, but always in a rather disorganized manner. He loved the never-ending contact with the media, as he flew from city to city and country to country to explain and defend the concept of surrogate motherhood to an endless series of talk-show audiences. He was a born scrapper and felt at his best in a feisty debate in which he used shock, cynicism, wit, or (less frequently) sympathy and reason to win his point. Bill was less enamored of the administrative aspects of running a surrogacy program. Calls for information sometimes went unanswered. Bill's West Coast operation seemed destined to run a poor second in volume to Noel Keane's surrogacy program. In actuality, Noel's program had more problems than Bill's—more disgruntled parties, more losing lawsuits. But Noel also had more couples, more surrogates, and, worse yet in Bill's mind, more firsts.

A year earlier, Noel had been responsible for the first IVF surrogate, a woman who had gestated another couple's embryo and then turned the baby back over to its genetic parents for rearing. The couple had created the embryo through in vitro fertilization of her egg with his sperm, but since the wife had undergone a hysterectomy, they needed to rely on a second woman (who had no genetic relationship to the child) to carry the pregnancy to term. Once this novel pregnancy was underway, Noel was faced with an equally novel legal issue. The law had always recognized the woman who gave birth as the child's legal mother. This was why the infertile wife in the traditional surrogate mother situation had to adopt the child. Yet in this case it seemed strange to think that the genetic mother would have to adopt her own child. In the seventh month of the pregnancy, Noel went to court and successfully reversed centuries of legal precedent. According to the court ruling, the names of the genetic mother and father (the couple who had created the embryo) would be put on the birth certificate. They would be the legal parents; neither would have to adopt the child. The birthing mother would be listed nowhere; she would have no legal claim to the child. The woman who had nurtured the baby for nine months, who had gone through the morning sickness and the varicose veins, the distension of her body and the pain of delivery—this woman had been rendered invisible.

Bill, who had been trying to arrange an IVF surrogacy for nearly two years now, had been pissed when Noel had beat him to it. Here it was a year after Noel's success and still none of Bill's embryo transfers had led to a live birth.

Bill was counting on Ralph Fagen to change his second-best status. He hired Ralph in May as his business manager to organize the surrogacy program. Bill's past hirings had not always been inspired. Big-hearted and a soft touch, Bill often populated his staff with people with whom he had a personal bond—old friends, high school classmates—who didn't always work out. Hiring

Ralph was not the result of an open personnel search either: Bill and Ralph's wife were friends. Ralph had never even been an office manager before, but Bill had a good feeling about him.

One big asset to Handel's agency was Hilary Hanafin, the program's psychologist. As a graduate student, she had written her dissertation about the personality traits and motivations of surrogate mothers. She got so fascinated by the women she talked to that she decided to make a profession of counseling surrogates. Hilary had an unshakable ground rule when matching surrogates and couples. She tried to pick people who, if they had met under other circumstances, would have become fast friends. To do so successfully, she needed to understand both sides' values and interests, as well as their expectations about the relationship. The results were often spectacular. That very month, May 1986, Jan Sutton and her two children were camping in Yosemite with a couple and the infant she had borne for them two years earlier as a surrogate mother.

While Hilary was trying to make surrogacy arrangements more responsive to the psychological needs of all involved, Ralph was trying both to reshape the program and to reshape Bill. Remaking Bill was akin to housebreaking a lion or domesticating a wild stallion, for the essence of Bill's personality was that he had no inhibitions. He would say or do whatever he felt like— dressing up for meetings like an Arab sheik or signing into a formal party as Bruno Hauptmann. Now, a certain disregard of conventionality was a strength in this business. Being a "surrogate mother lawyer" was not thought to have the same social merit as, say, representing AT&T. But Bill was always pushing things just a bit too far, acting the same way he had in grammar school when his role in life was to outrage classmates and embarrass the teacher. (Even as recently as law school, he had wanted to graduate in a chicken costume. His dad had cried, so he had opted for a giant chef's cap with *LAW* stenciled across it instead.)

A London tabloid ran a cover story on Bill, with the headline: "I Will Sell You a Baby for £23,000." The large photo of him on the first page was enormously unflattering; taken with a fisheye lens, it made Bill's nose look about the size of the space shuttle. Nevertheless Bill framed the newspaper and hung it in his office for all potential clients to see.

These were the sorts of antics that would turn Ralph pale. Dignity, dignity, dignity—Ralph tried to drum it in. And for the first time in his life Bill was ready to listen to that message. He wasn't angling to have tea with the queen. But he did want to run the best goddamn surrogate program in the world. If Ralph thought dignity and credibility were the ways to get there well, hell, Bill was willing to try anything once.

Noel Keane's practice, too, was about to change that month, although he had not intended it to. On the surface, May of 1986 seemed like another routine month. He spent most of his time at his Dearborn, Michigan, office with a few trips to the Manhattan program he had established, the Infertility Center of New York. He phoned and corresponded with the Florida lawyers who arranged many of the quick adoptions that were the culmination of the surrogacy arrangements. He celebrated the birth of the 105th child who had been conceived under his legal guidance. And so when the call came informing him that one of his surrogate mothers had changed her mind and decided to keep the baby, he was able to respond as a man with confidence in himself and his cause.

On May 5, Noel's clients, William and Elizabeth Stern, went to court to force the surrogate mother, Mary Beth Whitehead, to turn over the six-week-old child she had agreed to bear for them. Court order in hand and accompanied by Brick Township, New Jersey, police officers, the Sterns went to the Whitehead residence to retrieve the child. A panicked Mrs. Whitehead passed the baby out a back window to her husband, who fled.

Connie Binsfeld, a Michigan state senator, sensed that this incident was just the sort of ammunition that she was looking for. A longstanding opponent of surrogate motherhood, she was appalled that Michigan, due to Noel Keane's presence, seemed to be the surrogacy center of the universe. Almost since the beginning, she'd been looking over his shoulder, waiting for him to make some mistake. In 1983, she introduced a bill that would have banned surrogate motherhood. It had resoundingly passed through the state senate, but was defeated in the house. In fact, the knowledge that there was a strong pro-surrogacy faction in the house had provided an excuse for some otherwise liberal senators to vote in favor of the ban. This way they could curry favor with the right-to-life groups who opposed surrogacy, while at the same time doing little damage to the process itself, since the bill was bound to be defeated by their house colleagues.

Connie was sixty-two years old, a Republican, a former Michigan Mother of the Year, and a believer in the traditional nuclear family. When she entered politics seventeen years earlier, she told her husband that she would not let her job interfere with their home life. According to a staff assistant, Connie still made several days' worth of dinners in advance so that he would have something to eat if she got tied up with legislative duties.

The notion of a woman conceiving a child just to give it up was something that Connie just could not fathom. A staunch Roman Catholic, Connie opposed the use of contraception and abortion. She also followed the Church's view that reproductive technologies, especially those involving third parties (such as artificial insemination by donor), were sinful. Although at the time Mary Beth fled, the Church had not yet taken a formal stance against surrogacy, the practice went against everything Connie believed in.

With the Mary Beth Whitehead incident, Connie had something more than her personal moral and religious beliefs to bolster her arguments against surrogacy. She had an example of how the process could create a tremendous trauma for all the participants, especially for the child in question. She had the incredible image of a child being wrenched from its breast-feeding mother.

Connie had two decades of political experience and expertise to draw on. What would be the best approach? First, she would light a fire under the consultant whom she had caused the legislature to hire to assess the surrogacy situation. They would get background information and then put together a blue-ribbon commission to make recommendations for a proposed law. If the commission members recommended the ban that she wanted, she would introduce a bill to that effect with their imprimatur. If their suggestions did not directly overlap hers, well, they were just an advisory group and she could justify her bill banning surrogacy by claiming that they were just one of the many groups she had consulted on the matter.

Barbara Katz Rothman was also concerned about the policy implications of surrogate motherhood. In May of 1986, she was attending her fourth meeting of a national feminist group which had banded together to study the reproductive rights issues that would face this country in the 1990s, including late abortion, genetic screening, and reproductive technologies. Barbara was a natural choice for such a group. As a sociologist, she had devoted her professional career to studying the extent to which women actually control their own reproductive choices. As a feminist, she was committed to promoting ways in which women could gain greater control over these choices and developing procedures that would place their experiences at the center of legislative debates about reproduction.

Barbara had started in this area with a study of home births and had moved on to research about women's reactions to the often-used medical procedure of amniocentesis, the prenatal genetic screening of fetuses. At every juncture, Barbara had uncovered evidence about how men (and particularly male doctors) had controlled and redefined women's reproductive experiences. Barbara—and the rest of the Project on Reproductive Laws in the 1990s—were naturally suspicious of surrogate motherhood. In surrogacy, the issue of control seemed almost completely on the side of the male. Male doctors and lawyers had invented and marketed the concept. The male progenitor retained all legal rights to the child; the biological mother, even when she was also the genetic mother, had none. And the contract gave doctors and the father dominance over the woman's body during pregnancy. She could not smoke or drink. She must follow the doctor's every whim. She must undergo amniocentesis and abort or not, depending on the father's wishes.

Barbara Katz Rothman opposed surrogate motherhood, at least in its current form, in which the creation of a child became a matter of commerce and the profound gestational relationship between the mother and fetus didn't count for a whit. Ironically, she now found herself in the camp of those people who had been her adversaries on reproductive rights issues for years—religious groups, political conservatives. She had to be very careful about how she articulated her position. She supported abortion rights and nontraditional families. She thought the use of artificial insemination by an unmarried heterosexual or lesbian woman was a perfectly appropriate way to start a family. She needed to begin the difficult task of challenging surrogacy without leading to a political backlash that would wipe out all other reproductive rights in its wake.

Carol Pavek had also come to this issue with an interest in home births and women's reproductive freedom. But Carol, a midwife, had come to a different conclusion than Barbara. Carol saw surrogacy as a natural adjunct to other reproductive choices. Women's control of their reproductive choices should be unfettered, even (or maybe especially) when that choice meant surrogacy. One thing that midwifery had taught Carol was that women did not react to each pregnancy or each child in the same way. Surrogate motherhood was just another way of relating.

"I'm a strong feminist," Carol told Noel Keane. "I believe in helping other women, even to the extent of donating my body, if necessary.

"In time, I think surrogate mothering will become a very big thing. We still have a generation of women out there who were raised not with the concept of sisterhood but with the concept of competition. That's competition against other women. My generation has more of a sharing attitude. I guess many women still view childbirth as an ordeal. But there are also many, like me, who view it as the greatest gift women have. A gift that is meant to be used. But it will take time for surrogate mothers to become common."

Carol's belief in surrogacy was strong enough that she had agreed to serve as a surrogate mother herself, for three separate pregnancies. She gave up the resulting children with no regrets. But this May her mind was elsewhere. After years of saying that they did not want any more children of their own, she and her husband Rick decided to expand their family.

That month, in opposite circumstances, both Lorrie Jones and Carol Pavek conceived.

2

〜

BIRTH RIGHTS

To CAROL PAVEK, the people of Amarillo, Texas, were a lot like the climate. They were as dry as the dust that covered the roads. They seemed to drift aimlessly, like the tumbleweed she found when she began exploring the Panhandle at age eleven. Carol saw herself differently. She took control of situations, even when she was quite young. She read masses of books and always had plans afoot. Whenever she decided she wanted something, she would doggedly pursue it, even if the natural flow of her life seemed bent on pulling her in another direction.

Many people have a vague feeling that they were born in the wrong era, or the wrong place, or to the wrong parents. But Carol Pavek knew exactly why she was different from the people of Amarillo. She was adopted. She came, at least prenatally, from somewhere else.

That somewhere else was Washington, D.C., where her adoption had taken place. When she was in third grade, she began to imagine what her birth parents were like. She went to the encyclopedia to find out who had been president nine months before she was born—Eisenhower! She decided she must be the child of Eisenhower and one of his female assistants.

Adoption made Carol feel special. It was a source of comfort to her, like religion was to her Texas parents. Her brothers were adopted, too, but they didn't have her fantasy past. Their birth parents had tried to sell them for $100 each to Carol's parents at a roadside restaurant. Carol's parents said that they wouldn't buy the boys, but they would take them and give them a good home.

Carol felt no need to seek out her birth parents. She loved the couple who raised her, and felt she could get from them any help and advice she needed. But when she got pregnant with her own child, her link to her biological mother became crucially important.

It was her ninth month of pregnancy, April 1978, and her doctor was worried. The fetus seemed too big, indicating the possibility of a potential defect. "Did your mother always have big babies?" the doctor wanted to know.

Carol wondered how she could get the information. She felt awkward about asking her mother what she knew about the woman who had given Carol up for adoption. So she called a close friend of the family, a woman who had known her mother since before Carol's birth.

"Do you know any way I can get in touch with my birth mother?" asked Carol, after explaining the circumstances.

There was silence at the other end of the phone and then the woman began to cry. "I'm your birth mother."

Later on, Carol could look back on the incident with a little humor. "After all these years of thinking my mother was someone exotic, she turned out to be someone I'd known for years."

The family friend was able to explain that her babies had all been big—not only Carol, but the children she conceived after settling into marriage. This comforted Carol that her baby was not suffering from diabetes or any other disorder that would cause it to be abnormally large; she felt confident about going ahead with her planned home birth.

On April 14, Carol's labor pains began, intensifying over the next twenty-four hours. Carol's husband Rick called Judy, the midwife who would be supervising the birth. Carol moved to the comfort of the living room couch. For the next couple of hours, she sat, she laid down, she walked; Rick massaged her back and Judy monitored her cervix. It needed to be dilated to at least ten centimeters for the baby to be born, but it stubbornly stayed at seven. At 3:00 P.M., it was seven centimeters. At 7:00 P.M., it was seven centimeters. At 10:00 P.M., it was seven centimeters. The contractions were coming faster, now at two minutes apart. The baby was ready to make his debut. Carol was rushed to the hospital.

Her disappointment was crushing. She had been wrenched from the warm living room where she wanted the baby to start its life to an anonymous delivery room at the William Beaumont Army Medical Center. Birth had been transformed from an intimate experience, shared with those she loved, to a medical procedure under the control of a doctor she barely knew. It was as if a wall had been put up between her and the baby—a wall of medicine, equipment, and hospital staff. The nurses wanted to whisk the child away, put silver nitrate in his eyes, weigh him, and test him. Carol insisted on holding him and started refusing tests that she felt were unnecessary. The staff argued that they knew best. By the time she arrived home a few hours later, Carol was determined she would do it again—her way. She wanted a home birth.

Carol and Rick could not then afford a second child, but that did not stop Carol from finding out everything she could about midwifery and home births. She talked to local midwives, tracked down studies of how children delivered by home births fared, and read books about home birth principles, like *Spiritual Midwifery*, which explained how lay people in a commune setting in Tennessee had learned to deliver each other's babies.

Carol learned that Jimmy Carter was the first president of the United States to have been born in a hospital. Until the early twentieth century, most births occurred at home with the assistance of midwives. Then male doctors came to power in healthcare circles and births were moved into hospitals. The immediate effect was a huge increase in deaths of infants and mothers. Hospitals were breeding grounds for infection. Doctors who did not wash their hands carried fatal bacteria from contagious patients and corpses to women in labor. Their overzealous use of interventions such as forceps added to the dangers. A 1933 study by the New York Academy of Sciences of 348,200 births in New York City found that midwife-assisted home births had a significantly lower maternal mortality rate than did physician-attended hospital births.

By the late twentieth century, of course, hospitals had become cleaner places. In addition, they offered a range of consultants and high-tech machinery to aid in high-risk births and to provide care to premature babies. But 90 percent of the women giving birth did not need these medical miracles. And for those normal women who got swept into the technological whirlwind, the medical technologies actually increased the risk to them and their children rather than decreasing it. A large-scale study by the World Health Organization, replicated by many other researchers in the early 1980s, found that the battery of interventions represented by fetal monitoring, labor-inducing drugs, and Cesarean sections was being overused, leading, tragically, to higher infant and maternal mortality rates.

The World Health Organization lobbied for more births to be handled by midwives, outside of hospital facilities. At first, doctors argued that all births should remain in hospitals, so that the 10 percent of women who needed special care could get it. But subsequent research showed that midwives could correctly assess which of their patients could safely undergo a home birth and which needed more sophisticated hospital care.

At the same time that Carol Pavek was scouring used book stores in Amarillo for home birth books and obstetrical texts, Barbara Katz Rothman was completing a major study on the subject in New York. Some years earlier, Barbara had given birth to her son Danny at home.

"It was 1974 and New York and *nobody* had births at home, it seemed, except maybe people in communes in California—certainly not Ph.D. students married to computer programmers and living in Flatbush," says Barbara. Her desire to have a home birth had feminist roots. "It had something to do with control, power, and authority. At home, I would have them; in the hospital they would be handed over to the institution."

Barbara's own experience launched her into a study of doctor-managed hospital births versus midwife-attended home births. She found that the difference between the two was not merely one of location, but rather was based on profound differences in concepts about motherhood.

"It became clear to me that the medical model viewed pregnancy through men's eyes," explains Barbara. "The body is seen as a machine, and the male body is taken as a norm. Pregnancy and birth are at best complications, stresses on the system.

"The fetus, in the medical model, is seen as almost an adversary, the product of a man planted in a woman's body. That way of thinking creates a particular type of technology. There is a desperate search for a means to get the mother out of the way so that you can get to the other patient, the fetus."

In hospital births, evolving technology focuses almost entirely on the fetus, minimizing the importance of the woman altogether. "With ultrasound, the doctor turns away from the mother to examine her baby," observes Barbara. "Even the heartbeat is heard over a speaker removed from the mother's body. The technology that makes the baby/fetus more 'visible' renders the woman invisible.

"The midwifery model, in contrast, sees women's experiences through women's eyes and does not accept the male vision of pregnancy. The fetus and mother are an organic whole, the fetus being part of the mother's body. Childbirth is viewed from the perspective of the woman as a normal and healthy activity. The mother works to bring forth her baby, and whatever helps the mother in her work is believed to help the baby. As in pregnancy and postpartum care, the needs of the two are interrelated and interdependent."

The principles of midwifery resounded with Carol Pavek's own ideas of how children should be brought into the world. Until this point, she had been working as an office manager and studying psychology. She changed directions now, and began training with a group of El Paso midwives.

The more involved she got, the more disappointed she became that she hadn't been able to have a home birth herself. She wanted that joy, that test of her limits. She felt a part of her was missing without that experience. Just as she had studied psychologist Erik Erikson's theory of human development, which postulates that every individual needs to go through a stage of marital bonding and child rearing, Carol was convinced that women, and certainly she, needed that intense, painful, pleasurable, intimate experience of natural childbirth to develop themselves. Beyond her personal needs, Carol wondered how she could ever understand and meet the needs of her laboring patients if she hadn't gone through the experience herself. Did this mean that males should never be obstetricians? she mused. Probably.

Rick was disappointed about missing the chance to share a natural childbirth as well, especially as time passed and they decided they would not have any more children of their own. "We felt unfulfilled," says Carol. "We teased each other that we would keep giving birth until we got it right, only we would have to find families to give the children to."

When their son, Chris, was eighteen months old, their joking took a serious turn. That's when they first heard about the possibility of surrogate motherhood on a television show. The guest on the show was Noel Keane, the Dearborn, Michigan, attorney. Noel explained how, for decades, artificial insemination by donor had been used by couples when the husband was infertile. Now it was being applied in a new way to help couples when the wife was infertile. Her husband's sperm could be used to artificially inseminate a second woman, the surrogate mother. The surrogate would carry the pregnancy, give birth to the child, and turn the baby over to the couple to rear.

Noel is known as the father of surrogate motherhood, but the actual impetus for such arrangements came through requests from clients rather than from any creative legal thinking of his own. In 1976, a couple came to him and asked if he could help them find a woman to carry a child for them. The wife was infertile due to two ectopic pregnancies that had damaged her fallopian tubes. The husband wanted a child who was genetically related to him. "Maybe it's egotistical," he said. "Adoption leaves me cold."

At that point in his career, Noel knew little about family law. He had never done an adoption. He let the couple's request languish for months until his wife read a newspaper story about a California couple who had successfully advertised for a woman to bear the husband's child. With that precedent, Noel decided to go ahead with the arrangement. He called his law partner and said, "Chuck, is our malpractice insurance paid up? I'm about to do something different."

The idea of surrogacy was novel and Noel was trying to navigate a conservative course through existing laws on adoption, paternity, and artificial insemination. Existing adoption laws forbade payment to a biological mother in connection with giving a child up for adoption. These laws had been enacted before the advent of surrogacy and Noel felt they shouldn't apply, but he didn't want to run afoul of the laws before he could get a definitive court ruling about whether they banned payment to surrogates. That meant that Noel was in the position of trying to find women who would, with no compensation, agree to be artificially inseminated with the sperm of a stranger, carry the pregnancy for nine months, and then release the child to be raised by the stranger and his wife. It was no small task to prompt women to be this altruistic. It required a lot of imagination and a major media blitz. It required him to humanize infertility.

So Noel took to the talk shows with infertile couples. They were blue-collar workers. A butcher and his wife. A newspaper press operator and his wife. They talked about their dream of becoming parents and their years of fruitless attempts.

Infertile couples became the poster children of the 1980s. Unlike the March of Dimes toddlers with leg braces, the physical deficiencies of infertile couples did not show, but they felt disabled nonetheless. For our society is ferociously pronatalist. Childbearing is an expected facet of adult life.

For generations, infertility had been shrouded in secrecy. There were many social supports for a couple whose child had died, but virtually none when the "death" occurred before birth or even before conception, when it was the death of a dream rather than the death of an existing member of society.

Now infertile couples were coming forward. In 1977, they founded RESOLVE, Inc., a national self-help group for infertile couples. Within a decade it would grow to a major support group, with telephone hotlines, chapters in forty-four cities across the country, and a policy arm that lobbied for insurance coverage of infertility treatments and that filed a brief in the Baby M case.

Infertile couples were also speaking out to family, friends, and the public at large. Many viewed themselves as victims of social and technological change. They were seeing the dark underside of those otherwise positive developments that brought educational and career opportunities for women, sexual freedom, medical advances, and enhanced societal acceptance of alternative family structures.

The grueling legal quest that led ultimately to constitutionally protected access to contraceptives and abortion had affected fertility. If a woman has more than one sexual partner, her chances increase for pelvic inflammatory disease (PID), an infection that damages the fallopian tubes and is a major cause of infertility. Some contraceptives themselves sound the death knell for future fertility. The Dalkon Shield IUD, for example, sometimes caused PID and subsequent infertility.

Other medical and technological developments were likewise hazardous to reproductive health. Medicines were introduced into our lives and chemicals into our environment without sufficient thought about their effects on fertility. DES (diethylstilbestrol), given to women in the 1950s to prevent miscarriage, caused many of their resulting children to be infertile. Pollution lowers men's sperm counts, while certain pesticides and other chemicals lead to miscarriage and stillbirth.

At the same time that the problem of infertility has grown, the traditional solution—adoption—has become more difficult to achieve. Abortion limits the number of babies available for adoption. And enhanced societal acceptance of unwed mothers encourages many pregnant women to keep babies who in past years would have been given up for adoption.

So infertile couples turn to medically and socially complex means to have a child. Laser surgery. Superpowered fertility drugs like Pergonal. And newly emerging alternative forms of reproduction, such as in vitro fertilization and surrogate motherhood.

As Noel Keane and an infertile couple described surrogate motherhood to the television audience, Carol Pavek recognized how she could connect her dream of a home birth with a couple's dream of a baby. She and Rick talked about it. He said, "We can't realistically have a child of our own now, but here's a way that we can do it and don't have to suffer the negative consequences of raising a child. Granted, we don't get the beneficial consequences either, but here is a way to experience the child's birth."

Rick understood Carol well enough to know how much the experience would mean to her. "This was a way for Carol to express herself and do something for others," Rick said later. "There was a lot of altruism. In that period of time Carol was also mulling over the possibility of our going over to Africa to help people have babies."

It took six months' reflection before Carol actually began to fashion a letter to Noel expressing her interest. "It wasn't actually a letter," she says. "It was more like a book." In fourteen pages, she introduced Noel to herself and her ideas, then described how she felt a birth should be conducted. She covered her family and medical history. She talked about how, during pregnancy, she would abide by the requirements she gave her midwifery patients—walking several miles a day, avoiding prescription and nonprescription drugs, and eating natural foods (no caffeine, no white sugar, no flour, one yellow vegetable and three green vegetables a day).

Carol was candid in her portrait of herself, mentioning her receding chin, heavy hips, and nearsightedness. She was equally blunt about what she was looking for in a couple. They would have to agree, of course, to a home birth and the adoptive mother would have to be present. If possible, the father and any other children in the family should be present as well. Carol would breast-feed the baby for three to five days to pass on her immunities.

At the time Carol contacted Noel, in 1980, surrogate mothers were not being paid. It hadn't even occurred to Carol to ask for any money. Her main concern was the quality of the relationship she would have with the couple.

"The adoptive parents must be personally involved during the prenatal period," Carol declared. "They must be willing to exchange feelings with me, and they must be honest with friends and relatives about what they are doing. The parents should feel joy and anticipation, not guilt or doubt. The parents should have no wish to forget me after the birth. They must realize that I can never forget what I've done for them."

Noel received the letter the same day he received a desperate call from a couple of modest means who lived in a rural section of northern California. Nancy's first husband had died when she was pregnant with their second child. She raised their two daughters alone through childhood, then required a hysterectomy. When she later married Andy, it was clear that she would not be able to bear children. But now, in part because of his attachment to Nancy's two daughters, they were wishing they could have another child. Nancy's hysterectomy ruled out a biological child for the couple, and adoption agencies would not give a baby to a woman who already had children. They had seen Noel on a CBS documentary and were hopeful about the possibility of a surrogate arrangement to bring a child with Andy's traits into the world.

After listening to Andy's story, Noel picked up the letter he had received that morning and began reading Carol's background and requirements to Andy.

"Would you like her number?" asked Noel.

"You bet."

By sundown, Andy and Nancy had called Carol. Within a week, they had taken the tiresome three-and-a-half-day bus ride to the Texas panhandle to meet Carol and Rick face-to-face.

The trip left them totally exhausted, and the excitement and novelty of meeting the woman who might bear their child put them emotionally on edge. When they walked into the Pavek home, Nancy burst into tears.

Carol and Rick immediately took to the couple. "They were blue-jean/T-shirt/fast-food-type people," says Carol. The two couples were similar in personalities, financial worries, and attitudes toward children. Andy had red hair and nearsightedness, like Carol, and admitted that under his beard "there is a terrible receding chin."

"Great," said Carol, "if the baby gets a receding chin, we can blame it on you instead of on me."

Early in their visit, Carol took Rick out of earshot. "What do you think?" she asked.

"I think they're wonderful," he replied.

So they went back into the living room and made this offer: "Why don't you stay in our home with us? If you save the money you would have spent on a hotel room, you could afford to go back by plane rather than bus."

Their conversations over the next few days were not at all like a business negotiation; they were getting to know each other like new neighbors. Surrogacy is not like a merger of corporations. It is the creation of a relationship—and, as with any intimate relationship, it takes a certain level of compatibility to allow the relationship to flower.

"I think the issue that decided that, yes, we would be compatible was the issue of circumcision," says Carol. "It was something I was very strongly against. We were at the kitchen table and I tried to keep my voice very neutral and I asked, 'How do you feel about circumcision?' They said, 'Well, we feel it is the child's body and the child should make the decision when he gets old enough.' This immediately sold me. I felt that if they respected the child on that particular issue, they would respect the child in other aspects of child rearing as well."

Carol also got a chance to see how Andy and Nancy cared for a child. It was April 16, 1980, Chris's second birthday. The California couple was completely relaxed around him—offering to baby-sit and helping him splash in his new wading pool.

The two couples had timed the trip so that they would be together when Carol was due to ovulate. That day, Carol sent Nancy into town to buy a sexy nightgown for herself. "I wanted her to make love to her husband so that she could be a part of the start of the pregnancy," Carol says.

Nancy collected the sperm from her husband in a paper cup and brought it to Carol in the second bedroom. Carol inseminated herself, and Andy and Nancy returned to California.

The first insemination did not result in a pregnancy, so the following month, May of 1980, Carol flew out to their home in the California mountains. They lived out in the country in a cabin with a dog and horses, about four miles from an old mining town. Carol was immediately enchanted by the area as the perfect place to raise a child.

Andy and Nancy made her feel like a part of their family. Andy took her for rides on his motorcycle. The three of them went to a nearby town some evenings for strawberry ice cream. And, every other day for a week, Carol artificially inseminated herself. On Mother's Day, Andy brought both Nancy and Carol breakfast in bed.

"You're the mother of my child," he told Carol, "even though it's only temporary, nine months' worth." He felt that she must be pregnant; and it turned out she was, by a few hours at most.

During the pregnancy, the couples had to limit their phone calls back and forth, because of the cost. But there was still a lot of contact—at least a letter a week. As the pregnancy progressed, the two families began to ponder what would happen if there was a snafu in the complex legal proceedings that were to take place in

Texas and California. "Everyone agreed that we would never put the baby in foster care," says Carol. "Either we would keep the baby or they would keep the baby."

When she was growing up, Carol's parents had told her that she was not to draw attention to herself, not to run for school office. They had raised her with the old adage, "Fools' names and fools' faces are often seen in public places." So when reporters began calling her for interviews about her unusual pregnancy, Carol was at first a bit hesitant. But she believed in surrogacy as strongly as she believed in home birth, and wanted to take that message to other women.

Carol agreed to several media interviews. On one radio show, a caller likened surrogate motherhood to adultery. Although the allegation surprised Carol, the claim was nothing new. Decades earlier, when artificial insemination by donor came into widespread use for the wives of infertile males, an Illinois judge ruled that donor insemination was adultery, whether or not the husband had consented. A later court decision pointed out the absurdity of the notion that a sperm recipient commits adultery with the doctor or the donor. The judge wrote, "Since the doctor may be a woman, or the husband himself may administer the insemination by a syringe, this is patently absurd; to consider it an act of adultery with the donor, who at the time of the insemination may be a thousand miles away or may even be dead, is equally absurd."

"You cannot commit adultery with a syringe," says Carol. "Yes, my body is being used. When I die, my eyes are going to be used. My kidneys will be used. It is not my body in the first place. I come from a Christian philosophy which says we are our souls, the body is merely a vehicle we use while we are here on this planet. We shouldn't be so possessive about our bodies."

Carol also received letters, some supportive, some negative, some just plain weird. A nurse was irate that Carol had inseminated herself under unsterile circumstances; the nurse pointed out that even cattle breeders use sterile circumstances to inseminate their cattle. "I was tempted to write her back to ask her how long her husband boiled his penis before he inserted it," says Carol.

Every reporter who interviewed Carol was interested in talking to Rick. In fact, most were more interested in delving into his mind than into hers, because they couldn't understand why he approved of his wife carrying someone else's child. Often reporters told him "what an unusual, wonderful man you are."

"So much of the nation has the attitude that the female is the male's property," bristles Carol.

"How could you let Carol do this? Don't you care about her?" reporters would ask Rick.

"I care about her a great deal," Rick would respond, "but I realize that she's not chattel. She's not my property. I don't own her. This is a way for Carol to express herself and do something for others. Regardless of whether or not I support the concept, it is my moral obligation to support Carol."

Rick remained supportive, undertaking extra housework as Carol tired more easily during her pregnancy, and never having any second thoughts about what he considered to be their joint decision.

"The adopting mother typically liked to hear, and sympathize with, all the sordid details of the pregnancy," remembers Rick. "She didn't realize that I was going through a lot on my part as well, all of the things fathers go through during pregnancy."

Rick points out that mental preparation is necessary during a surrogate pregnancy, just as it is during a pregnancy in which the couple intend to rear the child. "During the nine months, one thing that really helps the process of surrogating is thinking 'that's their baby.' If you feel the least bit possessive, regardless of what your motivations are, you're going to feel bad when you give it up.

"Some people asked me, 'How could you stand to give up the baby?'" says Rick. "There weren't a whole lot of feelings in me toward the baby, because there was no emotional tie, no genetic tie. When I patted Carol's tummy, it was because I cared about Carol.

"I think the mental preparation is a big part of making it work, but they don't really cover it in the surrogate programs. I think they should test the women psychologically. They didn't test Carol."

Four days before the scheduled due date, Andy, Nancy, and the two teenaged daughters drove down to Amarillo in a motor home. The four of them rushed to Carol's house once her labor began. By this time, Carol had helped with thirty-five successful home births; she hoped her own would be the thirty-sixth. But, again, there was a problem with Carol's delivery and by midnight she was giving birth in a local hospital. This time at least, Carol knew a doctor whose techniques were more compatible with her childbirth philosophies. Andy and Nancy stayed with Carol through the labor, but once delivery began, they had to leave because no advance arrangements had been made for their presence. Rick was left to coach Carol through and oversee the birth of a ten-pound boy.

The doctor said that he wanted to lay the baby on Carol's stomach. "Have you forgotten, this isn't my baby?" she asked. She was worried that she might bond with the baby—which, after coming so far to have a baby for someone else, she didn't want to do.

"But, Carol," he continued, "it's the only warm place in the room."

The baby was gently lowered onto Carol's abdomen. She slowly opened her eyes, and was relieved to find that she didn't have any feeling of possession. Her only thought was "What a gorgeous baby."

Two hours later, Andy and Nancy wanted to give Carol the baby to breast-feed. A nurse took Nancy aside, saying, "Oh you must not let her breast-feed the baby, she will bond."

"I've trusted her this far, I'm going to trust her again," Nancy replied.

Carol fed the baby, then spent a peaceful hour watching Nancy hold her son. Carol thought of how, in traditional adoptions, the hospital staff did everything they could to keep the biological mother and the baby apart. It wasn't right to rip a baby away, Carol thought as she drifted off to sleep; the mother must have a chance to say good-bye.

The next day, back at home, Rick turned to Carol before she fell asleep. "You're already thinking of trying again, aren't you?" he asked.

Carol smiled, happy that her husband knew her so well.

3

PREGNANCY FOR PAY

OVER THE NEXT FEW MONTHS, Carol Pavek dedicated herself to her new professional venture, the establishment of a clinic with two other midwives, Ann Houghtaling and Lea Ann Gilley. They called it the Amarillo Lay Midwives Association. Its acronym, ALMA, meant "soul" in Spanish. They rented a wonderful old frame house, with a large porch and a widow's walk. They stripped away old wallpaper and brought to life a five-foot-tall brick fireplace in the living room, using its mantel as a shelf for their lending library of books about midwifery and childbirth. The finances of the three midwives in Carol's group were stretched to the limit in their renovation. They spent the bulk of their resources on the bedrooms where their "mothers" (they never referred to them as patients) would deliver. Ornately carved antique wooden beds covered with inviting spreads in pale blue florals seemed to promise a dreamlike passage into parenthood.

The state of Texas left midwifery virtually unregulated. The women had to register with the state and comply with certain laws about reporting births and deaths, putting drops in babies' eyes, and advising parents about certain diagnostic tests for newborns. The only time the law intervened was when midwives seemed to be crossing over into the unauthorized practice of medicine—and that only happened when a physician began to complain about the competition. As a new entity serving mainly poor women, ALMA was unlikely to be harassed.

"Midwifery is consumer-regulated," says Carol. "If a midwife has a bad reputation, no one will come to her. I would like to see the whole medical profession regulated in this way."

Carol's philosophy of health care paralleled that of the feminist women's health centers that had grown up around the country in the 1970s. The idea was that women could understand more about illness and health care than traditional doctors ever gave them credit for. At the feminist centers, women used a speculum and a mirror to assess whether they had a vaginal infection, joined self-help groups to swap effective remedies for urinary tract disorders, and even, at some centers, learned to perform their own blood tests.

Women were remarkable people, thought Carol, capable of much more than society usually acknowledged. Generations of legal precedents designed to "protect" women served often to hold them back. Carol felt that women as a class would never get ahead until individual women's decisions were respected. This was true even in the rare instance when a woman made a decision that was against her own interests. For any progress to be made for women, thought Carol, "women have to be allowed to make their own mistakes."

During the days, Carol worked on the transformation of the clinic. She added such humorous touches as a sign in the living room that read, "HOME DELIVERY—IT'S EASIER AND IT COSTS LESS," which was actually an ad for home delivery of the *Dallas Times Herald*. At night, Carol went home to letters and calls from couples who needed surrogates.

The opportunity for Carol to try again came almost immediately after the February 1981 birth. *Newsweek, Family Circle*, and a myriad of television shows from New York to Tokyo had reported Carol's successful surrogate pregnancy. Bags of letters from inquiring couples appeared on Carol's doorstep. She was overwhelmed by the sadness they represented. She began to look through them to see if there were any couples that she might feel as close as she had to Andy and Nancy. She was able to rule out about two hundred couples fairly easily. "I want to feel that I've personally selected a good home for my baby," she thought at the time. "I don't want to worry for the next eighteen years whether the couple is financially and emotionally stable."

Carol refused to serve as a surrogate for a couple who wanted a child just because they needed an heir, and for a couple who she thought would not spend enough recreational time with the child. In making her decision, Carol tried to picture the type of life the child would have. With one couple, she felt that they did not so much want a child as someone to pass the corporation on to. "I could see him in the Ivy League, maybe even in military school from the time he was six years old," envisioned Carol. "The couple didn't seem to have any warm feelings of 'Let's go make mud pies in the rain.'"

Rick helped Carol assess the couples and, ultimately, they settled on one in which the woman was blind. "I talked to her for a long time and felt very comfortable that she could raise a child without any problems, and I was excited about working with them," explains Carol. "They were comfortable with my doing the insemination myself, but, at the last minute, said that they wanted their doctor to do a physical and genetic testing. I said I would not submit to having a doctor go over my body to tell me what I already know." The couple would not go ahead without a genetic guarantee, so Rick and Carol moved on down the list.

When some of Carol's friends said that they, too, wanted to be surrogates, she shared the letters with them, along with the advice that women who think that they might want another baby should not be surrogates. "You should only be a surrogate if, at that time in your life, you do not want a child of your own," she cautioned. "If you have any interest in being a mother again, it's not for you." Ultimately, three of Carol's friends became surrogates, one for a couple who had approached Carol and two others for distant relatives who could not give birth. Carol happily served as their midwife.

The volume of correspondence was so heavy, and the stories of the couples so wrenching, that Carol and Rick rented a post office box and took out an ad in the paper to search for other surrogates. "We didn't get surrogates at the post office box," says Carol, "we just got more couples."

Noel Keane's mail reflected the same surge of interest in surrogacy. He had now arranged a dozen successful pregnancies; his media appearances around the globe brought letters to the Dearborn offices from countries he had never even heard of. The most significant change was that, now that it had been shown that surrogacy *worked*, wealthier couples were coming forward offering to pay for the procedure. Surrogacy had been gentrified. The blue-collar couples and surrogates who were the experimental vanguard were giving way to a new group of potential users who wanted to benefit from this reproductive alternative.

While Noel had used his media appearances to humanize surrogacy, a Louisville, Kentucky, doctor was seeking to glamorize it. Dr. Richard Levin—young, attractive, dark-haired— opened a competing surrogacy clinic. He drove a sleek car with the license plate "Baby 4 U." He traveled the talk-show circuit with good-looking, articulate surrogates, who viewed themselves as modern-day Florence Nightingales, ministering to the needs of infertile couples. And most important, he quite publicly admitted paying his surrogates $10,000 per pregnancy.

Levin had hired a sharp recent law school grad, Katie Brophy, who believed that surrogate mothers, employed in cases of female infertility, had just as much right to payment as those sperm donors who were hired in cases of male infertility. "Realistically, if you wanted to compensate a woman for her time as a surrogate mother, the fee would be phenomenal," said Katie. "A man who donates sperm anonymously receives twenty-five dollars for fifteen minutes of his time, with no risk to himself, physically or psychologically. A surrogate is pregnant twenty-four hours a day for nine months."

Katie found a loophole in Kentucky law that would allow them to publicly offer payment. Like other states, Kentucky banned payment to women in connection with giving a child up for adoption. However, Kentucky did not ban payment to a woman in connection with giving up her parental rights. Katie drafted a contract in which the surrogate agreed, for a fee of $10,000, to be artificially inseminated with a man's sperm, carry the pregnancy to term, and then terminate her parental rights. Once that was done, the child would automatically go to its father, the man who had provided the sperm. At their leisure, the man's wife would adopt the baby, but the adoption would not be part of the same transaction in which payment was made.

The existing Michigan laws did not give Noel that option. In 1978, he'd filed suit challenging the ban on payment to surrogates as an unconstitutional infringement on the couple's right to privacy to make procreative decisions. Noel pointed to the U.S. Supreme Court contraceptive and abortion cases, which held that people had a right to make decisions about whether or not to reproduce. He argued that, for men with infertile wives, the only socially acceptable way to beget their own children was through a surrogacy arrangement.

The key question in the case was whether existing adoption laws should apply to surrogate motherhood. When a couple decide to create their own biological child through sex, there is no legal red tape, no advance screening about their suitability as parents. When a couple decide to adopt a biologically unrelated child, a host of statutes comes into play, including ones requiring an assessment of their parental merit, forbidding them to pay money to the biological mother, and allowing the mother a certain time period after the child's birth to change her mind about the adoption.

But what about the hybrid situation? What should happen in cases of artificial insemination by donor, in which the wife has a constitutionally protected biological link to the child and the husband does not, or surrogate motherhood, in which the husband has a biological link and the wife does not?

When male infertility led to the widespread use of donor insemination starting in the 1960s, doctors advised the husbands to adopt the children because the husbands had no biological tie to them. Courts and legislatures rejected that approach and said the adoption laws should not apply. When donor insemination is used, the couple is not screened to see if they would be good parents. Payment to the donor is allowed. The donor does not have a right to change his mind after the child is born. The couple is treated as if they were having their own child in the old-fashioned way.

Noel argued that a similar approach should be taken with surrogate motherhood. He felt that the adoption laws were not appropriate for surrogacy. Payment to a biological mother in the context of a traditional adoption is prohibited to prevent the child from being given to an "undeserving" stranger, since mere ability to pay does not signify sufficient merit for being allowed to adopt a child. In contrast, in paid surrogacy, the child is turned over to the biological father. This biological bond has traditionally been considered to be a sufficient indicator of parental merit.

In January 1980, a Michigan trial court rejected Noel's claim. The judge insisted that "the State's interest, expressed in the statute . . . is to prevent commercialism from affecting a mother's decision to execute a consent to the adoption of her child. 'Baby-bartering' is against public policy."

Undaunted, Noel went on to file an appeal, arguing that the adoption laws were meant to protect *already pregnant* women from being coerced into giving up the child for a fee. He charged that "a surrogate mother exercises her choice to become a surrogate, prior to conception, and is, therefore, not subject to duress and anxiety which commonly attaches to an unexpected or unwanted pregnancy."

Attorneys for the state of Michigan, arguing in favor of the ban on payment, cautioned that allowing surrogates to be paid would thrust the court into the role of setting prices for children, perhaps allowing higher compensation for a bright, beautiful surrogate than for a less attractive, less intelligent one.

"The integrity of the court system and statutory adoption process," they said, "demands that the court be absolutely prohibited from deciding which individual has a Saks Fifth Avenue price tag and which individual has a K-Mart price tag."

The 1981 decision by the Michigan Court of Appeals, which came down three months after Carol gave birth to a son for Andy and Nancy, ruled that although a couple has a constitutional right to use a surrogate, they do not have a right to pay money in connection with an adoption to make the child legally theirs. In the eight years following this decision, courts around the country— including the courts in the Baby M case—would face the issue of payment again and again. Some would rule against paying the surrogate, others would rule in her favor.

Since surrogacy could not readily fit into the Procrustean bed of existing laws, Noel's next move was to attempt to convince legislators to adopt a special surrogacy law. A young lawmaker, Representative Richard Fitzpatrick, had already approached Noel with questions about how legislators should begin to deal with reproductive technologies. Fitzpatrick, who voted consistently for Medicaid support of abortions, supported a woman's right to choose what she did with her body. He also emotionally understood the couples' plight, since his own marriage was being challenged by infertility.

Fitzpatrick approached the issue of a surrogacy law with some trepidation. "I'm a firm believer that the less government involvement in matters of reproduction and parenting the better," he told Noel.

The track record of state legislatures in prescribing parenthood was a dismal one. Since the turn of the century, laws had been enacted which circumscribed reproductive rights in the supposed best interests of potential children and of society. Starting in 1907, state laws authorized the sterilization of feeble-minded people, prostitutes, paupers, and criminals—to protect their potential children from developing similar traits. Thirty-four states passed laws prohibiting interracial marriages—on the grounds that such marriages would result in defective offspring. Laws were adopted prohibiting the use of contraceptives and abortion—in order to preserve the traditional family. It wasn't until the 1960s and 1970s that this panoply of restrictions was ultimately laid to rest with legislative repeals and clear court decisions stating that a person's decisions about reproduction are protected by the U.S. Constitution under the right to privacy.

"Decisions about whether, when, and how to have children should be matters of personal choice, not government mandate," explained Fitzpatrick. "The less law in this area the better."

The paradox was, though, that by forbidding payment and indicating that the adoption laws should apply to surrogacy, the Michigan court had put barriers in the way of infertile couples' reproductive rights. If Fitzpatrick wanted couples to have the choice of creating a child with the aid of a surrogate, he would have to draft a law which specifically allowed it.

The law he developed spelled out in incredible detail the various parties' rights and responsibilities. The prospective biological father and his infertile wife would have to file a petition with the court asking for permission to enter into a surrogate arrangement.

The court would then order a full investigation of the couple, similar to the home study made in the course of a regular adoption. If the couple passed inspection, the artificial insemination of the surrogate could take place.

The bill also detailed nineteen provisions a surrogate agreement would have to contain. The surrogate would have to agree to undergo psychiatric, medical, and genetic evaluations. The father would be required to undergo genetic and medical evaluations, which would include venereal disease testing before each insemination. He and his wife would be the legal parents of the resulting child, no matter what the baby's condition. If either spouse died before the child's birth, the other would still get custody of the child. If both died, the surrogate would still be paid and she would have the choice of keeping the child or putting him or her up for adoption. The bill also set a limit on what surrogates could be paid—$10,000.

The last provision angered Carol Pavek. Even though she had not asked for a cent in her surrogate pregnancy, she saw no reason that women should be limited in what they could collect in this form of employment. "I'm just furious about the bill," she said at the time. "Either surrogacy is legal or it's not. Instead of setting limits on what the surrogate can get, they should set a limit for what the psychiatrist, attorney, and medical doctor can get. All of these people are making a killing in the surrogate situation for very little work. Once you get the precedent set, it shouldn't be that tough for the attorney to use the same papers in the next surrogacy adoption. Right now divorces have become standardized and are down to $30."

Rick, too, felt it was unfair to restrict payment to surrogates, but not to doctors and lawyers. Rick had a strong sense of fair value. Once he saw a toy train car for fifty cents at a garage sale. It was worth more than that to him, so he opened his wallet and gave the man two dollars instead.

It would be a while before any surrogacy bill got enacted into law. In the meantime, Noel's hands were tied with respect to paying surrogates in his home state of Michigan. But the United States is a crazy quilt of fifty-one legal jurisdictions, with each state and Washington, D.C., having its own law on adoption. He decided that he would affiliate with local counsel in Florida, a state with a more liberal law. In Florida, there was no residency requirement for an adoption. A streamlined adoption procedure applied when the wife of a biological father adopted his child; no inquiry was made about whether money changed hands. Noel would continue to arrange surrogacy agreements in Michigan, but the actual adoption papers would be filed in Florida. With this legal sleight of hand, Noel could, for the first time, offer compensation to surrogates. He called Carol Pavek to learn whether she was interested in being a surrogate mother for a couple in the Northeast who would pay her a fee of $10,000.

The possibility of women being paid to be mothers troubled Frank Kelley, the attorney general of Michigan, who worried that women might be coerced into serving as surrogates. How would women react to the $10,000 fee? Perhaps it would be as if a Brink's truck accidentally dropped a bag of money on your lawn. One part of you would want to follow all your previous principles, be a good citizen, and report the loss. The other part of you couldn't help but look around you and notice all the cracks in your life—the clothes that you wanted to buy for the children, the sink that needed fixing, the trip you had always wanted to take—that the $10,000 could plaster over.

In the actual surrogacy arrangements, the $10,000 was not as potent a lure as surrogacy opponents made it seem. The money was not given in a lump sum at the time the woman joined the program, but rather (as in other forms of employment) was spread out over her service in the program. Since it might take months for the woman to be matched with a couple, then more months of artificial inseminations for her to conceive, the $10,000 might be her payment for two years' work, with the bulk of the amount coming at the end. "Surrogacy is not for poor women," says surrogate Jan Sutton. The surrogates need to have enough money themselves to cover out-of-pocket expenses until they can be reimbursed.

But Attorney General Kelly argued that the fee was offered to get a woman to "conceive a child she would not normally want to conceive, carry for nine months a child she would not normally want to carry, give birth to a child she would not normally want to give birth to. Then, because of this monetary reward, she relinquishes her parental rights to the child that she bore."

Carol definitely was not in that position. She was a booster of the surrogacy concept and would be going ahead with another pregnancy, whether paid or not. But even for her, the possibility of earning money to carry the baby added a new dimension to the arrangement, one that Carol was not comfortable with. Rick and Carol had decided not to have another child because they could not afford one. So Carol was troubled by the idea of creating and carrying a child for a couple whose entry into the parenthood lottery was premised on their having $30,000 in their bank account—the $10,000 for her, the $10,000 for Noel, and an additional $10,000 for miscellaneous expenses.

Carol had loved being a surrogate because she was bringing a baby to a couple like her and Rick. "Andy and Nancy were a lumberjack and his stay-at-home wife," she explains. "She had worked at child care centers, but she was basically a housewife. There was not a lot of money involved with them at all." Andy and Nancy had paid Carol's minimal medical expenses and had paid $365 for the Texas portion and $250 for the California portion of the adoption. "That was a big enough bite for them and there is no way they could have had this baby if they had had to cough up the type of money Noel was now talking about. Yet it was a real good feeling that we had a lot in common and were very comfortable from the first."

Carol had reservations about the men who were now seeking surrogates. "The men who would be the best fathers," she said at the time, "are men who do not mind being spit up on, who will sit on the floor with the baby. They are not the aggressive, assertive attorneys or doctors who are the ones who were most likely to be able to track me down or who are the ones who could afford to pay a surrogate. The men who would be the best fathers might not be able to pay."

The mental impasse that daunted Carol about whether or not to accept payment was overcome by a physical accident. One day, Carol was backing her and Rick's old green Opal out of the driveway at the precise instant that the neighbor across the street was backing her car out of her driveway. Both cars were thoroughly wrecked. "Well, I guess, yes, we will accept money," Carol thought.

If you had talked to Carol around the time that this decision was made, you might have been struck by the complex interweaving of motives in her decision to go on to her second surrogate pregnancy. The articulate, feminist Carol talked persuasively about women's reproductive freedom and how surrogate motherhood was a pillar of that freedom. The Carol who was in touch with her own body spoke clearly of the "craving" she felt about doing it again in order to have a home birth. And a quiet, much younger-sounding voice from within Carol spoke almost wistfully about what the money would mean. "Just once, I would like to be able to go into a car dealership, be well treated, and pick out a car without them quizzing me about how I would ever be able to afford it," she said. These three sides came together as she telephoned Noel.

In August 1981, Carol agreed to talk to Rhonda and Jerry, the couple that Noel was pushing. Of course, like everything else Carol did, the final decision would be up to her. As with her first surrogate pregnancy, she had a checklist of things she did and didn't want. On the basis of her previous pregnancy, she had added a few more. She now wanted life insurance, so that her own child, Chris, would be protected if she died during her surrogate pregnancy. She also wanted decision-making power over the baby's medical care for the first twenty-four hours, so that physicians would not be confused about who to turn to if there was an emergency and so that she could refuse tests for the baby that she, as a midwife, felt were unnecessary.

Rhonda and Jerry started out with several strikes against them. Before Carol even met them, the differences between them and Carol and her husband were strikingly apparent. Both Rhonda and Jerry were professionals. They lived in what to Carol was a mansion. Rhonda was attractive and slim, five feet four inches and 110 pounds. "I can't stand women with good figures," Carol thought. "And here she's going to keep her figure, while I ruin mine for her."

The initial phone call did not go well. "They were very formal," says Carol. "They said they would get me a nice hotel room and the dad did not particularly want to meet me. He was very uninvolved, very cold, a workaholic. He felt that whoever his wife chose was fine."

When she got off the phone, Carol turned to Rick. "I have the impression that they have always been able to get everything they wanted," she told him. "And now the husband wants to buy her a baby."

Carol was anxious to meet Jerry since she felt that her surrogacy decision hinged on what kind of father she thought he would be. Carol described to Rhonda her first surrogate pregnancy and how Andy, the biological father, had brought her breakfast in bed for Mother's Day. Jerry wasn't like that, Rhonda replied. "He'd just work a lot harder so he could pay someone to bring you breakfast in bed," she explained.

Jerry certainly didn't fit Carol's vision of the perfect daddy. "My husband won't come to the birth," Rhonda said. "For him, babies don't even exist until they're six years old."

Carol was angry. "From the time he drops out of my vagina, the baby immediately needs a father. He needs a father's smell and strength. I want the father there to share."

Over the next few days, Carol went over an endless series of questions in her head. How would Rhonda and Jerry be during the pregnancy? At the birth? How would they treat the child?

Given Carol's fundamentalist upbringing, it was also hard for her to imagine her son or daughter in a Jewish home. On the other hand, Rhonda and Jerry could provide for a child in a way that she and Rick never could. "Rick and I are so poor and always will be," she thought. "I like the idea of my child going to a family where the child can go to whatever schools he or she wants and wear clothes that people aren't going to laugh at."

Talking to Rick helped her put this potential pregnancy into perspective. Carol fretted that she would be harming a couple if she took money from them to help them create a child. "I finally realized that Rhonda and Jerry would give ten times the amount they would give to me to charity each year," she says. "It was just nothing for them to write out a check for that amount. It took me a long time to realize that I was not hurting the couple, but it was still hard to turn people away who did not have the money."

In addition to Rhonda and Jerry, Carol talked to three other couples who offered to pay her. But all the couples who had that kind of money were of a completely different social status. Rick finally sat her down and said, "There is not going to be one that you will have the same feelings for that you had for Andy and Nancy.

It will not be as wonderful, because they are rich and you have never associated with the rich."

Carol finally decided on Rhonda and Jerry, in part because Noel would provide the legal work. Carol didn't feel that she needed a lawyer of her own. "All I have to do is sign the relinquishment papers," she said at the time. "It's just a two-minute thing."

When Rhonda met her at the airport, Carol was struck by how much she resembled Nancy. "I got off the airplane and a woman came walking toward me," recounts Carol. "She could have easily been a sister to the woman in California, they looked almost identical. She was wearing a Mickey Mouse T-shirt and blue jeans. I think that helped. If she had looked like a Junior Leaguer, I think I would have turned around and got back on the airplane."

On the drive from the airport, Carol warmed to Rhonda as she discussed how much she wanted a child. She had been trying to become a mother for seven years, had suffered through every test, and still had no diagnosis for why she had failed. She ovulated properly, her tubes were fine, her cervix produced the right kind of mucus, her husband had a high sperm count. Their infertility was, literally, inconceivable.

During dinner at a restaurant, Jerry was secretive about the nature of his work. Carol began to worry that it was something illegal. "You know the way you talk, it sounds like the Mafia," she said. It turned out that his dealings were aboveboard, but that he hadn't wanted Carol to know the extent of his wealth. "He did not trust a poor woman," observed Carol. "He was just not sure that I wasn't after all of his money."

After getting to know Carol better and learning more about her first surrogate pregnancy, Jerry became more comfortable. He and Rhonda decided to invite her home with them, instead of making her stay at a hotel.

There, Carol and Jerry fell into an uneasy alliance. The next few days passed in a running debate. Carol had studied psychology, as had Jerry before he turned to law. They would fight about child rearing, about private schools, and about whatever other topic came to mind. "I think we just played devil's advocate to each other," says Carol, "just for the sake of having somebody that could carry on a good verbal fight. I enjoyed him a lot, and he enjoyed me living there, and the fighting we used to do." On alternate days, Carol would artificially inseminate herself with Jerry's sperm.

A few weeks later in Amarillo, Carol realized that she had managed to get pregnant. When Rhonda learned of her impending motherhood, she was thrilled. "You're just going to have to trust me on this," she told Carol. "I know Jerry and I know that he won't be that involved with the baby as an infant, but once the child is a toddler, he'll be a great father."

During this second surrogate pregnancy, a Swedish reporter asked Carol, "Did you love the men?"

"Well," replied Carol, "if they were winos on the street, I certainly would not have considered having a baby for them. It was not love, but I certainly had very good feelings about them. Rick and I never would have done this for an anonymous couple. Love, no, but to the extent that I did not have Rick, would I be attracted to these men? To the extent that they were kind, compassionate, attractive, intelligent (and, in Jerry's case, money-makers), well certainly."

When Carol acts as a midwife for a woman giving up a baby for adoption, she has the adopting mother attend, wearing a button-front shirt and no bra. "As soon as the baby comes out, I lay it on the adoptive mother," says Carol. "That's the first thing the baby smells, the first skin it feels."

When she described the process to Rhonda, Rhonda was initially squeamish at the thought of ripping off her clothes in front of everyone to make room for a bloody newborn. But when the time came, Rhonda loved it.

It was three-and-a-half weeks past the baby's due date. Rhonda was a nervous wreck, but Jerry told her, "It's okay, I was very late." Carol was thinking, I'm not going through another day like this. Carol had been walking five to seven miles daily, and on this particular day, she went walking with Rick. As she tried to keep pace with his long strides, her water broke and her labor pains finally started. They slowed down for the trek back home, and Rick called Rhonda at her motel, while Carol tried to make herself comfortable in the bedroom.

"Don't call Rhonda until I'm sure I'm in labor and that everything is going to be fine," Carol told Rick. "I love her, but she is so nervous that she is driving me crazy. Wait until the head is crowning and then bring her in."

Carol reached inside herself and could feel the baby's head. "Oh," she thought, "this baby is actually going to succeed and I'm going to have a quiet home birth and it's going to be wonderful."

Rhonda came in the room. "This is your baby crowning," said Carol, "go ahead and touch it." She touched the baby's head just as it was emerging from Carol's body. Rhonda opened her shirt and held the baby against her.

Rhonda was so mesmerized by this baby, *her* baby, that she started to walk away.

"Wait, wait, come back," said Carol, laughing. "We have to cut the cord. He's still attached."

Carol was giggling so much that she couldn't find her glasses. Rick finally located them for her and she cut the cord. In that dramatic motion, she was making Rhonda a mother.

Afterward, Carol felt complete. She had finally succeeded at her home birth. When the money came, it was certainly anticlimactic. She did use it to buy a car, a 1982 Subaru. She is still driving it, and being more careful when she backs out of her driveway.

Rhonda's predictions about Jerry's parenting potential came true. When the baby was six months old, she walked past the baby's room and could hear Jerry talking and singing to him. She snuck away, knowing that if she said, "Aha, caught you, you do love that baby," he would have been embarrassed.

4

※

MOTHERLESS CHILD

In early 1983, Carol was again devoting her energies to her midwifery practice, but there were problems at ALMA. The responsibilities for running the clinic were supposed to be divided evenly among the midwives, but Carol felt she was doing a disproportionate share. She always seemed to be the one racing out to buy supplies when they were low and making sure that the couples paid their fee—$150—for the use of the facility. Carol felt that if she were doing all the work, she might as well just have her own private practice.

Noel Keane, too, was experiencing problems with his practice. Despite his attempts to formalize and systematize surrogacy (his contracts had changed from a twelve-line paragraph to a twenty-page tome), something had gone terribly wrong at the human level in the agreement Noel had arranged between Judy Stiver and Alexander Malahoff.

In her contract with Alexander, Judy had made more vows than she had when she married her husband, Ray. Judy had promised to undergo a complete physical and genetic evaluation, to be artificially inseminated with Alexander's sperm, to refrain from smoking, drinking, and using drugs during her pregnancy, and, upon Alexander's demand, to have amniocentesis and abort if the fetus had a genetic defect. She had agreed to follow a prescribed schedule of prenatal medical appointments and to follow any medical instructions given to her by the inseminating physician or her obstetrician. She and her husband agreed to see a psychiatrist, Dr. Philip Parker.

At the heart of her contract was her agreement to give custody of the child to Alexander after its birth. To further that goal, she and her husband signed statements that they would "not form or attempt to form a parent-child relationship" with the child she conceived.

Under provision 18 of the contract, Judy swore that she understood the contract and was freely and voluntarily entering into it. But Noel wasn't content to let a surrogate's participation hinge on this clause. He sent Judy to Dr. Parker to assure that she was capable of giving a voluntary, informed consent. Then, in a somewhat demeaning exercise, he had Judy copy over a paragraph in her own handwriting. It was reminiscent of writing on the blackboard a hundred times, "I will not chew gum in class." The paragraph read, "I understand that the child to be conceived by me is being done so only because the wife of the natural father is unable to bear a child. I, as the natural mother of the child to be born, acknowledge that it is in the best interest of the child for its natural father to have immediate custody. I agree to cooperate fully to place the child with its natural father as soon as possible after its birth." Judy, in her round, clear, sensible handwriting, copied the statement and dated it April 7, 1982.

To hammer home some of the risks Judy faced in being a surrogate, Noel provided a three-page list of the potential complications of pregnancy. "Pregnancy is by no means a condition to be taken lightly," it began, pointing out that there was a 1 in 4,800 risk of maternal death. The list then proceeded through each bodily system (the cardiac system, the respiratory system, the urinary system, the endocrine system, the nervous system, the reproductive system, and so forth), describing the many and varied disorders that pregnancy could cause or aggravate. It pointed out that a surrogate could lose her future reproductive potential due to complications of a surrogate pregnancy. It noted that she might contract a venereal disease, a viral infection, or a bacterial infection that was transmitted through the sperm insemination. Another three pages described the incidence of genetic defects in fetuses and the tests that were available to detect those defects. All in all, it was probably more information than most women had before they conceived a child.

On his part, Alexander agreed to undergo a physical examination, venereal disease testing, and a genetic evaluation. He also agreed to pay Judy's medical and travel expenses and to take out a $100,000 insurance policy on Judy. He agreed to pay $300 so that Judy could consult an independent attorney for advice on the contract. He consented to pay two-thirds that amount for maternity clothes.

If Judy miscarried after the fifth month or the baby was stillborn, Alexander's responsibilities were minimal; he would pay Judy $1,000, instead of the $10,000 that she would get for a live birth. If she miscarried before the fifth month, she would get nothing. Alexander also agreed that he would assume legal responsibility for any child who had genetic or chromosomal abnormalities (unless the abnormalities had been detected and Judy had refused his request to abort).

At the time Judy became a surrogate, she had been married for nearly three years. She was the mother of a two-year-old. Her husband, Ray, was a part-time bus driver. In explaining what she considered to be their joint decision for her to become a surrogate, she said, "We felt we needed the money and there were a lot of things we could do for our daughter with the money." Like many surrogates, Judy described how easy and happy her previous pregnancy had been.

Noel has been criticized for his rapid processing of surrogates, and Judy's case seems to support that critique. On March 22, she was accepted into the program. On April 7, Judy signed the contract and met with Noel, Dr. Parker, an attorney whom Noel said would represent her interests, and the doctor who would perform the artificial inseminations. On April 14 and 15, she underwent inseminations with Alexander's sperm. Less than a month after she had taken her surrogacy vows, she was pregnant. At that point, Alexander Malahoff had not yet even signed the contract.

In the early afternoon of January 9, 1983, Judy entered Lansing General Hospital. Twenty-eight hours later, she gave birth to a baby boy. The baby was born with microcephaly (a small head, indicating possible mental retardation) and was suffering from a life-threatening strep infection. Dr. Carla Smith asked Judy's permission to treat the baby with antibiotics. Judy disclosed that she was a surrogate mother, and that the doctor would have to seek Alexander's permission. Judy, having complied with the contract, said she felt "no maternal bond to the child."

When Alexander was contacted in New York, he refused to allow the baby to be treated. He wanted a child to hold his marriage together, but now his marriage was even more rocky. The thought of caring for a seriously ill child was apparently just too much.

Dr. Smith couldn't stand this parental ping-pong, with neither side taking responsibility for the child. So she took the matter to the Ingham County Circuit Court, where she convinced Judge Michael Harrison to temporarily declare the Stivers to be the parents so that they could authorize treatment.

The baby was treated, but Ray and Judy still asserted that they were not the real parents of the child. In court papers and newspapers, the child was referred to as Baby Doe. Unwanted by all four parents, he became a ward of the state.

While later surrogate cases, like the Baby M case, would involve surrogate infants that were wanted by too many parents, Baby Doe was wanted by too few. Unlike the usual state ward, the result of an unwanted or unplanned pregnancy, Baby Doe was the product of an intentional, deliberate attempt to conceive. Although he didn't have a name on his birth certificate, he did have a twenty-page contract reciting how and why he had come into the world. Who were his legal parents? While in another society this issue might have been resolved by wise elders, in our society it was put to the test of the Nielsens. Alexander, Ray, and Judy agreed to argue their case on the Phil Donahue television show. One of Alexander's titillating claims was that he was not really the father of the child.

In almost every surrogacy dispute, one side or the other raises the issue of nonpaternity. When the surrogate wants to keep the child, she claims that her husband, and *not* the man providing the sperm, is the biological father of the child. (Mary Beth Whitehead made this claim even though her husband, Rick, had undergone a vasectomy.) In the case of Baby Doe, since Alexander did not want the child, he claimed that the baby was not his.

The claim of nonpaternity rarely pans out, because at the beginning of the surrogate pregnancy, there is no dispute. Both sides have the same goal—to create a child for the contracting couple. And, at that early stage, surrogates follow their contracts to a tee in trying to meet that goal. But Alexander's claim in this case was provocative enough that the Donahue producers had arranged the show for the day that the laboratory would determine, through blood tests, who was the father of Baby Doe. Judy, Alexander, and Ray would get this news for the first time in front of millions of viewers.

The show aired February 3, 1983, with the laboratory phoning in. And the loser was . . . Ray Stiver. The blood tests fingered Ray, the surrogate's husband, as the father of the child.

The camera pan of the trio shows Alexander, the youngest-looking of the three, beaming under his bushy dark mustache. His hands are outstretched as if to embrace the audience for sharing in his good fortune. Judy, still slightly heavy and less than a month postpartum, is hunched slightly forward. Her hands hang low and clenched together. Her mouth is a straight line and, behind her glasses, her eyes are distant and unfocused. Ray, a solid-looking man with close-cropped dark hair, narrows his eyes. His mouth turns downward. Ray does not look like a man who wants to pass out cigars.

Apparently Judy had been told not to have sex with her husband for a month after the insemination, but had not been told to abstain immediately before the procedure. She became pregnant by Ray just before the insemination and carried the child, all the while thinking it was Alexander's baby.

The Stivers could have left the baby in foster care, or given him up for adoption by strangers. Instead, they pulled themselves together, gave him a name—Christopher Ray Stiver—and took him home to join Mindy, his three-year-old sister.

Within three weeks of the baby's birth, Alexander had filed a lawsuit against Judy Stiver, Ray Stiver, and Noel Keane. The well-meaning Stivers had done everything they could throughout the pregnancy to assure the best start in life for the child they thought was Alexander's baby. They had not yet recovered from the shock of unplanned parenthood and the trauma of a child with a serious illness. They weren't sure how they would be able to afford the medications and doctors' visits that young Christopher Ray needed; they couldn't even afford a phone so that they might be able to call an ambulance. And here came Alexander Malahoff suing them for $50,030,000. His claim: since Judy had not gotten pregnant with his sperm, he had been "denied the love, services, affection, and happiness" of the child that Judy had promised to bear for him.

Ray and Judy now had to find their own lawyer to defend them. When they did, the legal issues began to snowball. They sued the professionals associated with Noel Keane's program for not advising them to forgo sex before the insemination. They sued Noel Keane for not properly reviewing the procedures used in his program. And, finally, they sued Alexander Malahoff, claiming that his sperm had transmitted the infection that caused Christopher's illness.

The Michigan court system was not the only legal body affected by the *Malahoff v. Stiver* case. Its reverberations shook the legislature as well. Michigan State Representative Richard Fitzpatrick had also been a guest on the Donahue show. "I felt badly that surrogate motherhood was being treated as a sideshow, a question of 'who wins the baby' live on network TV, rather than being given the thoughtful, intelligent review it deserved."

In each of the previous two years, Fitzpatrick had introduced laws to regulate surrogate motherhood. Other legislators wondered if such laws were really necessary, since he could only talk about hypothetical problems. But now newspapers and constituents were asking why there hadn't been a law to avert the original erroneous conception and the subsequent confusion over who had decision-making authority with respect to the child. Shortly after the birth of Baby Doe, the *Detroit Free Press* editorialized: "Surrogate parenting, no matter how we feel about the practice, isn't likely to go away. Properly regulated by specific and careful legislation, it could help to enrich lives. Unregulated or bound only by loose guidelines, it could become the spawning ground for countless tragedies."

The Stiver/Malahoff debacle finally brought the attention of lawmakers to surrogacy. "The case was critical in getting legislation considered," says Fitzpatrick. "The fact that it happened in the backyard of the capital, in Lansing, made legislators think it was a serious phenomenon that they had to look at. Legislation gets bogged down by inertia. With surrogacy, the Stiver case started to move the rock. But there was still a long way to go. It's not abnormal for legislation about a new concept to take five or six years from drafting to passage."

In response to the case, which as of this writing is still in litigation, Fitzpatrick drafted a law which required medical and psychological testing of the surrogate and required the surrogate to adhere to medical instructions before and after the insemination and during pregnancy. Within twenty-four hours of the baby's birth, blood tests would be performed to determine who the biological father was. If the contracting man was indeed the biological father, he would assume responsibility for the child, no matter what his or her condition. At age eighteen, the child would be able to learn the surrogate's name, unless she objected.

Baby Doe affected Michigan State Senator Connie Binsfeld in a much different way, resulting in legislation opposing Fitzpatrick's. Connie had been in the chambers of Judge Donald Owen, at the Ingham County Circuit Court, learning about child abuse cases, when the call had come from Lansing General Hospital about Baby Doe needing medical care.

Connie was concerned that a man's payment to a stranger to bear his child would cause him to view the resulting child as a commodity. If the baby didn't meet his specifications, he might try to return it, like "damaged goods."

"As I walked out of Owen's chambers," says Connie, "I thought, how could the best interests of a child ever be served by allowing this kind of stuff?"

A few years earlier, according to Connie, a young woman on welfare—the daughter of one of her friends—had been accepted into Noel's surrogacy program. "She had nothing but problems," says Connie. Now here was yet another set of problems. "I wanted to prohibit surrogate motherhood before anyone else got hurt."

Surrogate motherhood was completely at odds with Connie's traditional homemaker background. Born in 1924, she quit her job teaching social studies when she got married, then mothered five children. Although she was interested in politics, she did not run for state office until 1974, when her youngest child entered college.

Connie sincerely felt that surrogacy was no way to bring children into the world. The bill she introduced made surrogate motherhood a crime and set jail terms for everyone associated with it—the couple, the surrogate, the lawyer, the psychologist.

"It is a fact that today Michigan laws prohibit natural parents from giving a child away without the process of Michigan's adoption laws," Connie asserted in a speech on the floor of the senate before her bill was put to a vote. "It is a fact that today Michigan law prohibits the exchange of money, buying or selling of a child, and the law prohibits making a child an article of commerce or a commodity. These both have criminal penalties under the present adoption laws that we are amending.

"Ask yourself why we have these laws. Certainly not to fulfill the emotional needs of infertile couples. Certainly not to contribute to the pro-choice of adults who wish to enter into arrangements, financial or otherwise, to use their bodies as they choose. No, we have arrived at that public policy and those laws because the emotional and physical desire of adults have been superseded by Michigan's 'best interest of the child' argument. Then why are we discussing today an amendment to that law? Because today a scientific process called 'surrogate mother' leaves some children outside the protection of our present laws. . . .

"The very important point that has received very little discussion or consideration is the misrepresentation of the term 'surrogate.' 'Surrogate' means substitute, and that she isn't. In these arrangements, it is her ovum that is fertilized; her genes; it is her child. Ask the maternal grandparents. Speak with some of them as I have, who have been victims of surrogate arrangements, and you will soon be concerned too that the surrogate child is their own maternal grandchild. . . .

"A human 'surrogate' in these arrangements is the natural mother and the word surrogate is a misrepresentation. I think the most vital question is: Shouldn't the children born of these natural mothers have the same protections of children born of other natural mothers? Those children can't be sold or given away. A hundred years ago we did away with that. We said slavery was wrong; it was wrong to sell a human being."

Connie's bill banning surrogacy passed the Michigan senate, but got deadlocked by supporters of Richard Fitzpatrick's bill in the house. Even though the Stiver/Malahoff case had brought the issue of surrogate motherhood to legislators' attention, interest in the matter died down quickly. Because the baby turned out to be the child of the surrogate's husband, lawmakers did not count it as a surrogacy tragedy. They went back to ignoring the issue.

The best that Connie could do was to get the legislature to hire a consultant to prepare a report on surrogacy. Connie had already gone on record as saying that surrogate motherhood was against the best interests of children. Since Connie picked the consultant, it seemed fairly clear how the study would come out.

Opposition to surrogate motherhood was also growing from another corner—that of adoption agencies. Bill Pierce, executive director of the National Committee for Adoption in Washington, D.C., a nonprofit amalgamation of adoption agencies and maternity homes, had been monitoring surrogacy since the late 1970s.

Noel's surrogacy arrangements angered Bill. "What we had here was a fellow who was doing this thing by the seat of his pants," says Bill. "That really bothered me, because of the lives involved, not the least of which were the kids." When he read that surrogates were getting paid, Bill's first reaction was, "This is baby selling."

In 1982, Bill sent a questionnaire to the 115 member agencies of the National Committee for Adoption, asking their views on surrogacy. Ninety-four percent opposed surrogate motherhood and 89 percent felt it should be outlawed. An overwhelming majority—93 percent—felt that the National Committee for Adoption should play a role in setting policy in this area.

Many of the agency heads had voiced their concerns about surrogacy by writing comments on the survey form: "Surrogate motherhood is a further step toward the merchandising of human life." "I believe that there is something intrinsically immoral about regarding a woman as a baby-factory who provide a product for a fee." "This could be devastating to the children in the surrogate's family and the husband." "What about the infertile wife of the sperm donor and her real feelings?" "Surrogate motherhood makes human reproduction commercial. It is intentional adultery. It could give rise to all types of fantasies on the part of the sperm donor and may be hard for his infertile wife afterward to accept that another woman carried her husband's sperm." "Surrogate motherhood is subject to all the hazards of independent adoption and many additional ones."

Bill felt that surrogate motherhood was bad for the children involved. He was concerned that some of the couples entering into surrogacy arrangements would not tell the children about their unique origins. "We learned later than we should have through experience in adoptions that sharing the fact one is adopted is critical to one's mental health," says Bill. In addition, Bill worried that "the child subject to an expensive contract could be stigmatized, could think that he or she was a piece of goods."

Beyond his concern for the child, Bill felt that surrogacy would adversely affect traditional adoption. "Surrogacy represents a real crisis in terms of adoption," he says. "If surrogacy prevails, it will be the end of ethical adoption.

"Surrogacy besmirches adoption," continues Bill. "It's a perversion of something that's really great, just as commercialized sex besmirches legitimate marital intercourse."

An official at one of Bill's member agencies, however, pointed out how the National Committee for Adoption might be seen as having a conflict of interest if they came out publicly against surrogacy. "This seems to be a no-win situation," he wrote. "If we support regulating the practice, we seem to approve it. If we oppose it we are seen as protecting our turf."

Despite these cautions, Bill Pierce was determined to put a stop to surrogate motherhood. When he first arrived in Washington, D.C., over a decade earlier, he had carefully studied how public policy got made. In nineteen of the twenty issues he followed, the media played a pivotal role in getting legislation passed. To prevail his anti-surrogacy position, Bill Pierce would have to beat Noel in his use of the media.

Bill began dogging Noel's footsteps—he wrote rebuttals to favorable newspaper articles about surrogacy, debated Noel Keane on television shows and on university campuses, and presented a strong anti-surrogacy position in legislative hearings. More and more, reporters began to rely on Bill for a counterpoint to Noel.

Whenever a state legislature considered a bill to allow surrogacy, Bill could be counted on for a quote condemning "wombs for hire."

Bill tried to enlist other organizations in his challenge to surrogacy. He wrote to Concerned United Birthparents (CUB), the national organization of people who had given up children for adoption. In the past, CUB and the National Committee for Adoption had locked horns on a number of issues. The agencies that were members of Bill's organization were committed to making adoptions work and CUB was committed to deterring and overturning adoptions to allow children to remain with their biological parents. Yet Bill felt it would be to their mutual advantage to discourage surrogacy. But the woman leading CUB at the time would not take a position against surrogate motherhood. "Since I am personally oriented to women's choice," she wrote, "I am uncomfortable with telling women not to share their fertility."

Bill Pierce was bringing out the seamy side of surrogacy. Earlier media articles had glowingly referred to surrogate motherhood as "the gift of life," but in the wake of the Stiver/Malahoff case and Bill's efforts, journalists started to raise cautionary concerns about the practice.

The controversy surrounding surrogacy did not deter Carol Pavek's couple, Rhonda and Jerry, from wanting another child. By spring 1983, Rhonda and Jerry were trying to persuade Carol to have a second baby for them. Carol was ambivalent, although she knew that the money would help in the new clinic. Having had the home birth that she wanted, she no longer had a craving to be a surrogate. And this time around, there was an additional concern. Carol and Rick's son, Chris, now five, was asking for a baby brother of his own.

Rhonda, who had spoken to Chris a number of times, asked for him to be put on the phone.

"I'll come to Amarillo and I'll take you to the toy store and buy you anything you want, anything," Rhonda told Chris.

"Okay, she can have another baby," he said.

Carol reports on that visit. "They went to the toy store together. I stayed home, cringing with terror, because she quite literally would have bought him anything," explains Carol. "He picked out a $25 or $30 G.I. Joe airplane. There were things in the store that cost $400, $500, and $600 and my son only spent $30. Maybe I was a little disappointed, I don't know, but I was so proud that he didn't try to wring her for all she was worth. That airplane was his pride and joy."

In May 1983, Carol conceived again with Jerry's sperm. She spent the summer renovating a new clinic of her own. In September, Carol was on a scaffold, putting the finishing touches on the painting of the clinic. Her father walked in and realized that she was pregnant again. He just rolled his eyes and didn't say a word.

"My parents didn't say much about my being a surrogate," recalls Carol. "They never made negative comments or said, 'It's our grandbaby.' I have a feeling that if surrogate motherhood had been allowed twenty-eight years ago, they would have done it."

Carol remembers this third surrogate pregnancy as an awful time. Her mother was dying, so Carol was running to the hospital four or five times a day, working on the clinic renovations, and responding to her patients throughout the Texas panhandle for each false and true labor. Carol's own water broke two weeks early. Her doctor was out of town. But since she had suffered two major hemorrhages in the two weeks after the birth of Jerry's first baby, a partner of her doctor cajoled her into the hospital. He promised that she and the baby could leave after the birth, as soon as she could put her clothes on.

Rhonda was on an airplane en route to Amarillo this time when the baby was born. To Carol, the baby looked fine even though he was a wee bit premature. She and her partner midwives had delivered many babies like this, who were all still alive and well without ever having had to go to the hospital. But the delivery-room staff panicked. A nurse grabbed the baby off of Carol's stomach and took him to the neonatal intensive care unit. She came back and said, "Your baby's on a respirator. If you had had the baby at home, it would have died."

Carol got the readings on the baby's blood gases, got dressed, and left the hospital. At home, she began calling neonatal specialists around the country to ask whether a baby with those vital signs needed to be on a respirator. She was worried that unnecessarily treating the infant like a high-risk newborn would lead to lasting damage. She knew that children put on respirators were later more prone to allergies and respiratory disorders. Some became respirator-dependent and were still on a respirator at age three or four.

In the meantime, Rick had called Jerry to tell him that he was a father. Something in Rick's voice must have indicated there was a problem, because Jerry contacted Rhonda en route and said, "Something is wrong and I don't know what it is, but whatever it is stay calm. We are going to love the baby and accept it no matter what it is."

Rhonda was pale when Rick picked her up at the airport, but he assured her the baby was fine. The baby was on a respirator, but otherwise he was physically perfect.

Over the next few days, Carol and Rhonda were together at the ICU. Although technically only parents were allowed in to the unit, they had pleaded to the nurses, "We're both his mother." They stood silently, one on either side of the Isolette, each holding one of the baby's hands.

They were in constant touch with Dr. Robert Mendelsohn, a Chicago physician who had spoken out against unnecessary pediatric treatments. They gave him reports on the baby's blood tests, which indicated that the baby was healthy, with no signs of an infection. "This is a bunch of baloney," he concluded. "That baby shouldn't be on a respirator."

Carol and Rhonda desperately wanted to take the baby out of the hospital, but were concerned about the effects of abruptly taking him off the respirator, rather than slowly weaning him off. Three days after the birth, they went to the hospital and requested seven copies of the baby's records.

"What do you want that for?"

Carol named the seven people they were consulting—four notable physicians, Carol's attorney in Amarillo, and Rhonda's attorneys in New York and Florida.

The hospital began weaning the baby off the respirator, but refused to make plans for the baby's release. Carol and Rhonda worried about the damage to the baby that might be caused by each additional day in the ICU. Finally, they decided, "We've tried to reason with them, and it's not working, let's just steal the baby out of ICU."

Rhonda, Rick, and Carol set out for the hospital at midnight in two separate cars. The car Rhonda was driving had an extra blanket and a legal car seat for the baby. The baby was off the respirator by then. In her purse, Carol carried an alcohol swab and Band-Aid, so that she could take the intravenous needle out of the baby's arm.

The three of them scrubbed and checked in to the ICU and then said calmly, "We are taking the baby home tonight."

One nurse yelled to another, "Call security." Within moments, alarm bells were going off.

Carol took out the baby's IV, grabbed the naked little boy, and ran. She slipped into an empty room to dress the baby, listening as hospital carts and guards went past. When the noise died, she ran out the back door of the hospital.

Rhonda and Rick had not fared as well. Guards were detaining Rick. They had also caught Rhonda and were in the process of searching her car.

So there were Carol and the baby, stranded in the parking lot. It was an unseasonably cold December day for Amarillo, around forty-five degrees with a bitter wind blowing. Carol frantically looked for Rick's car, which he never locked, but of course he had locked it that night. So she did the only thing she could think of. She began trying car door handles for an open car, found one, and hid the baby behind the seat.

"People generally don't think they have any control over situations against large bureaucracies," explains Rick. "Here was a case where we were challenging a large bureaucracy to strike a blow for freedom. We had conviction. We knew we were right.

"It was some of the most exciting stuff I've ever done," says Rick about the baby snatching. "There was a tremendous amount of fear, apprehension, and just feeling, 'Oh shit, are we really doing this now?'"

Eventually Rick came out of the hospital and they drove the baby to a midwife, Carol's former partner, Lea Ann Gilley, who had been standing by. Lea Ann had oxygen on hand for the baby, but he didn't need it. Since the baby had only been fed intravenously, Carol used an eyedropper to see if he would tolerate feeding by mouth. The little one grabbed the eyedropper and sucked the whole thing down. He moved on to a bottle of breast milk, which Carol had been storing in the refrigerator for the past few days.

Carol was thrilled at the baby's vigor. She called Rhonda at the Sheraton and joked, "I've got your baby. How much ransom do you want to pay?"

Rhonda, not having seen the baby since his flight, was not in a joking mood. So Carol took the baby to the hotel, where the three of them spent an exhausted night.

By now, Carol and Rhonda were being sought as if they were fleeing felons. The police arrived at Carol's house and threatened to take Chris away. By morning, the Department of Human Services was in on the case, calling midwives, birthing centers, and other people and places that might be harboring the fugitives.

The department staff left the message for Carol that all they wanted to do was see the baby and verify that he was not dead. "I will never, ever believe a person from the government again," says Carol about what subsequently ensued.

Carol's first inclination was to have Rhonda get a plane home with the baby, but Rhonda was tired of running and hiding. So Carol took the baby to the Department of Human Services. Before even examining the baby, the woman from the department said, "We have to take it back, you have to surrender it."

Carol called her attorney, Betty Wheeler, who joined them in less than ten minutes with a stack of law books in tow.

"It says right here," Betty pointed out, "that unless the baby is in imminent danger, you can't rip it from the parents. You have to prove there is some harm, and there is no harm here."

So while one Human Services staff member left to get a court order to take the baby away, another offered a compromise. If Carol would have the baby examined by a physician, they would abide by what the physician said.

Lea Ann Gilley, the midwife who had examined the baby, had already spoken to the department. "I'm a midwife, but I am also a registered nurse and, take my word for it, the baby is fine," she said. Lea Ann took her work seriously. She hadn't been willing to accept Carol's word that the baby was in good health. Instead, she had performed a full physical, listening to the heart, listening to the lungs, examining the tiny limbs. But the word of a midwife was not good enough. The department wanted an examination by a physician.

Carol started phoning physicians all around Amarillo. They had all already heard of the case and refused to examine the child. They simply did not want to get involved. Her only option was to have him examined back at the hospital he had been liberated from.

Carol had no idea what the doctor would say. He was not personally involved in the case, yet the hospital's own position on the matter was clear. Betty was there, the child abuse and neglect statute in hand, as he looked over the child.

Finally, he reached his conclusion. "Well, he's obviously fine," the doctor reported.

The next day, Jerry flew down to meet his second son. They all attended the court hearing in which Carol relinquished her parental rights, and by the end of the week, the baby was at home in the Northeast.

Just as the birth of Carol's first child, Chris, had launched her into a study of midwifery, the circumstances surrounding the birth of this, her fourth child, also pointed her in a new direction. She read extensively in the medical literature about premature babies, made contacts with other people around the country who were doing work in this area, participated in candlelight vigils outside the local hospitals protesting the unnecessary use of respirators and neonatal ICUs, and even helped orchestrate a few other baby snatchings by parents.

Absolutely all the money she earned from the surrogate pregnancy went into the establishment of Carol's new midwifery clinic. The expenses were enormous; even though the house she had chosen for the clinic had perfectly good wiring, she had to have it totally redone—at a cost of $4,000—since the building code required a different type of wiring for a building put to commercial use. She also started a prenatal service as part of the clinic. She was particularly concerned about women who were in the gap between those poor enough to be eligible for indigent care and those wealthy enough to afford private physicians. Many such women were getting no prenatal care. She contacted all the pharmacies around Amarillo and persuaded them to donate urinalysis sticks and urine sample cups. With those simple tools, Carol and another ex-partner, Ann Houghtaling Wylie, were able to offer free prenatal care to otherwise unserved women.

Carol's midwifery practice flourished. While she had started out delivering one patient every two to three months, she was rapidly moving to ten a week. As more prize patients—middle-class women with low-risk pregnancies—came to her, physicians in town began to take notice. Some complained to the prosecutor's office that she was practicing medicine without a license by using physicianlike tactics during home deliveries.

The battle lines between the physicians and the midwives were drawn. Physicians began refusing to provide medical backup for patients of midwives. When babies delivered by midwives were taken to hospitals or to physicians for subsequent care, they were examined intensively with any deviation from normal being reported to the police or prosecutors.

These investigations seemed particularly mean-spirited in light of midwifery's overall safety record. A 1984 law review article pointed out that Texas was a state "where midwives attending normal births are completely unregulated with no adverse impact upon the quality of care women and their infants receive during labor and delivery."

"We had started getting really good publicity about the clinic," says Ann Wylie. "That publicity is what brought the doctors down on us."

Carol again found herself in the media and in the courtroom. This time she was not defending her personal decision to become a surrogate, but rather her professional decisions, such as whether to induce labor or not. A midwife colleague attending a home birth was actually charged with murder when a baby died. People supporting midwifery picketed the grand jury proceedings with babies and signs. They sent to the district attorney the obituaries of all the babies who had died in hospitals.

Prosecutors pressured Carol's patients to testify against her. In one case, Carol was charged with breaking a woman's water to induce labor.

"Did she break your water?" the prosecutor asked the woman on the stand.

Carol's patient looked the lawyer straight in the eye. "I was in hard labor," she said. "I don't know if she broke my water or not."

The prosecutor threw her papers up in the air. Carol's attorney asked for a directed verdict. The judge held that she was not guilty.

Carol tired of the legal melodrama. She couldn't stand the fact that the nightly news would show pictures of her or of the clinic, recite a litany of charges against her, but never report when she was acquitted. She was also tired of the harassment by police and prosecutors.

In April 1986, Carol took a trip to California to clear her mind. The midwifery prosecutions had daunted her, even though she could tally up the good things she had done—the many infants who would have died if not for her, the women she saved from forced Cesarean sections, the women who wouldn't have otherwise known about nutrition.

She was staying with a midwifery student in Carmel, and it was there that she began to contemplate her own pregnancy. After five years of pregnancies for other people, she and Rick again had the desire to bring a baby into their own family.

She thought a lot about being a mother, and being a midwife, on the long trip back to Texas. "The bus ran downhill and that's how I felt," says Carol.

But within a month of returning to Amarillo, her feelings were soaring. She was pregnant with her fifth child. And this one, like Chris, she was going to keep.

"Our desire for a child was so strong that we would not have another child as a surrogate until we fulfilled that desire," explains Carol, who views her surrogate experience as a joint activity with Rick. "It would be extremely difficult to want a baby and to give it away."

5

※

FOR LOVE AND MONEY

Wᴴɪʟᴇ ᴄᴀʀᴏʟ ᴘᴀᴠᴇᴋ was in Carmel, Lorrie Jones was heading for an interview in a modern ten-story office building in Beverly Hills. Lorrie was a superb secretary, typing upward of one hundred words a minute, but the job application she had mailed in did not ask a single question about her office skills. It focused instead on such personal matters as her past pregnancies and her relationship with her husband. It included a photo of her—a pretty, willowy blond smiling over at her two young sons. By filling out this five-page form, Lorrie had applied to be a surrogate mother.

As she rode the elevator to the seventh floor, a series of questions raced through Lorrie's mind. "Maybe I'm too short, maybe they'll think I'm too small. What if they don't like me? What if I'm too ugly?" she asked herself. She had heard that they turned down 80 percent of the surrogate applicants. She was certain that they were going to turn her down.

The suite of offices that made up the Center for Surrogate Parenting further intimidated her. They were uniquely elegant. Windows on three sides showcased the Hollywood Hills sign and the splendor of Beverly Hills. The receptionist's desk appeared to be carved out of a large gray and white block of granite, as did the massive desk and built-in bookshelves in the corner office occupied by attorney Bill Handel. A large russet marble conference table was complemented by gray leather chairs with russet piping. The flowers, the art, and the furniture in psychologist Hilary Hanafin's office were mixtures of beiges, apricots, and pale greens, matching the silk suits and blouses that she often wore.

What Lorrie was seeing, though, was a far cry from Bill Handel's roots as a surrogacy lawyer. Only three years before, his office was a tiny building in North Hollywood next to a doughnut shop and across the street from a deli. Its former owner had been a distributor of porno films. When Bill moved in, the bathroom had shag carpeting and tracks to run a camera for filming in the gargantuan walk-in shower.

When he first went into practice, Bill tried to make his work as much fun as possible. He hired a lawyer who had been his best friend since elementary school. He hired as a secretary a buddy from high school. He put a gumball machine in the waiting room. The jovial carryings-on reminded visitors more of the set of "Happy Days" than an environment where legal problems could be identified and solved. It was Bill's way of rebelling against being a lawyer.

"I had absolutely no desire to go to law school," says Bill. At age twenty-five, he had his own construction business. But his mother insisted that he go to law school "to have something to fall back on." He did not search out a law school that would best prepare him for a career as an attorney, but instead enrolled in the only institution that would admit a student the day before classes began. All through law school, he focused his attentions on construction. Instead of apprenticing at law firms during the summer, as most students do, he worked at his construction business. "I didn't know the address of the court," he admits.

His last year of law school, 1979, brought with it a national building recession. One of his projects was a house for an infertility specialist, Dr. William Karow. In the course of construction, Bill ran $250,000 over budget. That spring, he said to the doctor, "You could sue me for that amount, but I don't have any money. I am graduating from law school this week and would be willing to make this up to you by doing your legal work."

Astoundingly, Karow took him up on the offer. Three months

later, a couple approached Karow with a request that he insemi-nate another woman with the husband's sperm. "Soon I had a pregnant surrogate on my hands and I didn't know what to do with her," says Karow. "I knew this was apt to be of major signifi-cance and there were no specific laws on it."

Karow phoned Bill. "Bill, I want you to draw up a surrogate-mother contract," Karow said. "Do you know anything about these things?"

At that point, Bill was a struggling young lawyer, trying to get his practice off the ground. "Do they have the money to pay for this contract?" he asked.

"Sure they'll pay your fees, there's no problem."

"Then I'm an expert and I know everything there is to know," replied Bill.

Bill hung up the phone and went to the dictionary to look up the word *surrogate.*

Over the next few months, as he worked with the couple and the surrogate, Bill got drawn into the issue of surrogacy. He sympathized with Karow's patient, who had myriad infertility problems—fallopian tube problems, adhesions, fibroids. After her sixth unsuccessful surgery, Dr. Karow had told her that she couldn't have a child. She refused to take no for an answer. She and her husband ran an ad in the *Los Angeles Times* revealing their plight and asking if there were any women out there who would be willing to undergo artificial insemination with the husband's sperm.

Two years earlier, in a pediatrics law text, attorney Angela Holder had described surrogate motherhood and had suggested that "only a woman who was so poor that she had no other way to survive would deliberately rent her body for nine months of preg-nancy followed by labor and delivery." However, the woman who responded to the ad did not fit that description. She was artic-ulate, bright, and living in a stable, loving marriage. She was the middle-class mother of two. Bill enjoyed the time he spent talk-ing to her, and to the couple. Here finally was an area of law that interested him.

For Bill, there was nothing shocking about a woman having a baby for an infertile couple. Bill himself had no qualms about ask-ing people for help when he needed it. He was generous to a fault with people he barely knew—doing hundreds of hours of free legal work for a Jewish community leader, offering his spare bedroom to distant acquaintances who couldn't afford a hotel room, giving money to clients who were in a financial pinch.

Bill's parents had moved to the United States when he was five. They lived initially in a garage, sharing a bathroom with four other families. Perhaps it was that early experience of relying on people outside of his family to get by that had led Bill to say, "When I'm in need, I have no problem asking other people to help."

Bill is outgoing, informal, and unpretentious. He'd rather spend time with people than with law texts. In fact, one of the most noticeable things about the offices he has inhabited is the almost complete lack of papers and books. Unlike the crammed bookshelves and stacks of files and texts on the floor of a typical lawyer's office, Bill's shelves are virtually empty, except for mementos like the photo of him graduating from law school in his giant chef's cap, a large ceramic replica of a sperm with a slot in the front (a "sperm bank"), and several dozen photos of the children created through surrogacy arrangements. In Bill's office, the paper chase is barely a saunter.

Surrogacy appealed to Bill because it was a hands-on area of law, with a wide potential for Bill to provide comfort and camaraderie, not just legal counseling. As a novel area of law, it had the advantage of few legal precedents for him to familiarize himself with. Unlike, say, corporate or tax law, where there were thousands of confusing rules to follow, surrogacy had no hard-and-fast guidelines. In the vast majority of cases, surrogacy was nonadversarial. It was just one big happy family. Bill was on a first-name basis with his clients. He began to socialize with most of the couples and many of the surrogates.

Bill was hooked. He threw himself into the development of the surrogacy contract, working sixteen hours a day for seven months to develop a document that he felt covered every possible situation that could arise when a couple use a stranger to create their child. (The vast majority of the time was never billed to the clients, who were asked for $2,000 for his efforts.) He read the right-to-privacy cases, and studied the principles of contract law and constitutional law. He wrote an article on surrogacy for a legal publication. Within three years, he went from being a law student who attended classes when it didn't interfere with his other activities to a lawyer who was honored by the school as the Alumnus of the Year and asked to teach a seminar on reproductive technology. He so motivated students that a group joined together under his tutelage to draft a model surrogacy law that was introduced into the California legislature.

Bill was excited by the possibilities of mapping out new legal strategies in surrogacy and getting people to reconceive how they thought of the family. To Bill, the insemination of that first surrogate mother for Dr. Karow's patient was analogous to the 1957 launching of *Sputnik #1*. "At that point," says Bill, "5,000 years of common law had to be thrown out with the idea that we couldn't own space." An equally radical reconsideration of parenthood was now in order.

Across the country, in New York, Barbara Katz Rothman stood poised and ready to begin that reconsideration. "The new technology of reproduction offers us an opportunity to work on our definitions of parenthood, of motherhood, fatherhood, and childhood, to rethink and improve our relations with each other in families," she advocated. "Freed from some of the biological constraints, we could evolve better, more egalitarian ways of relating to ourselves and each other in reproduction."

"Earlier technologies *could* have revolutionized the family, but were incorporated instead into the existing family," she wrote in her 1982 book *In Labor: Women and Power in the Birthplace.* "Think of how formula might have changed women's and men's roles in child-rearing."

Barbara was following the developments in reproductive technology with great interest. She believed that the use of sperm donors, egg donors, and surrogates could expand, in a healthy way, the nuclear family. Barbara saw surrogacy as providing the basis for a revolutionary way to form families—"a reproductive communism, with each giving according to his or her ability." Rather than being paid providers of a genetic or gestational component of reproduction, donors or surrogates could become part of the family itself.

"We do not have to be 'donors' and 'hosts' and 'surrogates'— we can be mothers and fathers and aunts and uncles," she wrote in the July 1982 *Ms.* "We are coming to understand this with social parenting, that several people, including fathers and other men, can 'mother' a child. Perhaps we will learn the lesson for physical parenthood too."

To Barbara, surrogate motherhood raised the same issue as did the two competing views of childbirth: Would the surrogate and fetus be viewed as one entity or would they be viewed as separate and adversarial? In Barbara's view, the surrogate and fetus should be viewed as a unit and the surrogate should have a right after the birth to decide whether to keep the child.

Even if the surrogate gave the child up to the couple, Barbara could envision a new family structure in which the surrogate took an auntlike role. Under such an approach, the traditional nuclear family could be expanded to include continued involvement of the surrogate mother. Barbara's concern, though, was that surrogate motherhood would be co-opted by doctors and lawyers, with the creation of a child being viewed not as the evolution of a relationship of the birthing mother, but as the manufacturing of a product.

Bill Handel's desire to change parenthood through surrogacy ran along more traditional lines. The surrogate would create a child to be reared by a married couple, thus replicating the nuclear family. Once he realized how much he enjoyed surrogacy law, Bill was ready to take that message to the streets in an attempt to find clients. He approached a law professor who had a local radio show and spent a few hours one Sunday debating surrogacy on the air. Within a month, his story was picked up by the *Los Angeles Times,* then "60 Minutes," then the "Today" show.

The growing notoriety raised Bill Pierce's ire. The adoption specialist wrote to Dan Rather, complaining, "You've given a free commercial for 'surrogates.'. . . Your interviewer, valiant as he may be, wasn't playing hardball." Pierce criticized the "60 Minutes" segment interviewing Bill Handel for not emphasizing the alternative of traditional adoption and for not exposing the fallacies of the contract.

"The major tactic used by the surrogate promoters is a 'contract' which, by their own admission, is not enforceable," wrote Pierce. "It's therefore not a contract and is instead a legal trick meant to ensnare the unwary—surrogate mother and adoptive couple alike. It's also, as was clear from their hopes, meant to 'convince' the courts that a practice with the cosmetic covering of a contract is acceptable."

But word was out. Potential clients began calling Bill Handel from all over the country, all over the world.

Back in North Hollywood, however, Bill's practice lacked the administrative organization to deal with surrogacy on any sort of mass scale. He hired a psychologist to handle the screening aspects, but did not have any procedures in place to handle the recurring minutiae—setting up doctors' appointments, responding to inquiries, sending out expense checks to surrogates, following up with adoption officials once a birth took place.

The practice limped along for several years in this chaotic state, even as the office moved from North Hollywood to Beverly Hills. By the time Lorrie Jones applied to the program, Bill had finally admitted to himself that his administrative style was a disaster. He spent long hours gossiping with and reassuring clients and surrogates, little time assuring that the files were in order. When a talk show in London or Australia phoned, he was only too willing to let some administrative detail slip and hop on an airplane. He was well known, but he was actually making little money from surrogacy. He had to take in personal injury cases to cover his overhead. When a *Los Angeles Times* reporter suggested that he was in surrogacy just for the money, he pulled out his ledgers and showed her that he had $128.00 in his general account. Bill was a terrific promoter, a great facilitator, but he was no administrator. He finally broke down and hired Ralph Fagen.

Once Ralph was brought on board, things got done on time, weekly staff meetings were instituted in which the status of each of the seventy or more pending surrogacy arrangements was discussed, accountability was held across the board, and staff people were hired according to strict criteria of technical skills. Now every call that comes in from a couple or a potential surrogate is handled professionally and efficiently, with the answers recorded on special forms. The couples are asked about their ages, how long they have been married, whether they have children, and what their infertility history has been. The surrogates are asked questions about their motivations, their previous pregnancies, and their income level. Surrogates below a certain income are rejected at this initial stage of contact; the program does not want to be open to the charge that it is exploiting poor women.

There is concern about exploiting the couples as well. Bill's program is set up so that couples cannot sign up to contract with a surrogate at the initial consultation. "If they pull out a checkbook at that point, we say no," explains Bill. "It's just too much information at that point. They need time to sit back and think about it." In Noel Keane's program, in contrast, couples are told to bring an $11,000 cashier's check to the initial appointment.

Bill's surrogacy program is one of about two dozen around the country. In some programs, such as Harriet Blankfeld's Infertility Associates, Inc., in Chevy Chase, Maryland, the parties never meet—the surrogate carries a child for an anonymous biological father and his wife. In his Louisville, Kentucky, program, Richard Levin, too, discourages meetings between the surrogate and the couple. In other programs, the parties meet under the watchful eye of a psychologist or social worker.

Noel Keane takes a casual approach to the matching of parties. In his program, groups of couples and surrogates meet on Saturday mornings in his Dearborn, Michigan, office. The couples sit in various waiting rooms as a bevy of surrogates, one by one, pass through. With the awkwardness of a first date, the parties tally up each other's physical attributes (some surrogates refuse to gestate the child of a man who is too tall; a number of couples turned down a surrogate with a large nose) and ask each other personal questions. The surrogates search for couples who will provide decent homes for their children. "I don't want to have to worry for the next eighteen years about whether my child is being mistreated," says one surrogate. The couples labor to find a surrogate who will honor her word and give up the child. "I failed at becoming a mother through natural reproduction and through in vitro fertilization," says one infertile woman who sought a surrogate. "I do not want to fail again by having the surrogate keep the child."

In Bill's mind, programs in which the surrogate and couple do not meet do not make sense. "Inevitably and in the end, the program is really the surrogate and the couple," he explains. "It is a woman or a woman and her husband committing to a man and a woman to carry their child. That is such a fundamental commitment. Not meeting each other is almost like getting married without knowing who you're marrying. It doesn't make sense. It happens, there are arranged marriages in the world, but it doesn't make any sense."

The participants in the surrogacy arrangement do not have years of courtship to get to know each other. For that reason, Bill has also put great emphasis on the role of the psychologist. He or she narrows the field by initially screening the couple and the surrogate to determine what type of relationship each is looking for. Some surrogates want to be able to visit the child as he or she is growing up, for example; others do not.

"To be honest with you, I think that almost any lawyer can do this, almost any administrator can do this, but it takes a real special, magical kind of psychologist," says Bill. "People who say that a psychologist is not necessary are out of their minds. As a matter of fact, that's the only person that's completely indispensable. Anybody else can be replaced. In our program, if Hilary were to leave, I don't know what I would do. I wouldn't have a program."

Thirty-year-old Hilary Hanafin, Bill's polar opposite in terms of dignity and professionalism, is a most unlikely person to be involved in a controversial field such as surrogate parenting. The third of six children in an Irish Catholic family, Hilary grew up as the peacemaker, the caretaker. She hated confrontation and eschewed controversy, specifically avoiding a bioethics course in college out of a reluctance to debate divisive issues.

Hilary first heard of surrogate motherhood when she was a psychology graduate student with joint interests in research and clinical practice. She couldn't fathom how women could do this. Researchers in psychology had just gone through a decade-long study of mother/infant bonding.

"There were shelves of books like *The Maternal Instinct* and *Separation and Attachment*," says Hilary. But here came a group of women challenging traditional notions about how mothers relate to the children they bear. Hilary was intrigued by "a group of women who decided to challenge some of our societal notions— basically white Anglo-American notions—about motherhood, about what women are capable of, about the maternal attachment issue, and about what makes a family."

Hilary's interest was sufficiently keen that she sought permission from Bill Handel and his cooperating psychologist to study the surrogates in Bill's program. Hilary was fascinated by what motivated them to become surrogates, how they felt about their pregnancies, and how they coped with separation from the children.

On the one hand, Bill was reluctant to let an outsider have full access to all aspects of his program. On the other hand, he was curious himself about the motivations and personalities of the women who agreed to bear children for others.

The typical couple contacting Bill were thirty-eight to thirty-nine years old, had been married an average of seven years, and had dual careers. Their motivation—wanting a child—was easy to fathom. But what made surrogates tick?

At that point, Bill was receiving about fifteen letters a month from graduate students wanting to do studies at the center. The psychologist working with Bill talked to a number of them and decided that Hilary was the best.

Hilary ultimately studied eighty-nine surrogate mothers. She found that the average surrogate was twenty-eight years old, married, and the mother of two, had completed two years of community college, and had full-time employment. Most surrogate mothers were Christian, with 25 percent being Catholic.

The idea of reproductive choice was not new to these women—many used contraception and over one-third had undergone an abortion in the past. "The women saw surrogacy as expanding the definition of what women can be and feel and think and do," says Hilary.

"I don't think it's a coincidence that we have surrogate moms, abortion, and people choosing never to be parents in the same decade," continues Hilary. "I think what we're looking at is women saying it is not absolute that every woman has to have children and not every woman feels the same way about every child she has. I don't think that every woman could be a surrogate mom and feel good about it. But those who can are saying, 'Hey, listen up, women don't have to feel absolutely 100 percent attached to every child we carry. Our behavior, women's behavior, is much broader than we ever thought it was before. Don't define us only by our reproductive systems, define us by who we are and how we feel and what we think and give us, give women, a little flexibility here.'

"It is accepted that the desire to have children is variable in men, yet there seems to be a need to perceive the maternal instinct as a constant and as a given in women."

For her dissertation, "The Surrogate Mother: An Exploratory Study," and for follow-up research, she administered a battery of tests—the Minnesota Multiphasic Personality Inventory, Hansburg's Separation Anxiety Test, Mehrabian and Epstein's Emotional Empathy Scale, Snyder and Fromkin's Uniqueness Scale, and a Likert Scale Questionnaire that she herself had developed. But she also got to know the surrogates in less clinical ways. She talked to them. She attended their monthly support-group meetings. And she found that these women were nothing like what she had imagined. "They appeared to me to be the most lovely, healthy, functional group of women I had ever seen," she says.

Hilary had expected to find women who put little value on motherhood—what else could explain their willingness to get pregnant and then turn the child over to someone else? Instead, she found women for whom motherhood was a central focus of their lives. They couldn't imagine life without children and therefore felt sorry for infertile couples. And, since they viewed bringing a child into the world as a valuable activity, they saw pregnancy as a creative, important experience. Many confided to Hilary that they had been drawn to surrogacy because they wanted to be pregnant again.

The lure of pregnancy is difficult for many people to understand. The sensations and significance of pregnancy have not been highlighted in popular culture. Novels and plays do not seek to convey what it feels like to be with child. The academic world, too, has ignored the experience. There is little scholarship on the philosophy of pregnancy, the psychology of pregnancy, the sociology of pregnancy.

"The problem is illustrated by considering some of your own experience," says philosopher Caroline Whitbeck of the Massachusetts Institute of Technology. She asked a conference audience, "How many of you have seen films or read novels about men's experience in war? How many have seen or read at least four such works? How many of you have seen films and read novels that deal with women's experience in pregnancy and childbirth? (I do not count Lamaze and other childbirth training films any more than I count combat training films.) My contention is that of those people who have not borne children, more have identified imaginatively with Lassie than with a pregnant woman."

Pregnancy and childbirth can mean many things. They can be a source of comfort, an avenue of power. They can be a chance for spirituality, an affirmation of femaleness.

What is it like to be pregnant? Though each woman experiences pregnancy differently, they are all profoundly challenged, physically and psychologically. Some women approach it almost as a religious experience. They are creating life, giving a new individual a chance to live, changing the face of the earth by bringing forth the next generation. Other women see it as a test of strength and will, relishing the physical experience for the sense of skill and mastery it gives them, similar to competing in sports.

Pregnancy is a mirror that allows a woman to view herself in many new ways. It puts her slightly out of sync with her own body, forcing her attentions from the world outside to the world inside. She notices parts of her body that had been silent in the past.

At the same time that pregnancy is luxuriously narcissistic, it is also overwhelmingly other-directed and giving. Pregnancy demands a unique level of responsibility; it is rare among experiences in that only one person—the pregnant woman—can meet the needs of the developing fetus.

Pregnancy is a study in contrasts—debilitating yet exhilarating, narcissistic yet giving, unifying yet separate. When labor begins, new sensations occur. At the first stunning pain of contractions, the pregnant woman may want to call off the baby's debut. But then, she begins to triumph, she finds a way to cope. Hours go by with every contraction having its own unique feel, but she rides each one out and even as her body tires her confidence grows. Finally, it is time to push—the hardest, most gratifying part of the process. For one hour or two or five, she concentrates all of her energies on moving the baby down through the pelvis, out through the birth canal.

The actual moment of the baby's arrival passes much too quickly. After the nine-month prelude, the lengthy labor, and the superhuman pushing efforts, the slide of the baby from its world to our world seems to happen in an instant. In the concentration of pushing, the woman may not even notice that it has occurred, until the infant's wet, warm body is laid upon hers. She may want to push a pause button, replay it again in slow motion, and live over and over the moment when the baby she has been holding on the inside becomes the baby she is holding on the outside.

To the surrogate-mother applicants Hilary was interviewing, pregnancy and childbirth were rich enough experiences in their own right. They did not have to be followed by parenting—an entirely different set of experiences—to be worth reliving.

The desires to be pregnant again and to help a couple have a child motivated many of the surrogate applicants. About half of the women also thought that surrogacy would be a good way to earn money, but the money became less important as they became more closely involved with the couples and the program.

Listed starkly, such rationales for having a child sound strange. But are they any more strange than most people's reasons for conceiving children? For example, because they want someone to love, they're lonely, they want to hold their marriage together, they want an heir, they want to continue bearing children until they have a boy, or a girl, or because they feel parental or social pressures to have children? "Needless to say," observes Hilary, "people have children for all sorts of healthy and unhealthy reasons."

The personality tests Hilary conducted for her dissertation revealed two types of surrogates: empathetic, sensitive women who emphasized the importance of motherhood in their own lives, and active, independent women who adapted well to novel circumstances and to separation. The tests showed that none of the surrogates had a personality disorder or any psychological problem that might have led them to become a surrogate for pathological reasons. The surrogates also had a history of feeling confident in their decisions.

Most of the surrogates felt that their knowing and liking the couple would ease their separation from the child. One-quarter of the surrogates said they would feel sad about saying good-bye to the couple. About one-quarter of the surrogates had a special scenario planned for saying good-bye to the child. One had made a special quilt for the baby, while others had written letters. Some had a special farewell speech planned.

"The vast majority of surrogate mothers are not noticeably unique outside of the fact that they've chosen to be surrogates," concluded Hilary on the basis of their responses to the Snyder and Fromkin Uniqueness Scale. "One-third of the group are housewives. These women were able to expand their worlds without venturing much outside of the home or outside of their traditional role into new careers and new jobs. Being a surrogate mother simultaneously allowed them to be independent, adventuresome women who could make a contribution to society while maintaining a somewhat traditional role."

The women who have become surrogates have often been housewives or women in traditional occupations, such as nurses or teachers. They are mothers themselves and put a high value on having a family. Being a surrogate mother is a way of making what they feel is a dramatic contribution to the world, to alleviate a problem—childlessness—with which they can sympathize. And it's a contribution they can make while still remaining within the surroundings of their own family.

"I couldn't feed the hungry. I couldn't stop war, but by being a surrogate mother I could make a contribution to the world," Janine Dodson explained a week after giving birth to a surrogate child. Janine's life was not like a puzzle, with one piece missing; she did not seek out surrogacy to fill a hole. She already had a feeling of completeness. Her marriage was complete. Her family was complete. Instead, she wanted to share, to give, to leave her mark on the world. "I know I've done that with my children," says the twenty-seven-year-old, "but I wanted to do more."

For many surrogates, the accomplishment of bringing a child into the family of a childless couple gives them the confidence to make further changes in their own lives. Janine, a Chicana from a low-income California town, says, "I'm planning to go to college. I want to change the world in other ways. You haven't heard the last of me yet."

The reactions of these surrogates are common, says Hilary Hanafin. "There is a funny dynamic," she explains. "When you get a working woman in her thirties together with a pink-collar woman in her twenties, they help each other. And it's fascinating. We find the surrogate moms pursuing further education and making career advances after they are finished being a surrogate, while the infertile couple de-emphasizes career once they have a family. They sort of switch places."

Hilary was interested in how the relationship between the couple and the surrogate progressed over time. "Support is mutual," she says. "Surrogates support couples as well. I didn't suspect that when I started the study."

"Being a surrogate may not be a good idea for all women, but for some women being a surrogate may be a positive, functional way to do something very important, to feel good about it, and to reach personal goals that they have," says Hilary.

While working on her surrogate-mother dissertation, Hilary studied how other cultures handled the issue of infertility. "We are judging surrogacy by our culture, our definitions, and our biases," says Hilary. "There are other countries and there have been other times in our history where surrogate parenting was the natural solution to infertility. If a sister or a woman in the community was infertile, someone volunteered to be the surrogate. Sometimes this involved sexual intercourse with the husband, but more often it involved the volunteer conceiving with her own spouse and turning over the child to the infertile woman. That is a natural solution in a society where there is a shortage of babies. It occurs in Vietnam, in Greece, in some nations in Africa, and in some parts of Asia. It has only been since industrialization, about 1880, that our society began to think that all women must be moms and must attach to each child, that this was their primary role and it was bad if they did not fall in love with each child.

"In undertaking surrogacy, we may be going back to basics, not doing anything new."

To put the responses of the surrogates she interviewed into perspective, Hilary found an equal number of women who had become mothers in the normal fashion and gave similar psychological tests to them. She found that both groups had comparable views on motherhood. But the surrogates had experienced their past pregnancies more positively than women in general. They had felt prouder, prettier, happier, and healthier. In contrast, about half of the comparison group of nonsurrogates felt moody, anxious, self-conscious, and confused during pregnancy.

The surrogate group reported that in their current surrogate pregnancies, they felt even better. Since they did not have to worry about long-term commitments to the child and financial readjustments in rearing the child, they relaxed and enjoyed the pregnancy even more.

One of the surrogates Hilary interviewed for her dissertation was a thirty-four-year-old pediatric nurse from San Diego, Jan Sutton. Jan personified the trends that Hilary was finding in her research. Jan loved being pregnant. Her own children, Jeff and Kris, had been born when she was in her mid-twenties and now some of Jan's friends were getting pregnant for the first time. "I was jealous of them," she says. "I had felt good during my pregnancies. Very good. I was happy. I think it simply has to do with the fact that you know you're carrying life."

Jan was comfortable with being pregnant for someone else. She had known all her life that a woman did not need to be a biological mother to be a good mother. Jan's own parents had thought they were infertile and had adopted two children before having Jan. "Surrogacy is a way of saying thank you for giving my parents my brother and sister," says Jan.

Jan wasn't afraid of new experiences; she had always volunteered for experiments when she was getting her college degree at the University of Michigan. In pursuing surrogacy, she did not need the money. Besides her husband's income, she was making $42,000 a year as a pediatric intensive-care nurse.

Jan entered the program at the time Bill had his unorthodox office in North Hollywood. "I drove past it a few times," says Jan, "thinking, 'This can't be the right office.'" When she got the courage to go inside, she was not at all comforted. "What sort of sleazy thing am I getting myself into?" she wondered.

Before coming to the center, Jan had called other surrogacy programs. "I was a good consumer and did some investigation," she says. "I knew exactly what I wanted." Once she began talking to Bill and Arlene Westley, the program's psychologist at the time, she knew she was in a place where she could be comfortable.

"The program had strong supports and would allow me to

choose and have contact with the couple," explains Jan. "It would have been too nebulous for me to help a couple without knowing who they were."

But Jan did not want to participate in the program without the assent of her eight-year-old son and five-year-old daughter. After she had visited the center, she sat them down. "How would it be if I had a baby for another couple who can't have a baby?" she inquired.

"It sounds okay," replied Jeff. "How are you and the man going to do it?"

After hearing the explanation of artificial insemination, Jeff and Kris thought the arrangement was "neat." They talked proudly about it to their young friends—and were able to brush aside the occasional rude comment at school.

"How come your mother is giving her baby away?" a school-mate asked Jeff.

"It's not our baby, it's the couple's baby," Jeff replied.

Jan told Jeff and Kris that "someone gave Grandma and Grandpa two children to love and I'm doing that for someone else."

Although Bill's center encourages meetings between surro-gates and couples, the policy of the clinics that perform the artifi-cial insemination of the surrogates is to depersonalize the actual conception by trying to prevent the surrogate and the father from running into each other. But since Jan was ovulating on a week-end, there was a skeleton staff at the clinic.

"The dad ran into me at the elevator," recalls Jan. "He went in to give the specimen, while the mom and I sat chatting. Then I went in for the insemination."

During the pregnancy, Jan sent the couple Mother's Day and Father's Day cards from the baby.

"I never felt I was being put into the background during the pregnancy," says Jan. "They wanted to hear about every ache and pain."

Sometimes the wife would kid Jan, "I'm glad it's you and not me." But Jan would joke back, "I'll be saying that when you're up at night."

When Jan felt the baby move, she was eager to share that with the couple. They met at a Los Angeles restaurant and caused more than a little attention when Jan, the wife, and the husband were moving all six hands over Jan's belly, applying pressure here and there to try to get the baby to kick.

When the baby was born, the mother-to-be was in the delivery room with Jan, along with a friend of Jan's who was serving as a Lamaze coach. "Tears were streaming down the mother's face," recalls Jan. "I was paying so much attention to her joy that I didn't pay any attention to the birth." Jan immediately decided to be a surrogate again.

"The hardest part was saying good-bye to the parents, not to the baby," says Jan. "I went right back into the program as soon as I got my next period."

Elizabeth and John, the second couple to work with Jan, live in northern California. Elizabeth could not bear a child because her reproductive system had been damaged as a result of the DES her mother had taken—on doctor's orders—when she was pregnant with Elizabeth. John and Elizabeth considered undergoing IVF surrogacy, in which an embryo conceived with John's sperm and Elizabeth's egg would be implanted into a second woman, but decided against it. Since there had been no studies yet on how DES affected the third generation, Elizabeth painfully decided that it would be too risky to the child to pass on her genes.

Concern for the child also led the couple to rule out adoption. They felt that it would be better for the child to live in a home with a genetic link to at least one of the parents. And they were worried about any inherited psychological problems that the adopted child might have.

"If you accept that there may be a genetic component to psychiatric problems," says John, "and it is clearly becoming more and more evident in the literature that there is, [choosing an adopted child of unknown parentage] was a gamble that I really didn't want to take. If I was going to have a kid, I could have cared less about skin color, eye color, hair color. But I wanted to maximize having a normal kid from the psychological standpoint."

After ruling out IVF surrogacy and traditional adoption, there was but one place to turn. "That, by elimination, left surrogate motherhood," says John.

According to John, the baby boomers like himself and his wife are not willing to take no for an answer when it comes to having a child. "We're the generation that has discovered technology," he says. "We're the generation that has the biological knowledge to apply the scientific method in dealing with these issues. We're not willing to accept infertility without looking for a solution."

At Jan's fertile time, Elizabeth flew down with her husband's sperm sample in a lunch sack. She refused to put the bag through the airport x-ray machine.

"What's in it?" asked the guard, unfolding the edges of the bag.

"It's my future child," she said.

He refolded the edges and handed it back to her without a word.

In San Diego, Jan met her at the airport. "This is a little odd," Elizabeth said. "This is not how I pictured the creation of my child."

The couple had many relatives in the San Diego area near Jan's home. After the insemination, an aunt met Jan and the mother-to-be for lunch. The aunt asked only briefly about Jan; she spent most of her time telling Jan friendly and humorous stories about the family the baby would be born into.

Jan's family also met John and Elizabeth. "Jan's daughter was particularly interested," recounts Elizabeth. "She very clearly wanted to spend the day with us to know what kind of parents we would be. She considers herself a sister of the baby, which she is.

"My fear throughout the whole pregnancy was that we wouldn't be able to keep the baby," says Elizabeth. "It was an irrational fear, knowing Jan. But I could not imagine why anyone would really want to give up a baby."

John had his own dilemmas. "When we learned Jan was pregnant, the biological and emotional issues from my standpoint became very real," says John. "The actual nine months of pregnancy was the most difficult part of the whole thing. It was a bitch. The concept that someone you know on a handshake level is carrying what is going to be your kid was daunting."

John was intimidated by the prospect of "having to deal with the fact that you're going to be a parent from a purely emotional level, without getting the psychological warning of watching your wife's belly grow and all the other things that go with it. The only analogy I could think of is a sailor who goes out to sea and comes back to the biological child he fathered.

"All the support structures that are in place are for the adoptive mother," says John. "It would have helped if I had someone else to share experiences with. But there was nobody. If you have a root canal, you have three people telling you, 'Well, in my root canal they did this . . . .' If you get in a car accident other people say, 'Boy, when I had a car accident . . . .' Even when you go through a divorce, there are males in your circle of friends and you sit down, have a couple of drinks and cry on each others' shoulders.

"But here I had a woman down in San Diego carrying a kid for me, we were about to be parents, my wife was going into a nesting cycle," says John, "and I had no idea of how I was supposed to think or feel or act."

As a father-to-be, John was not sure how to relate to Jan. "Here was this very attractive, very intelligent woman that under vastly different circumstances would have been somebody I would have dated—and she was bearing my child," says John. "I had to detach from that. It's not that I wanted to have an affair or anything like that. I have a wonderful wife. I am happily married. I don't want anything mucking that up. It's just that way down in the older brain, where sex and reproduction are connected, we get into some pretty delicate territory. In the subconscious, it's all inter-twined. That's another reason why I think it would be helpful to talk to other men going through the same experience."

During the pregnancy, Jan turned thirty-five, the age at which physicians usually recommend amniocentesis. Jan had specifically asked to work with a couple who, like her, favored amniocentesis and abortion of a seriously disabled fetus. Because of her daily dealings with such children in the pediatric intensive-care unit, Jan decided, "It's not fair to the children to sentence them to such a difficult life."

The amniocentesis results came back in a gray zone. One of the samples suggested the child was completely normal. Another in-dicated that the child had an extra chromosome 17. Jan talked to doctors at her hospital and elsewhere. They said that every fetus with that anomaly had died before birth. An abortion did not seem appropriate since the child might be completely normal. But Jan went through the rest of the pregnancy wondering if, after all her efforts, she would miscarry.

Elizabeth and Jan spoke every week. Jan told her everything that was happening—from what she ate to what she did. "For me, it was as close to being pregnant as it could be," says Elizabeth, "particularly since Jan is very much like me. She looks like me physically. We have the same personality traits. We both know ourselves very well and are both nurses. She was like a representation of me.

"At the amniocentesis, when I could see the baby on the screen, it made the baby very real," continues Elizabeth. "It was after that point that I was finally able to go into a baby store and go shopping. I was comfortable that I would actually have a baby."

During the pregnancy, Jan put together a scrapbook for the child. It explained who she was and why she wanted to be a surrogate. It contained pictures of Jan, including some of her as a baby.

As the delivery neared, Elizabeth took a Lamaze course, so that she would be able to help Jan through childbirth. "It was very awkward," Elizabeth explains. "It was a small group and I was the only woman there who wasn't pregnant. But once I told everybody about my situation, they were really supportive."

John admits that there were times during the pregnancy when he felt that he had done the wrong thing. But he also adds that he thinks such a reaction is fairly normal for any individual who is radically changing his or her life.

"I felt that way before I got married, before I applied to grad school, before I made any life change," says John. "I don't think my feelings were different or unique, but I couldn't tell because I didn't have anyone to relate to. I'd look at my friends and think 'I'm not a daddy like you guys are. It's great you get to pat your wife on the stomach and get to bitch about morning sickness.' I don't have those as reference points. This is still an intellectual concept. There's a lot of hope and dream, but it's kind of like getting married. Even if you've lived together, you're not married until you're married."

John told Elizabeth he did not want to be in the delivery room. "It would be too painful for me," he explained. "Although I care about Jan and am thrilled about what she is doing, I would rather have the woman giving birth be you."

"There was a definite decrease in the tension in my relationship with Jan once she had given birth," says John. He gingerly held his daughter Anna within moments after her arrival. "When Anna grabbed my finger, that was a metaphysical experience." In that one touch, all the emotions that had been hovering over John during the pregnancy ignited an overwhelming bond.

After this second surrogacy birth, Jan felt satisfied. "I didn't want to do it again," says Jan. "If I had done it a third time, I would have felt I was more in it for the business." Out of the first fee, she took her family to Hawaii. She was adamantly against using any of her surrogate fees for bills; she clearly had not become a surrogate out of financial need.

Jan and her children had grown close to Elizabeth and John. Because they live in different parts of the state, they joked about taking a joint vacation, along with the baby, in order to spend some uninterrupted time together.

"Why not a camping trip?" suggested John. So, Mother's Day 1986 found a most unusual family together in Yosemite. The fifteen-month-old baby was the focus of attention of her father, her half-siblings and, of course, her two mothers.

This was only the second time that Jan had seen the infant since the hospital. Jan took a deep breath and moved toward the child. She was a round-faced, honey-colored blonde, closely resembling Jan's own daughter Kris. Jan smiled—and the little girl ignored her. Jan realized that she had no desire to take the baby home, nor did the baby show any desire to be with her.

6

⚘

CONCEPTIONS BY CONTRACT

IN 1984, when Bill Handel's psychologist left his program, he offered Hilary Hanafin the job. She agreed—on the condition that she be allowed to maintain a small private practice on the side in which she could counsel birth mothers in traditional adoption situations. She felt her work with surrogates would be benefited by understanding the similarities and differences between them and other birth mothers.

Since then, Hilary has interviewed all the applicant couples and potential surrogates who have come to the center. In the screening process, Hilary asks herself, "If I allow this woman to be a surrogate, am I colluding with some unhealthy, maybe even pathological need or am I supporting a very functional, healthy step in her life?"

Hilary turns down about 80 percent of potential surrogates, but she will also turn away couples—something that is almost unheard-of in other programs. She will not work with a couple who insist on amniocentesis or drug testing of the surrogate. She turns away couples if she feels that one spouse is pushing the other into the arrangement—if the husband is insisting that he will only raise a child of his genes or, alternatively, if the husband is comfortable with adopting, but the wife is so guilty about not being able to have his baby that she wants to make it up by finding another woman to have his child.

If the couple view surrogate mothers as mere vessels—anything less than incredible human beings—she will send them away. "Some couples want to pretend the child just came to them out of the blue," says Hilary. "They don't acknowledge that the surrogate will be a part of their lives for the next year, the next generation. I don't want to support that line of thinking."

She has turned people away who seem to be having a difficult time with their own relationships. Bill notes, "We have a bitch of a time with foreign clients in terms of relating. Hilary has sent people away to therapy simply because the man has treated his wife like a piece of chattel and she wasn't about to let him treat a surrogate like a piece of chattel."

Bill and Hilary make many joint decisions about the program, with Bill continually shooting from the hip and Hilary being primly analytical. "We have run-ins all the time," says Bill. "My tendency is to go forward, take cases, and she's the one that says, 'Hang on a second, Bill, maybe that's not such a good idea.' She's the conservative conscience of this program and slows us down where we need to be slowed down. On the other hand, I give a lot of impetus and energy to what we do. It's a good mix."

Ever so slowly, Bill and Hilary have begun to influence each other's professional personalities. Bill is becoming more cautious. When Hilary suggests turning away a client whom Bill wants to keep, he'll yell, "Hilary, you think clients drop out of the sky! You don't understand what happens out there. You don't just open your door and people rush in." Nevertheless, Bill almost invariably trusts Hilary's good sense on such matters.

And Hilary, having learned to defend her ideas over Bill's brashness, has become more comfortable with defending her ideas in the larger societal debate. "Part of me would love to crawl back into my clinical work and work with my surrogates and my infertile couples and the children and not be involved in the larger debate at all," she confesses. "This field has made me face controversy. It's forced me to be not a peacemaker, but a challenger, and that's real different for me, *real* different for me."

Bill limits participation in the program to married couples. "I was called by a single, gay doctor who wanted a child," says Bill. "He had been in a relationship for the past five years and was the most stable, together, warm human being I've ever met in my entire life. But I wouldn't let him enroll in the program.

"It's not a moral decision we make," continues Bill. "It's a policy decision. Morally I'm in full favor of anyone who wants children having them. But we are now trying to get legislation passed that allows surrogacy, so we cannot let it look bizarre or unusual."

In matching particular couples and surrogates, Hilary searches for the right chemistry. She brings together people who have similar expectations about the relationship, similar values, similar priorities. Whether a couple is outgoing or shy, warm and affectionate or analytical and businesslike, close to or distant from their feelings, she wants to find for them a surrogate with a similar style. It often takes months to find out enough about both sides to suggest a match. She grills them about how they develop solutions in crisis situations, what they think about aborting the fetus during the pregnancy, how they would handle the child wanting to make contact with the surrogate.

At their initial consultation, which costs $400, the couples spend an hour and a half with Bill and up to three hours with Hilary. They also watch a videotape which explains the contract in detail. Bill's part consists of an explanation of parental rights in IVF surrogacy (in which the couple's embryo is used) and regular surrogacy (in which the husband's sperm and the surrogate's egg are used).

"I used to take a long time explaining the legal aspects of IVF surrogacy," Bill tells the couple, "but now it takes about five seconds. Are you ready for the explanation? Here it goes."

He looks the husband in the eye. "You're dad," he says.

Turning to the wife, "You're mom.

"There," continues Bill, "wasn't that worth $400?"

Bill, whose program had its first IVF surrogacy birth in July 1987, tells the couple how he went to court and was able to obtain a ruling in advance of the birth that the genetic parents were the legal parents. "It's just one court and it didn't go up on appeal," he cautions. "But we feel pretty safe."

Bill then goes on to explain the high failure rate of IVF surrogacy and how its application is limited to situations in which the wife produces an egg, but cannot carry a pregnancy. He encourages couples to consider regular surrogacy even in those latter situations. "Surrogacy works," he says. "You take home a baby. There's no such guarantee with IVF surrogacy."

Bill also explains to the couple how, once the surrogate is pregnant, they must put the full payment in an escrow account. "That money will be hers no matter what you decide to do," he warns. "If you divorce, die, or move to Pakistan and adopt eleven adorable Pakistani kids to make your own baseball team, the money is still hers."

At such a session, Sandra and Hillel responded to Bill's hard sell for regular surrogacy. He was quick to point out to them, as he does to all couples, that the consultation fee was not just for that day's session, but covered any questions that they might have for him and Hilary in the future. Often couples ask Hilary to meet them in the less intimidating surroundings of their home for another discussion of whether surrogacy is right for them; there is no additional fee charged for the session. Sandra and Hillel thought it over for two months and then asked to be considered for participation in the program.

The nearly $30,000 that the process would cost was a lot of money for them. They could have tried to do it less expensively by advertising for a surrogate on their own or by asking a friend or relative to bear the baby, but they wanted the psychological screening and other safeguards that the center seemed to offer. "I'm not in a market," Sandra said. "This is serious. I want everything to go smoothly."

Sandra and Hillel had been in the program for a year when Lorrie Jones first came to see Hilary. Sandra was a shy woman, but when she relaxed she had a warm sense of humor. Hilary had noticed a similar trait in Lorrie.

Surrogate applicants undergo a two-hour interview and follow-up phone calls with Hilary. Lorrie passed the initial screening requirements that "a surrogate mother already have children, a financially stable situation, the full support of her family, a good pregnancy health history and good self-esteem. She also must be between the ages of twenty-four and thirty-five and be bright enough to handle a complex forty-page legal contract and sophisticated psychological dynamics."

Hilary looks for signs that a surrogate is responsible. "If the applicant is a half-hour late for an appointment, tells me she is using the rhythm method of birth control, and does not have auto and health insurance, I question whether she is responsible enough to be a surrogate," says Hilary. "Her lack of planning might indicate a belief that bad things don't happen to her. She may not be prepared for the risks involved in being a surrogate."

Unlike Noel Keane's surrogates, who are scattered around the country, most of Hilary's surrogates are within driving distance of the program. Every month they meet for group counseling. In the process, a sense of community develops among the surrogates. They phone each other and Hilary between meetings to puzzle out developments in their relationships with their children, spouses, employers, relatives—and the couple—as their pregnancies progress. Before being accepted into the program, a potential surrogate is required to attend two of these support groups.

Hilary's first sessions with Lorrie focused on analyzing what motivated Lorrie to become a surrogate, whether Lorrie would be a good surrogate, and whether surrogacy would be beneficial to Lorrie. Lorrie was typical in having a friend whose life was marred by infertility. "She tried for five years and then her husband divorced her because she couldn't have kids," explained Lorrie. "He said the main reason he got married was to have kids and if she couldn't have them, he might as well be messing with the world."

When Lorrie had been pregnant with her second child, her friend barely talked to her for the nine months. "She treated me very badly," Lorrie told Hilary. "She apologized for it later, but I understood. I understood. So I know about the pain from this friend."

Among Hilary's concerns were the effects on Lorrie's two children, of their mother being a surrogate. She explored with Lorrie the extent to which they would be involved in the procedure. "I'm adamant about not keeping your other children in the dark," Hilary told Lorrie. "I've had women apply and tell me that they are going to keep the whole process a secret from their four-year-olds. But children at two and three years old know that mommy has a baby inside. And that's one of the reasons I'm very supportive of having an open relationship with the couple—so the children can be in touch with, meet, check out the couple. Because otherwise they don't have any visual or tactile or other evidence to help them understand how the baby got there or where it went."

Some surrogates put a picture of the couple up on the refrigerator door at home. "Everybody knows that's Mary and her tummy's broken and so we're going to carry a baby for Mary," says Hilary. "And they meet Mary and talk to Mary and have that information up front if they're over two years old.

"We have one couple who is very cognizant of the fact that the surrogate had an 11-year-old who was very interested in how the baby was doing," she continues. "So that 11-year-old gets his own separate set of pictures and letters from the adoptive couple on a regular basis so that he can keep posted on the child's development. I certainly think that is more healthy than pretending that if the kids don't get involved they won't have any feelings about it."

Hilary admits that her—and Bill's—feelings about involving the surrogate's children in the program have changed radically in the past five years. They used to fear that if the surrogate's own children saw the new baby, they would bond to it and be upset about the relinquishment—much as adoption authorities used to suggest whisking the baby away before the biological mother could see him so that she wouldn't become attached. Now Hilary encourages both the surrogate and her children to spend time with the baby in the hospital and have at least some contact afterward, whether by mail or in person.

"There are people who run surrogate mother programs who aren't mental health professionals who would like to think that once the baby's home with the couple and the surrogate says everything is okay, then no one thinks about it anymore or really considers that there is an important relationship," says Hilary. "I'm of the school that we have to deal with this very cautiously, but that if we all pretend what happened didn't happen, we may be creating rather than avoiding psychological scarring."

Consequently, Hilary is not afraid to ask tough questions of the surrogate long after the birth, such as "Are you missing the child?" Naturally, this line of inquiry makes Bill Handel very nervous.

Lorrie was surprised by the probing questions Hilary raised in the initial interview. "Hilary really tries to talk you out of it," she says. "I mean she sat there and said, it's going to ruin your marriage, it's going to wreak havoc in your life and you could die by complications. She really laid it on the table and really gave you something to think about. And I think if you had any qualms whatsoever, her talk would probably make you change your mind."

Not that Lorrie totally approved of everything Hilary did over the course of the program. "When you come to her with a problem, she'll help you work it out, but she plays the devil's advocate too well," says Lorrie. "She worries about everybody under the sun. When you approach her with something, she's got to sit down and think about it, who it's going to affect. 'Well, gee,' she'll say, 'I don't know about that. What would your son's grandchildren think about it if you were to do that?' Who the hell cares about what my son's grandchildren are going to think!"

After meeting with Hilary, Lorrie was introduced to the balding, heavyset Bill. She vividly remembers this first encounter, in which he explained how the surrogate, couple, psychologist, and physician were a team when things were going smoothly, but how he would make her life miserable if she decided to keep the baby.

"If I changed my mind," recounts Lorrie, "Bill said he would drag me through the courts, sue me, and take everything I had. He said he would buy me a dog and let my kids fall in love with the dog and then he would kill the dog."

Ralph constantly campaigns to get Bill to act in a more dignified manner, but Bill loves to shock. When the person in the next seat on a flight is reading the *Wall Street Journal,* Bill will pull out a tabloid with headlines like "Chimp Pregnant with Human Baby" and "Heroic Mom Gives Herself Cesarean with Can Opener." But part of Bill's success in surrogacy comes from the fact that he isn't a stodgy or pretentious lawyer, but a regular guy to whom surrogates can relate. Although Ralph has been successful in getting Bill to tone down some of the statements he makes to the press, Bill is reluctant to tamper with the blunt, tough, sometimes outrageous way he talks to surrogates and potential clients.

Bill tells surrogates and couples that the contracts he drafts do not have the force of law behind them. "I don't have contract law on my side in the sense that if any other legal contract were breached, you could always sue for breach of contract," says Bill. "I don't have the assurance that I could win a custody battle because a court, using a best-interests analysis, could simply decide that a mother could take better care of an infant than a father. It's a real possibility in this day and age. Parental rights are supposed to be equal—but they're not."

Because Bill is concerned that the contract will not be enforced against the surrogate, he has created separate legal grounds—the intentional infliction of emotional distress—upon which to sue the surrogate. Such a suit will not get the child back, but, by threatening to plunge the surrogate into financial ruin, could make it less likely for the surrogate to try to keep the child.

Bill tells each surrogate, "The only protection we have is my ability to sue you for destroying two human beings by taking their child. And what you do is allow yourself in this document to be sued for exactly that." The surrogate signs a statement that says she understands that the baby is the couple's child and that she is their last resort for a child, and that she and her husband understand that if she tries to keep the child, they will have intentionally inflicted emotional distress on the couple.

"If you change your mind, I will nail you to the wall," warns Bill. "I will sue you outside of the contract for destroying two human beings in a lawsuit that will probably garnish millions of dollars in judgments and is not dischargeable in bankruptcy. I will follow you the rest of your lives. You will not have a job, car, or house that I will not go after. It will be the most expensive child you've ever decided to keep.

"What I would tell the jury is that the issue here is not who is mother to the child, nor who is a better parent, nor what you think of surrogate parenting. It doesn't matter what you think of surrogate parenting," says Bill. "The only issue is that the surrogate entered into a relationship where she knew that if she followed a certain course of action, she would totally destroy two human beings. If I came into your home and took away one of your kids and you couldn't do a damn thing about it, how would you feel? Because that's what happened to this couple. Unfortunately, all you can give us is a monetary judgment, you can't return the child to their home, but you can tell us what this hurt means in monetary terms."

Bill is criticized for these strong-arm tactics, which take place at the time that a surrogate is making her initial decision about whether or not to enter the program. "Believe me, I get a tremendous amount of flak for that," says Bill. "But I think it's the most honest thing you can tell a surrogate. I think it protects everybody. I'm surprised no other program does it.

"I look at the surrogates and threaten them, saying that if they destroy one of our couples, I'm going to nail them," says Bill. "I would and they all realize that. But that's been accepted before any contract is signed. Our ground rules are established and there's nothing that stops us from becoming friends." And they do; surrogates speak with a genuine fondness for Bill.

Elizabeth and John, the couple who worked with Jan Sutton, had called several surrogacy agencies around the country before deciding to sign up with the center. They were impressed that Bill was active in drawing up surrogacy legislation but, most importantly, says Elizabeth, "I knew Bill would be a real fighter if anything went wrong."

When the couple and surrogate have separately navigated the initial psychological screening and understand the legal ramifications of what they are doing, they are ready to meet each other. Hilary presides at all the initial meetings of surrogates and couples "to see what is being said, how they're working together, and whether any surprises are coming up." She introduced Lorrie Jones to Sandra and Hillel at a restaurant. Hilary knew that Lorrie's relatives had mixed feelings about the surrogacy arrangement and that Lorrie's husband Casey would be away for much of the pregnancy, pursuing a new job. She had specifically chosen this couple because of the support she thought they could provide for Lorrie.

Sandra and Hillel described how they had tried every treatment, including in vitro fertilization and egg donation, for their infertility. "I felt so sorry for them," said Lorrie. "How many years they'd tried for something that had come so easy for me. All I could think was *don't let them down.*"

All surrogates have at least some idea of the type of home they want the child to go to. However small or large the emotional bond they feel for the child, they want to make sure that he or she is parented well.

Every parent makes changes and concessions in their lives to accommodate what they perceive as the needs of their children. Some potential surrogates need to know that the couple will be making the same trade-offs they would make (for example, giving up outside employment during the child's early years). Because Sandra and Hillel would be living part of each year in the United States and the rest in the Middle East, though, Lorrie talked to them at length about the potential dangers in that war-torn area and got their assurance that once the child was born, they would travel on separate planes to avoid the possibility that they might both be killed in an act of terrorism.

Lorrie wanted to work with a couple in which the wife was heavily involved in the pregnancy, which was precisely what Sandra wanted. "I wanted her to bond with the baby," says Lorrie.

Sandra and Hillel decided immediately that they would work with Lorrie. But Sandra couldn't help but feel somewhat jealous. She was angry that her husband had jumped so quickly into wanting Lorrie to have a baby with him. "I felt pissed off," says Sandra. "But I realized that I wasn't really angry at her or him, but at the fact that I couldn't have a baby myself. Recognizing that, I realized my reaction was pretty normal."

While the psychological portion of the program was well conceived to protect the surrogates and the couples, other aspects of the program fell short. The surrogate received $300 to obtain legal advice from an attorney of her choice, or from one of four attorneys that Bill recommended. Lorrie chose one of the recommended attorneys. According to Lorrie, he did not view himself as an advocate for the surrogates—he would not represent one if she changed her mind and wanted to keep the child. He spent his time explaining what her legal responsibilities were under the contract. He certainly did not actively negotiate each clause of the contract, as in most business deals, with changes to benefit his "client."

Surrogates in other programs encountered the same problems. "The program provided $200 or $300 for me to consult an attorney to advise me about the contract," said Kyle, a surrogate in Harriet Blankfeld's program in Maryland. "But it was a 30-some page contract and no one would touch it for that amount. I finally ended up having to go to a lawyer recommended by the program. He told me that as a surrogate, I had no rights."

Nor were the procedures particularly protective of the couple. Once Lorrie was matched with the couple, the doctor examining Lorrie diagnosed an infection and prescribed a ten-day course of antibiotics before she should attempt to get pregnant. "It was a vile medicine," says Lorrie. "I called Bill and I said, 'I will drop out of the program before I take another pill. I've taken them for three days and I'm in the middle of the month right now.' And so they went ahead and inseminated me and I got pregnant."

As the pregnancy progressed, Sandra joined Lorrie at every doctor's appointment, every ultrasound. They grew close, breaking outside the normal shell of their private lives. They talked about sex, filling out a women's magazine quiz on the subject.

"I never doubted that Lorrie was going to give us the child," says Sandra. "It was like I was pregnant. I had dreams about the child, and about whether it would be okay, similar to the dreams of pregnant women." But Lorrie didn't have these traditional dreams: she dreamed that no one would come for the child.

"What do you want the baby influenced with?" Lorrie asked Sandra one day. When she had been pregnant with her second child, Lorrie had listened to John Cougar through her headphones. For this baby, she followed Sandra's wishes and listened to classical music. "But every once in a while," she grinned, "I mixed in a little John Cougar."

Lorrie talked to the fetus as well. "You're a lucky baby," she said. "You're going to have two great parents. Plus I love you and I always will."

She didn't think of her conversation as mother to son, but felt like she was talking to someone else's baby. "I felt like I was carrying the baby for them."

Lorrie's reaction is typical for surrogates, says Hilary, and contrasts greatly with that of traditional birth mothers in the adoption situation. Hilary sees up to five birth mothers a week in her private practice and points out the dramatic differences.

"With birth mothers, they're already pregnant, there's no turning back," says Hilary. "Most birth mothers certainly consider, plan, and evaluate whether or not they should relinquish or keep the child. A surrogate mother generally doesn't entertain those thoughts because she would not have volunteered to be a surrogate if she had wanted a child of her own.

"When I work with birth moms, what we are really dealing with is the depths of their pain and how to cope with an incredible loss in their lives," Hilary explains. "When I am working with a surrogate mom, that's not what we're talking about. We're talking about what being a surrogate means to her, why it's important for her to be a surrogate and what self-growth she has accomplished by virtue of being a surrogate.

"Birth mothers are in a crisis in their lives and are trying to make the best out of a crisis situation," observes Hilary. "And during that crisis much of their thoughts and feelings about their past and themselves and their future are surfacing and coming out. The birth mother is reevaluating her life, her relationships, what she wants for herself. With a surrogate mother, you're dealing with a woman who is at a stable time in her life, who is content, self-satisfied and is not in any way, best as we can assess, being forced into a crisis situation.

"So in one sense, you're seeing a woman voluntarily, intelligently, after much consideration choosing to do something that she very much wants to do," summarizes Hilary. "And on the other side, you're seeing a woman who had unconsciously or accidentally found herself thrown into a crisis, a painful situation. These women talk about the child that they are carrying very differently, their degree of attachment, their fantasies, their fears and their concerns.

"The birth mothers in the traditional adoption situation are much more apt to have an attachment to the child and to be very worried about who the parents are going to be. The birth mother is selecting a couple to raise a baby that she may desperately want to keep, but she's sixteen years old or twenty-two years old, can't afford to raise a child, and the father's taken off.

"The surrogate mom sets out to deliberately create a child for another couple. She too is concerned about who the parents will be, but her feeling about how to select them tends to be different. A surrogate mother is often looking for a couple she will enjoy working with, be able to relate to and have a positive experience with. *And* be good, loving parents. She is not looking for someone to raise *her* baby. That's a very different perception." The surrogate-couple relationship in some ways is like a marriage; even though people marry, in part, to have a child, they generally don't pick a spouse exclusively because of the person's child-rearing potential.

While Lorrie was in her fourth month of pregnancy, the media first broke the story of Mary Beth Whitehead. In one woman, the emotions of a surrogate and the emotions of the traditional birth mother came together. Lorrie first heard about it at one of her surrogate group's monthly meetings.

Lorrie could empathize with Mary Beth's position. "If I were to take a baby home from the hospital for a while, you'd have to come with guns to take it away," she said. Nonetheless, she felt that Mary Beth should give the baby up.

"If she really cared about that baby, the best thing for that baby would be to let it go," said Lorrie. "I love this baby with all my heart and because I do, if I had any inkling of wanting to keep it, I would think about what such an action would do to the baby. It's not fair to the baby. Mary Beth should just get out of her life. I think the baby would probably respect her a lot more, probably thank her in eighteen years for allowing her to have a normal life."

Hilary recounts the reactions of the other surrogates in Lorrie's group: "Their first reaction was immense sympathy. But many felt that if Mary Beth had made a mistake, that she was a consenting adult who must deal with the error and not make everyone else pay for it.

"When Mary Beth came out and said all surrogate parenting should be banned," continues Hilary, "she lost the surrogates' sympathy and support. Because they felt that was a direct intrusion on their rights and their experiences. They began to blame her and become very hostile toward her."

Carol Pavek, too, reacted angrily to Mary Beth's comments about surrogacy. She was particularly critical of the implication that hormonal changes during pregnancy gave a surrogate a right to renege on the contract. "A contract is a contract," says Carol. "It's dangerous to say that we are ruled by our hormones, rather than our brains. You don't have a right to damage other people's lives because of your hormones. That would be like a man saying, 'I had a right to rape that woman because I had such a high testosterone level that I couldn't help myself.'"

Legitimating the surrogate's right to change her mind, says

Carol, "creates the same bubble-headed view of women that was used to deny women the right to vote."

Carol is equally suspicious about the argument that Mary Beth had been coerced into being a surrogate. "I'm smart, I'm educated, I did what I did, I certainly was not coerced into it," says Carol. "I can't imagine coercing anyone into it. I'm certainly not there for every conversation that Mr. Keane has with his potential surrogates, but from just the little contact I've had with him, I cannot imagine that happening. You know she had to have written, or called, or showed up at the office in the first place. He is not going out on the streets to find surrogates.

"Surrogates are not coerced. Nobody forces their legs apart for them to be inseminated.

"It's not that we're saying it's good for everyone to be a surrogate," Carol explained. "Those women who are saying it's bad, well, it is bad for them." But Carol sends this message to Mary Beth: "Please don't plead my case."

At the meetings of surrogates at the Center for Surrogate Parenting, conversation inevitably turns at some point to Mary Beth Whitehead.

"Mary Beth's situation has come up at every group meeting since the media first covered her change of heart," observes Hilary. "I try to neutralize the hostility and elicit empathy."

These surrogates' withdrawal of support for Mary Beth came at a time when there was growing support for her in society at large. Hilary attributes that outside support to people's innermost wishes about their relationships with their own mothers, as well as people's concerns about whether they themselves are being adequate parents.

"I think surrogate parenting, let alone Mary Beth giving up a baby and changing her mind, really is a direct threat to each individual's notion about their own relationship with their mother," explains Hilary. "We all want to feel that our moms would fight for us to the death and our moms would never give us up and our moms would love us no matter what we do and our moms are perfect people. Surrogate parenting is a very threatening concept in the sense that it questions whether or not a mother's attachment to her child is absolute. If some women don't form a strong bond with the children they carry then maybe our moms felt ambivalent about us too. And I think it hits us at a real personal, emotional, very primitive—and I think that's probably the best word for it—a really primitive level.

"Surrogate parenting and Mary Beth really threw people into a tizzy because it hit us head on," observes Hilary. "Those who are afraid that the nuclear family in America is disintegrating were appalled, those who have strong fears of abandonment in their own psyches were threatened. Women who were insecure about their own ambivalence toward their children had what is called a reaction formation: It was fear that they were not properly attached to their own children that made them feel protective toward Mary Beth. It hit us at a whole lot of levels.

"The role of the mother in society has served a lot of different purposes, depending on the culture, the time, and the religion. What's important here is that the role of mother in our society has been reevaluated for the last twenty years and surrogate motherhood provided a head-on confrontation of that issue."

The Baby M case brought the discussion of surrogacy into the mainstream. At a mock government weekend for high school students, one of the bills for discussion was a surrogate mother bill. Fourteen-year-old Rick Morales was a particular expert in the area. His mother had served as a surrogate two years earlier and was thinking about doing it again. "At first I thought it was a little weird and then I learned more about it and I liked it," he said. "The couple were really nice people and it was fun to see the baby when it was born. Surrogacy is okay and people shouldn't be putting down on it when it helps couples who can't have kids."

The news of the conflict between the Whiteheads and the Sterns, so prominent on the television, reached Lorrie's young boys. They were able to discern that the lady, like their mom, was having a baby for a mommy whose tummy was broken. Surrogacy was a concept that they completely accepted. When they were at the supermarket and someone remarked on Lorrie's pregnancy, her five-year-old was quick to point out, "Oh, we're not keeping this one."

7

※

REGULATING REPRODUCTION

THE WALL STREET AREA of New York lacks the color of
other parts of Manhattan. It is not a Times Square, a Fifth Avenue,
a Village, a Chinatown. Visitors are not greeted by a colorful eth-
nic variety of faces, costumes, smells, and sounds. The people
around Wall Street are not street people. They do not linger.
They walk purposefully into solemn-looking buildings that
house powerful investment brokerages, multinational banks,
massive law firms, extensive courts—mammoth institutions that
invisibly shape the lives of millions of people.

Wall Street seems an unlikely stopping point for a first-time
visitor to New York, a young woman with less than twenty-four
hours to spend in this urban cornucopia. A young woman whose
only other destination, after a brief television interview, was
Macy's, to buy souvenir sweatshirts for her two children. But
Lorrie Jones was curious to see what was happening at 14 Vesey
Street, where the New York Legislature was holding hearings on
surrogate motherhood.

The hearing room echoed the formality of the surrounding streets,
dominated by a raised dais where seven New York legislators—six
men and one woman—and their counsel were seated.

The one woman was New York Senator Mary Goodhue. Her involvement in surrogate motherhood had begun two months earlier, in August 1986, when Senate Majority Leader John Dunne roused her at her vacation house, interrupting her plans for a visit by her grandchildren. He had just heard from a judge on Long Island. Judge C. Raymond Radigan described a most unusual case. A couple had come to him wanting to adopt a child conceived with the husband's sperm and born to a surrogate mother. The stand-in mom had no objection. "The adoption laws just don't fit the situation," Radigan explained to Dunne. "Why should a man have to adopt his own child?"

Radigan, who had presided over twenty-five hundred adoption proceedings in his career, gave judicial approval to the arrangement. His published court opinion pointed out how the availability of contraception and abortion had reduced "the number of available children for adoption by loving and wanting parents." Science had responded with developments like in vitro fertilization and surrogate motherhood, to allow the conception of children with a biological bond to one or both members of the couple.

Although Radigan's opinion expressed his personal discomfort with surrogacy, he saw nothing legally amiss with the arrangement. Following a decision made earlier in 1986 by the Kentucky Supreme Court, he held that existing laws prohibiting baby selling were not meant to ban payment to a surrogate mother.

He acknowledged fundamental differences between surrogacy and traditional adoption. In surrogacy, the agreement to bear the child is entered into before conception. In surrogacy, the child will be reared, not by a stranger, but by its biological father. "The process is not biologically different from the reverse situation where the husband is infertile and the wife conceives by artificial insemination," wrote Radigan, echoing the Kentucky Supreme Court.

After rendering his opinion, Radigan called Dunne, the chair of the Senate Judiciary Committee, seeking legislation to guide judges handling surrogate mother cases. "My personal beliefs are not important," he said. "What is important is that the judiciary is in need of some guidelines."

When an adoption takes place, explained Radigan, it is as if the judge "transfused into the adoptive child the blood of the adoptive parents." The question raised by surrogacy was whether that imaginary transfusion should take place at the moment of conception, with no need for an adoption to take place after the child was born.

John Dunne immediately called Mary Goodhue, a four-term Republican state senator and the head of the senate's Standing Committee on Child Care, which dealt with all issues affecting children's welfare. Through her committee work, Mary had frequent contact with infertile couples and adoptive parents' groups.

Before Mary, there hadn't even been a child care committee. But Mary's presence in the capitol—as the only female majority party member in the senate—forced her fellow lawmakers to rethink some of their policies about families. Lots of politicians gave lip service to their concern for children—like kissing babies, it was de rigueur and had no political downside. Who, after all, was against helping children? Mary, though, knew that issues concerning children and issues concerning women were inextricably linked. Women were tethered to children not only during pregnancy, but before conception and even after birth. But unlike policies regarding children, policies regarding women were a constituent and legislative minefield.

Mary believed that the key to a woman's social, economic, and legal freedom was her reproductive freedom. Her pro-choice stance seemed, to some, remarkable for a conservative Republican senator from wealthy Westchester County. When Mary first ran for election, that stance had cost her the backing of the conservative party. Her effectiveness in office won them over by the next election and, ten years later in the 1984 race, she won the general election by more votes than any other senator.

The years had not softened her pro-choice stance. She didn't minimize it to curry political favor. She voted for Medicaid funding for abortions each time the issue came up and in 1983, a decade after the *Roe v. Wade* abortion decision, she allowed her picture to be used in an ad by Westchester Planned Parenthood with her statement that the Supreme Court decision "has no doubt been responsible for saving the lives of hundreds of women who otherwise would have obtained illegal and dangerous abortions." A framed copy of the full-page ad hangs in the reception area of her modest Mount Kisco, New York, office, in the midst of more traditional political decor—her photo with Ronald Reagan and dozens of brochures about how to obtain state benefits, save on energy bills, and make the most of a visit to the state capitol. Her inner office sports a more colorful poster of two babies with the caption, "Children: Our Investment in the Future."

Mary is a contradiction in other ways as well. Always described as a lady, she nonetheless uses salty language, is a tough adversary, and has a bellowing voice like Ethel Merman's. "When she calls," says one staff member, "we hold the phone out to here."

The types of bills Mary has nurtured into law include programs to prevent child abuse, directives to divorce courts to take into account the contributions a housewife has made to the family when dividing up assets, and a prohibition on forcing pregnant women (such as schoolteachers) to take a pregnancy leave when they don't want or need to. She successfully enacted a program providing funding for comprehensive prenatal care to low-income women. She supports laws that authorize court orders to protect battered women and that give tax credits to businesses providing day care to employees. She promotes women's rights, but not at the unjust expense of men. When she learned that women were fraudulently reporting their ex-husbands to the child abuse hotline in order to assure that the men were not granted custody of the children, Mary stopped that practice with a law that made such reports confidential and inadmissible in custody cases except when they were substantiated.

"I didn't think of myself as a women's rights advocate before I was elected," says Mary. But being in the legislature not only brought women's problems to her attention, it gave her the means to do something about it.

Mary's own background was of a comfortable (some would say cushy) existence as part of a caring, intact family. Raised in the wealthy Detroit suburb of Grosse Point, she was advised by her father to learn to support herself. "He never saw working as the primary thing women should do, but rather as something they should be able to fall back on, if they became widowed or divorced," says Mary. But after Vassar College, Mary found no jobs that interested her, and consequently turned her thoughts to law school. In those days, Harvard did not accept women, so she returned to the Midwest, to the University of Michigan.

"I was discriminated against," says Mary. "I couldn't eat or sleep in the law quad." She probably wouldn't have gotten a law job at all, but the year she graduated—1944—was the middle of the war. There was a shortage of young male attorneys to keep the Wall Street legal machinery grinding along and so a prestigious firm (now known as Dewey, Ballantine) took her aboard. Although she was permitted to do their legal bidding (to the extent that clients would tolerate a woman), she was shut out of their traditions. Only male attorneys were invited to the firm Christmas party.

In 1948, she married a fellow attorney, Frank A. Goodhue, and settled down, as other women of her generation, to be a wife. "That lasted for about six months," says Mary, until her boredom plunged her back into work at the firm. When her son Randy (Frances A. Goodhue III) was born, she again thought she would retire from law to be a full-time homemaker. This time she lasted two years until one day she confessed to Frank, "This is it. We've got to do something about it."

John Harlan (who would later become a U.S. Supreme Court justice) had left Mary's former law firm to become chief counsel to Governor Dewey's New York State Crime Commission. She took a job with him, spending part of her days with her innocent toddler and the rest deposing alleged crime-world figures.

"Frank Costello," she recalls, "took the Fifth Amendment even when he was asked his name."

In the course of the job, Mary honed skills in strategy, from bluffing to negotiation, that now serve her in her work in the back halls of Albany. They are skills she values—and wants to pass on. One Monday, her public relations director Robin Bergstrom asked her what she had done for the weekend. Mary explained that she had taught her six-year-old granddaughter to play poker—not just the rules of the game, but the strategy. And boy can that kid bluff!

In the Mount Kisco office, Robin describes life with the senator. "When constituents come to her and say they want a law that does such-and-such, she asks them, 'How would you do it?' " says Robin. Mary patiently sits down with people and, with a lawyer's precision, helps them craft the type of law they're interested in. Along the way, she will help them see the economic and social implications of what they are proposing.

Law has been called the fabric of society and Mary views the various laws of a state as woven together. The changes made in one area cause stretches and pulls in another. Rarely can you talk about a particular issue in isolation. The action taken on surrogacy, for example, will reverberate in traditional adoption laws, in society's view of the family, and in the respect given to women's decisions in other areas. To parse out the effects of a suggested law, Mary is constantly asking constituents and other lawmakers to "be specific." If there is a phrase identified with Mary Goodhue, "Be specific" is it. As a result, the laws she crafts are not one-line declarations of opinion or moral judgment, but intricate statutory schemes to assure that the *intent* of the law can actually be put into play and that the law won't cause unanticipated problems in related areas.

After their August introduction to the issue of surrogacy, Mary Goodhue and John Dunne set staff members to work on learning everything there was to know on the subject. Under the guidance of Mike Balboni, John's staff counsel, the staff reviewed medical and psychological articles touching on surrogacy, tracked down legislation in the other states on the subject, and called experts around the country. Mike made many of the calls, but he was beginning to feel frustrated. Each lawyer, sociologist, religious official, feminist, and surrogacy participant he talked to added new facts to the regulatory equation. He would often hang up, only to think of additional questions he should have asked. He wondered if he'd missed things that John or Mary would have picked up.

Since surrogacy had not embedded itself into many people's thoughts until they read that past spring of Mary Beth Whitehead's change of heart, some of the people and groups he called had not yet formalized their positions on the multitude of issues that now faced the New York legislature in regulating these arrangements. Mike felt he needed a better method for soliciting what promised to be a gamut of views on surrogate motherhood. He convinced John and Mary that they should hold a hearing on surrogate motherhood. They chose New York City as the setting, and October 16, 1986, as the date.

When Lorrie Jones arrived at the hearing, she was asked to sign an index card with her name, her affiliation, and whether she was willing to speak. She hesitated for a moment, used her maiden name, wrote "surrogate," and enthusiastically offered to answer any questions. Ironically, she would never be asked. The witness list had actually been formalized days before. Of the sixteen speakers, nine had "Esquire" after their names, two had "Doctor" before them, one was a judge, one a legislator, two were professors, one the head of an adoptive parents' organization. Judge Radigan, who had ignited the legislative activity by his call to John two months earlier, gave the first testimony.

Lorrie was shocked. Here was a group of legislators, mainly men, who wanted to draft a law to protect poor, exploited surrogates. And they hadn't bothered to invite a single surrogate to ask if she even wanted a law and, if she did, what problems that law should address.

The hearing was terribly uncomfortable for Lorrie. She heard surrogates like herself called "reproductive prostitutes." One witness argued that surrogate contracts violated the Thirteenth Amendment against slavery. Another witness argued, "The exploitation of women as depersonalized breeders takes quantum leaps forward under surrogate parenthood." The process was faulted as harming the surrogate, harming the child, and harming the surrogate's husband. A representative of the Catholic Church asked, "Can a surrogate's husband really feel happy about having his wife's womb loaned out, an indignity analogous to that once forced on slaves?"

The future of surrogacy was painted as equally bleak. Surrogacy was criticized as leading inevitably to "violations of natural law and genetic tampering."

One witness, a psychologist who had fathered a child through a surrogacy arrangement, took issue with the pejorative terms that other witnesses had used—baby selling, reproductive prostitution. "We're trying to relate surrogate mothering to available experiences that we know about, that we're familiar with," he said, "and there is a definite danger that we'll lose sight of the possibility that this is a new phenomenon where those terms don't apply." In terms of baby selling, he pointed out that in surrogacy, unlike adoption, the father is paying money for the conception and birth of his own baby.

The speakers mainly represented institutions (such as the courts, the Catholic Church, a national Orthodox Jewish organization), talking to another institution (the legislature). For those who did have a personal experience to recount, it was almost peripheral: the adoption lawyer whose children were adopted, the woman who ran a surrogacy center who had herself contracted with a surrogate. More commonly, the witnesses represented groups—such as the Catholic Church—that had little contact with surrogacy but nevertheless had a position on the subject that they thought should govern the actions of the rest of society.

Lorrie thought this an odd way to create a law. It did not start with the personal—the needs and expectations of the couples and surrogates that led them into these relationships, the problems and hurts that could occur. Rather, it started at such a high level of impersonality that it could have been a hearing on corporate insurance rates or highway construction.

The fourth witness, Noel Keane, tried to change that. In any setting, whether the talk show or the courtroom, Noel felt the best arguments in favor of surrogacy could be made by the infertile couples themselves. So, when it came time for him to speak, he pulled an unusual stunt. He talked briefly about how he had gotten involved in surrogate parenting and how, just the previous day, his program's 128th child had been born. Then he brought to the podium Roger and Mary, a couple who had a seven-month-old daughter who came into their lives through the womb of a surrogate. The couple pointed out how strange the surrogate process looked from the outside.

"We were both a little skeptical," explained Roger.

His wife was more blunt. "I'm a born and raised New Yorker and I have a healthy dose of cynicism," she explained, "so when I was told that some women do this because they wanted to make a charitable contribution in their life I really didn't believe it. I didn't believe it until I met the two possible candidates."

Roger agreed. "The crossover point to us in terms of comfort level was when we met the surrogates," he said. "They were very intelligent, articulate and, no question, humanistically oriented. It was not just the money. They had children of their own. They loved their children. They had families. They wanted to give the best gift they could to some people like ourselves who really wanted a baby badly and to whom the genetic link was important."

The surrogate they chose, testified Mary, "said that it was

something that she wanted to do, that she felt good about doing it, that she thought of me like a sister, and that she had a very good marriage and didn't want to keep a child by some other man."

"The whole process is a very positive one," Roger continued. "It's completely different from an adoption situation where a baby has been born into an uncomfortable situation for one reason or another and there's a tremendous emotional turmoil.

"Here, by and large, there needn't be that turmoil. You're making a decision together as a couple. You know, it really is our baby before the conception because we started the process together, we went through it together, we selected the surrogate, we talked to her. We really lived through it, so outside from carrying the child my wife obviously had a substantial involvement in the whole process."

Roger's wife turned to him. "If I could just interject something here," she said. "To anyone who has concerns about the child and how the child will be cared for, whatever, I can only tell you that I remember the time our surrogate called us up and told us she felt the baby kicking. I mean, I still get emotional now when I think about it. It was my baby. It was my baby she was carrying. I never felt that she was carrying her baby that she was going to give us. This was my baby that she felt kicking. It was my baby that she was taking care of every month and that kind of feeling just continued all through the pregnancy right up until the birth." When the surrogate gave birth, she handed the child to Mary. "She said, 'Here's your baby.' And she gave me the baby. She gave me my baby."

And it was their baby in every sense of the word. Roger testified that if the baby had been born with a defect, it would still have been their baby, the same as if it had been borne by Mary.

Mary and Roger stay in touch with the surrogate through letters and photos, said Mary, "because she did a wonderful thing for us and I couldn't just turn around and walk away and say, well, all right, here's your money, you did your part."

Their daughter, she continued, has "been a joy and the money that the surrogate received could not begin to compensate for what she's given us. And I know she got her compensation that morning in the delivery room also when we all cried."

Lorrie considered their testimony. This was closer to the reality of surrogacy as she knew it. But even the testimony of Mary and Roger raised questions about the process. Roger said his sperm had been screened for potency: "I had my sperm tested before we started the whole process to make sure we weren't on a wild goose chase, so to speak, but aside from that there was no other physical testing of me." Didn't this create an unnecessary risk to the surrogate? wondered Lorrie. Shouldn't he have been checked for venereal diseases and even AIDS?

Mary had mentioned that they hadn't felt the need to submit the surrogate to psychological testing. "We both have pretty good antennae and we felt very good about her and the support that she had at home from her husband." Personally, Lorrie felt differently. She thought that intensive sessions with a psychologist like Hilary could help a surrogate clarify her own needs—and protect a couple against a surrogate who might change her mind.

Mary had referred to the resulting child as *her* own baby. Yet other speakers at the hearing, such as sociologist Barbara Katz Rothman, thought this was absurd.

"To my way of thinking," said Barbara, "the woman who is standing there with the belly, the pregnant lady, the woman with child, is the mother of the child. If she's pregnant, it's her baby and she's the mother. Biological motherhood is not a service, it is not a commodity, it is a relationship. It is true that a mother, any mother can abdicate her motherhood, can give away a child, but it is *hers* to give." This led some speakers to advocate that the surrogate should have a short period of time, say twenty days after the birth of the child, to change her mind and assert her rights as the child's mother.

"We're moving toward buying babies in kits," Barbara told the legislators. "You buy the pieces and put the components together."

Barbara also voiced concern that women would be coerced into serving as surrogates out of economic need. In contrast, Yale Medical School attorney Angela Holder, who, like Barbara, opposes surrogacy, nonetheless disagreed that women were more susceptible to coercion than men.

"I think we have come in this society to the point where you cannot presume that a competent, adult woman who gets into a contract didn't understand what she was doing to any greater degree than the man did," said Angela. "I sit here and tell you, I think women have as much sense as men."

Janet Gallagher, a women's rights attorney, was also hesitant to let potential coercion be the reason for banning surrogacy. "I don't accept the proposition that the real possibility that women may experience economic pressure to serve as surrogates should lead us to legal prohibition of the practice," said Janet. "People, women and men, find themselves under economic pressure in the making of deeply private, crucial decisions all the time. Our solution to that should be one of movement towards economic justice and expanding people's options, not outlawing people's rights to make decisions as best they can within the limits of the social and economic context in which they find themselves."

"From a strictly ethical standpoint, I can see no reason why the practice of surrogate motherhood should not be permitted," asserted witness Lisa Newton. Lisa is the director of the Program of Applied Ethics at Fairfield University, as well as being a professor of philosophy. She had been invited to the hearing to provide a reading on the morality of surrogacy that was not colored by a religious or a traditional legal perspective.

Some witnesses had charged that surrogacy was baby selling, but Lisa dismissed such a claim. "If it is permissible and customary to pay a baby-sitter until the child is old enough to care for himself," said Lisa, "it certainly should be permissible and customary to pay the surrogate mother for these services provided before the child is old enough to survive outside the womb."

"Nothing is 'sold,'" Lisa would later tell a philosophy conference in describing surrogacy. "The microscopic genetic material of the egg is 'donated,' after the custom of blood or organ donation, and the baby already 'belongs to' the father who takes it home—there is no need for him to 'buy' it." In Lisa's way of thinking, the payment to the surrogate is the payment for a service—the service of caring for the father's child.

Newton also addressed the concern that surrogacy did not provide children with a secure enough future—both biological parents might fight for the child as in the Baby M case, or both sides might reject the child who was born with a defect. These problems, Lisa told the panel of lawmakers, "resolve once the position is adopted that the child is the child of the father and the father's wife from conception on."

The questions that had been raised by the end of the day seemed endless: What sort of women should be excluded as surrogates? What types of couples should be allowed to enter a surrogacy arrangement? Should counseling of the parties be mandated? If the couple got custody of the child, should the surrogate have visitation rights? If the surrogate kept the child, should the biological father have to support the child? Should compensation be banned or limited? What should happen if the child is born with a disability?

The ball had been tossed back to the legislators to go off and draft a bill that covered these disparate issues. Most of the questions focused on the appropriate protections for the parties, including protection for the resulting child. But a few speakers stepped outside the bounds of the surrogacy contract to ask a much broader question: How will the existence of surrogate motherhood affect society's view and treatment of women in general?

The answers they gave were varied. Some viewed the legalization of surrogacy as giving greater strength to the argument that women should control their own bodies and as giving recognition to the economic value and societal importance of childbearing. They viewed a ban on surrogacy as embodying a perspective that women were children and needed to be protected from their own decisions.

Others, like Barbara Katz Rothman, saw surrogacy as demeaning and restricting women. "Once we put a price tag on pregnancy we change and ultimately devalue the meaning of the relationship," she testified. "Once we allow some people to hire and thus inevitably control some women's pregnancies, we move closer to controlling all women's pregnancies."

Although there was no consensus about the answer, the mere question of the effect of surrogacy on women's roles put the process in a new light for Lorrie. Surrogacy, to some degree, had been orchestrated by men—the Noel Keanes and Bill Handels of the world. And now, up on the dais, a committee of mainly male legislators would decide surrogacy's fate. Throughout the witnesses' testimony, Lorrie had watched with particular interest the reactions of the one woman up there, Senator Mary Goodhue. Lorrie wondered what had piqued her interest in this area.

Though much of the focus of the hearing was on finding the

best way to protect women who wanted to be surrogates, not a single surrogate had been called to testify. Lorrie Jones, who attended the hearing and offered to answer questions, was never called upon. "It's amazing that so much effort was going into protecting my interests," she says, "without ever asking me what those interests were."

Janet Gallagher was summing up: "We can't build a livable society with a legal system based on our worst fears of one another. We can't anticipate and lock into law all the reasons why men and women might make certain very individual and private decisions. Life spills over the edges of legislation."

Lorrie mused that the proper regulation of surrogacy would require women talking to women. And a place where she could start would be with a smaller group, more personally affected— surrogates talking to surrogates. Then they could begin talking to legislatures.

PART II

MAKING DECISIONS

WHOSE CHILD IS IT, ANYWAY?

WHILE LORRIE JONES was in New York, five months pregnant, the "CBS Morning News" asked her "to give the other side of the Mary Beth Whitehead story." The interviewer, Faith Daniels, was herself pregnant—and couldn't quite fathom how Lorrie could describe pregnancy as an easy, happy time. But a key to surrogacy is that not all women experience all pregnancies in exactly the same way.

"I have no doubt I will be able to give up this baby," explained Lorrie. "I enjoy being pregnant. But my husband and I have all the children we wish to have. You go into this with the idea that you're doing it for the other couple. It's not my baby, it's theirs."

Lorrie could see how hard it was for Faith to relate to this approach to motherhood. When Lorrie returned to California, she described to other surrogates her experiences at the legislative hearing and in the television studio, imploring them to help: "We've got to find a way to help people understand what surrogate motherhood means to us."

At the same time, Jan Sutton, who had been away from the program since the birth of her second surrogate child two years earlier, was calling Bill Handel and Hilary Hanafin to see what she could do to counteract the impression created by Mary Beth Whitehead that all surrogates were exploited and regretful.

Over the next two months, Lorrie, Jan, and over sixty other surrogates organized the National Association of Surrogate Mothers (NASM), which they launched at a December 1986 press conference. "Our purpose is to educate and enable the general public to make informed decisions about surrogate parenting," said Jan, "and to lobby for legislation to protect both the mother and the family.

"NASM was formed as a result of the Mary Beth Whitehead case," explains Jan. "We really did not want to have her represent surrogacy. We wanted to show people it could be a situation in which everybody wins, rather than everybody loses."

Jan Sutton and Lorrie Jones wanted to counter ideas, just beginning to surface in the press, that surrogate motherhood was antifeminist and antifamily. "We should have a choice to do with our bodies what we want," says Jan. "Don't tell me I can't be a surrogate if I want. If they outlaw surrogacy, they are saying that we are incapable, that we don't even have the right to make that decision.

"Women do have a right to make that decision. In many ways it's a much better decision than abortion."

Lorrie Jones agrees. "In most states, you can legally kill a child until six months of pregnancy," she says. "You can kill a child, but you can't create one."

At the press conference, Jan described how surrogacy programs should meet certain minimum standards regarding psychological screening, medical testing, financial and insurance protections for the surrogate, separate legal representation for the surrogate, and assurances that the women were giving noncoerced, nonexploited, informed consent to be surrogates. Until such legal standards were in place, women like Mary Beth could be tragically harmed by the process.

Jan had to look no further than her backyard in San Diego to see the problems with unregulated surrogacy. A case was erupting there which brought to light more of the dangers of surrogacy than did the Baby M case.

The San Diego case, which went before a judge on the eve of the Baby M trial, raised the same central issue—what happens when a surrogate mother changes her mind? Yet the media virtually ignored the case. The Baby M case took place in New Jersey, abutting the communications capital of the world. It involved white, middle-class participants, including an articulate surrogate who was a valued talk-show guest. The arrangement had been made through a high-volume surrogacy clinic run by the king of surrogacy entrepreneurs, himself a media regular, Noel Keane.

The California case, in contrast, was a do-it-yourself arrangement involving three Mexican nationals. The surrogate spoke no English; she had entered the country illegally. Here was a case that truly demonstrated the dangers of surrogacy. There were allegations of fraud, coercion, and exploitation. This case, not Baby M's, should have been the focus of discussions among the public and among lawmakers about how surrogacy should be regulated. But hardly anyone heard of the case. National newspapers were calling the Baby M case, scheduled for a January 1987 trial, the first of its kind, even as Judge William Pate opened his chambers on December 18, 1986, for a hearing in *Muñoz v. Haro*.

The spotlight on the Baby M case was so bright that at times it blinded both the observers and the participants to the central issue. In the context of Baby M, the media plumbed the backgrounds of the judge, the attorneys, the guardian for the child. Reporters stalked Betsy Stern to learn if she was working as a physician when she should be at home playing mother. They scrutinized Mary Beth Whitehead to see if the strain of the case had gotten to her, calling into question her ability to mother. And most of all, they fueled the conflict between the parties, making it appear that each side was questioning the other's ability to parent. They pointed to clauses in the contract—see! He could have made her abort—as evidence of how William Stern had put his needs over those of Mary Beth's. They seemed to ignore that the contract was a standard document, designed by Keane, not something that Stern had drafted for weeks on end just to stick it to Mary Beth.

In the Muñoz case, the parties were in conflict. Their relationship was tense. But the principals hadn't been inflated into symbols, the size of Macy's parade balloons, of their respective positions. Consequently, Judge Pate had a luxury that Judge Harvey Sorkow in the Baby M case did not. Rather than having to act as Solomon himself, Pate could bring the parties together and cajole, direct, shame, and persuade them to come to their own Solomonesque decision about what should be the fate of the child.

According to court documents, the initial path of Nattie and Mario Haro was similar to that which leads many couples to choose surrogacy. In 1968, Nattie, then age seventeen, gave birth to a daughter, getting married shortly after that. A decade later she separated from her first husband, and in January 1984 she married Mario Haro. Because two tubal pregnancies required emergency removal of her fallopian tubes, she could not create a child with her new husband. So, in their first year of marriage, when most couples are getting to know each other better and establishing a home together, the Haros instead invested their emotional energy and financial resources in the high-tech world of infertility treatment. Three times that year, Nattie Haro put her hopes into an in vitro fertilization clinic. The surgeons were unable to remove any of her eggs.

The Haros had the chance to adopt a child of a fifteen-year-old mother, but they were not ready to give up their dream of a biologically related child. Mario was the fourth of nine children. He lived with his parents until, at age thirty, he married Nattie. He works with children, as a junior-high math and science teacher in the Sweetwater Union High School District.

Thwarted by in vitro fertilization, the Haros veered yet further from traditional baby making by including a third party in their reproductive plans. That's when Alejandra Muñoz came into their lives.

In June 1985, the Haros explained their infertility problem to relatives visiting from Mazatlan, Mexico. One of the relatives, Natividad Muñoz, speculated that her grandchild, Nattie's second cousin Alejandra Muñoz, might be willing to help. Alejandra, who lived in Mazatlan, Mexico, was nineteen at the time. Alejandra's background was similar to Nattie's, with Alejandra also having become a mother as a teen. In 1983, she had begun living with her boyfriend and, late that year, had become pregnant. She thought hard about the relationship and decided that her boyfriend was too irresponsible. Abortion was not an option for her. So she returned to her parents' home to continue the pregnancy. On July 9, 1984, she gave birth to Nayele Esmeralda

Nuñez. To support her new family, she got a job cleaning a bank. She quit that job to travel to California to help the Haros.

The initial agreement between Alejandra, Nattie, and Mario is much in dispute. The Haros claim that Alejandra volunteered to be a surrogate mother. According to Alejandra, she had agreed to be inseminated with Mario's sperm, carry the embryo for two to three weeks, and then have the embryo transferred to Nattie for the remainder of the pregnancy. This technique was not unheard-of. Not far from the Haros' home, in Long Beach, California, Dr. John Buster had used such a technique successfully with several infertile couples. Under his guidance, the inseminated women only carried the embryos for five days.

Alejandra had not realized initially that the embryo transfer technique could be used in humans. But she was not afraid. In Mazatlan her relatives owned ranches, so she knew that embryos could be transferred between cows.

The Haros arranged for Alejandra and her young daughter Nayele to cross the border illegally into California and to live with them. For the first two weeks, Alejandra cried each day from homesickness. During the same period Nattie gave Alejandra a syringe of Mario's sperm and the pregnancy began.

Two years later, Alejandra gave this account of the events to a congressional committee: When Alejandra was one month pregnant, relatives—including Nattie's mother, half-sister, and an aunt also named Alejandra—came to the house and "wanted to know if we had been to the doctor yet so the baby could be put into Nattie.

"Nattie said: 'That's not going to happen. It can't. I can't carry the child. Alejandra will have to carry the child.'

"That's when the big fight broke out." As Alejandra describes it, Nattie called her a whore. Alejandra began to cry. "Tia Alejandra [Aunt Alejandra] told Nattie: 'How can you call her that? You yourself gave her the sperm and she impregnated herself. How can you call her that?'

"Tia Alejandra asked the Haros why they deceived us all. She said, 'You don't do this to family.' The Haros said they were willing to give me $1,500. Mario Haro said he thought that was enough money for what he called an 'uneducated, uncivilized ignorant woman.' Angela told him that here in the United States, surrogate mothers are paid up to $10,000. He said, 'For that price, I could have gotten someone intelligent.'

"I was very depressed and angry that they deceived me. I had never agreed to accept money to bear a baby and then turn my baby over to them.

"Nattie Haro wrote something on a small piece of paper. She read it to me while everyone was shouting and upset. Mario Haro didn't want Angela or Tia Lupe or Tia Alejandra to read it. I can only read printed Spanish, not handwritten Spanish. Later, Nattie said the piece of paper was a contract."

The paper read: "11-4-85. I, Nattie Haro, agree to pay the amount of 840,000 national currency to Alejandra Arellano when she gives birth, in other words, after delivery. I, Alejandra Arellano Muñoz, grant all rights to the boy or girl and I accept this amount."

The money at issue—$1,500—seems like a modest amount. Yet it was the equivalent to what Alejandra would make in six months in her six-day-a-week bank job in Mexico. And, unlike in the bank job, she could stay at home with Nayele or undertake other employment at the same time she earned this money.

"Mario said 'Sign it' and I signed it," explains Alejandra. "It was very confusing to me. I had just found out that I had to carry the child and that was a big shock. Then Nattie called me a whore. I was crying and everyone was yelling at each other and then he came out with this paper I couldn't read and said, 'Sign it.' "

Alejandra felt that she couldn't afford to continue the pregnancy without the aid of the Haros, so she agreed to their demands. She continued to live with them. "I felt they had a responsibility to see me through and make sure I got good care since they had deceived me and put me into that situation."

The deceptions were not over. According to Alejandra, Nattie wanted Mario's family to believe that Nattie was the one who was pregnant, so she went out with a little pillow under her clothes, pretending that it was a normal pregnancy.

"When I first began to go to a doctor during my pregnancy, the Haros told me that I would have to use Nattie Haro's name because I was an illegal alien and for insurance regulations," says Alejandra. "In this way, their insurance paid for the medical bill and Nattie was able to falsify the birth certificate."

Other than her doctor's appointments and Lamaze classes, Alejandra remained a prisoner of the house. She had no money to go out. She spoke no English to make friends. "The Haros never took me anywhere—to a park or anywhere—and they didn't want me to leave the house. They told me that immigration would pick me up. . . . I think Nattie treated me so badly because she resented me carrying her husband's child."

By her sixth month of pregnancy, Alejandra had become profoundly depressed. "Finally, Angela said to Nattie that I was going to get sick if I didn't leave the house," Alejandra explains. "She said, 'If she's carrying that child, don't you care that she's mentally well too? She has to get out.' " So Alejandra began to baby-sit daily, from 7 A.M. until 5 P.M., for Angela's sister-in-law. For this, she received $40 a week.

When Alejandra was seven months pregnant, she told Angela and the Haros that she couldn't go through with giving up the baby. Alejandra was calm, because she was convinced that she would be able to keep the baby. Nattie and Mario were equally calm because they didn't believe she had the smallest chance of making a legal claim to the child. Both sides had their own plans.

Alejandra's plan was based on what she knew about registering a child's birth in Mexico. When a mother leaves the hospital there, she and the baby's father visit a government official and register the child. Alejandra schemed: "Mario and I would go together to register the baby. I was the mother and he was the father. Then, I thought, I would get the baby. Because mothers always get the babies."

Of course, it didn't work that way at all. Alejandra checked into the hospital under Nattie Haro's name. On June 25, 1986, she gave birth to a baby girl by Cesarean section. At the hospital, when Alejandra was asked to sign a document, Nattie took Alejandra's hand in hers and guided the signature, carefully writing "Nattie Haro." The Haros took the baby, Lydia Michelle Haro, home from the hospital. Alejandra went to live with Nattie's half-sister Angela, who was expecting her fourth child. Alejandra waited for the day to register the birth, only to learn that this was not the procedure in the United States. She had already signed Nattie's name to the birth certificate at the hospital.

"I grieved for my child," Alejandra explained. "I begged for help. I told Mario that I wanted my baby. He said that I would never see the baby. He said: 'If you try to get the baby from me, you're going to sink.'

"When I found out about the insurance fraud, he told me that I was guilty too. He did that to put fear into me. But I told him: 'I don't care. We'll both go down.' "

This was not just a dispute between two biological parents, but rather a family crisis that reverberated from San Diego to Mazatlan. Aunts, uncles, cousins, grandparents—mostly women in the family, but a few men as well—tried to figure out how to mend the family fabric and bring peace back to Alejandra, Nattie, and Mario. Most hearts focused on Alejandra. Even Nattie's mother, Maria Buono, and Nattie's half-sister, Angela Garcia, felt that Alejandra had been mistreated. They took her and Nayele into their home to live—which only served, it seemed, to aggravate the Haros' animosity against Alejandra.

Angela tried to persuade Nattie to have compassion for Alejandra. "I believe that you will *never* be able to repay this gesture that Alejandra has done for you, but you could at least be fair and try to compensate her for all she has done," Angela wrote to Nattie. "I hope that out of gratitude and goodwill you pay Alejandra at least 5,000 U.S. dollars, which is less than half of what you would have paid a surrogate mother here. Once before Mario said that he would not pay a penny more, but Alejandra was already pregnant, for that matter Mario said, 'I could have gotten someone more intelligent.' I am not trying to be disrespectful but I don't believe Mario's parents are highly educated and neither is mom and your father, yet the both of you claim to be intelligent, so please don't use this as an excuse, saying this is the reason Alejandra deserves less, she feels pain, and hurts just like all of us! I know this is a reasonable amount and not impossible for you to pay. Alejandra will always carry the scar and memory of the child you have, a child that has brought happiness to your home."

The letter brought no resolution, nor did the efforts of Nattie's brother to mediate and to draft a new contract for the three principals to sign. Anger was beginning to replace conciliatory suggestions. One relative contemplated turning the Haros in to the FBI for exploiting an alien. The family had failed. It was time to turn to the legal system.

"Angela tried to help me but because the birth certificate was falsified, things were complicated," Alejandra told the congressional committee. "She began to search for a lawyer to help me, looking through the yellow pages. Everyone wanted $1,000 to $2,000 right away. We didn't have it. It took about three months to find a lawyer. The lawyer said he would help us for $700. Angela got the $700 from friends and from people in the church.

"By the time we had a lawyer, the Haros had already been with my baby for three months. It was three and a half months before I could see my child."

When Harvey Berman accepted Alejandra's case, he pondered the numerous legal actions that he could take, based on his client's allegations, including one for fraudulent misrepresentation by the Haros. But there were several stumbling blocks to an all-out legal war.

First, Harvey and Alejandra didn't speak the same language. Angela translated, but it was clear at many points that Angela was going beyond what Alejandra was actually saying and embellishing the story. Second, even though there seemed to be many misdeeds on the part of the Haros—not the least of which were possible immigration violations and insurance fraud—Alejandra was arguably a willing party to them as well. Third, Alejandra was still in the country illegally. If he rocked the boat too dramatically, that boat might be taking her right back to Mazatlan.

The one thing that Harvey had going for him was a California statute that created a presumption that there should be joint custody between the biological parents of a child. Courts automatically had to grant that arrangement, unless it could be shown that one of the parents was unfit or that the tension between the parents was so great that the split custody would be damaging to the child. Fueling litigation between the parties might backfire and keep his client from achieving custody. So, despite the extraordinary allegations in the case, Harvey initiated a very ordinary lawsuit. He filed suit on Alejandra's behalf against Mario to establish Mario's paternity to her child and to force him to share custody. He also got Alejandra a temporary visa.

Since Lydia was living with Nattie and Mario, they were establishing themselves as her psychological parents. Nattie had quit her job five days before Lydia's birth in order to be a full-time mom. "I knew I had to get to trial before the child was a year old or we were lost," said Harvey.

The judge assigned to *Muñoz v. Haro,* the Honorable William C. Pate, had been on the bench for less than a month. The attorneys trusted him with this landmark dispute in part because they felt that, as a novice, Judge Pate would be particularly conscientious. Harvey had another reason for wanting Judge Pate in the case. Alejandra's only hope was if the case was tried as a traditional family law case, rather than as a straight contract matter. Harvey felt that Pate, who was married to a domestic relations lawyer, was apt as a result to know about family law.

In Judge Pate's mind, the case broke down into two issues: Was the surrogacy contract enforceable, thus cutting off Alejandra's maternal rights? If not, how should legal custody be distributed between the biological parents? To help him decide, the judge asked an attorney, Marlene Allen, to represent the child in the case.

On December 18, at a meeting in chambers with Harvey Berman, Marlene Allen, and Merle Schneidewind, the Haros' attorney, Judge Pate prepared to address the question of whether any surrogacy contract could be enforceable in California. Harvey argued that surrogate mother contracts were inherently exploitive and, therefore, impermissible. "The irony in all of this argument," countered Merle, "is that the masculine counterpart to surrogate motherhood, the 'surrogate fatherhood' of a sperm donor, is apparently lawful in all jurisdictions . . . despite the fact that the semen is usually paid for."

Judge Pate recognized Mario's strong constitutional claim to the right to create a child through a contract with a surrogate mother. "The issue of the permissibility of the contract," said Judge Pate, "appears to be an issue that can be resolved fairly readily." He then described the U.S. Supreme Court precedents about reproductive and family autonomy and related them to the surrogacy issue.

"The Supreme Court of the United States has addressed the concept of the right to procreate in several decisions, and in those decisions the Court has essentially always held that the right of procreation is a constitutional right of privacy and is one which everyone is entitled to, and is not one that is subject to interference by the state without some compelling state reason.

"With that in mind, the court has no problem with the concept that the surrogate parenting contract, as a concept, is not constitutionally void in the state of California, and, in fact, that there is a constitutional right to enter into such contracts."

Even though the making of such contracts is constitutionally protected, noted Judge Pate, each particular contract raises its own legal issues "as to what influence, promises, course of efforts or anything of that type that might have occurred that might have affected the parties in entering into such an arrangement."

Harvey argued strongly that a contract could not be enforced if it was a result of duress, fraud, undue influence, or mistake. He alleged that each of these had occurred in the Muñoz case.

Judge Pate was particularly troubled by the issue of payment to surrogates. He felt the law was clear in forbidding payment to a biological mother in connection with her giving a child up for adoption. "If in fact, the evidence is such that the contract was really for an adoption of the child, then the contract is going to be for an unlawful purpose and would not be valid in this state."

The judge noted that Judge Radigan in New York, as well as the Kentucky Supreme Court, had held that the laws banning payment to mothers giving their children up for adoption did not apply to surrogates. Pate said that he was specifically deciding not to follow these decisions. He also pointed out that the contracts at issue in the Kentucky case were radically different than the one that the Haros allegedly had with Muñoz. "Parties were represented by counsel, they were written in detail, the process was handled through the supervision of doctors and whatnot, plus Kentucky has certain laws which hold that any contract that's entered into prior to five days after the child is born is voidable at the discretion of the parent," explained Pate.

Although Judge Pate felt that surrogacy contracts would be valid if entered into with appropriate safeguards, he was so clearly leaning toward finding this particular contract invalid that the Haros withdrew their contract claim.

"Although Judge Pate felt that as a general rule surrogacy contracts are valid, this particular contract had some other complications," said Marlene Allen. "Muñoz said that she couldn't read or write. She thought she'd be carrying the embryo only for a certain amount of time. When the contract was signed she didn't have a choice, she was already pregnant. She was under duress when she signed. She had no money to have the baby delivered or reared. She didn't have anyone to explain her alternatives. No one said you could be financially helped to have the baby and Haro would have to support it. If she'd had her alternatives explained and *then* gone ahead, Judge Pate probably would have upheld the contract."

With no contract as a guidepost, custody and visitation would be determined by family law. To help in that assessment, Judge Pate asked Marlene to consult with William Sheehan of the Family Counseling Services of the Superior Court in order to determine what parenting arrangement would be in the child's best interest.

Once a parent travels through the looking glass of a child-custody assessment, a team of experts scrutinizes his or her life like the judges in a gymnastic meet. Points get added or taken away depending on how you've negotiated the parallel bars of your existence. Alejandra bore her daughter Nayele out of wedlock (points shaved), but so had the competition, Nattie Haro. Alejandra was not a U.S. citizen (rather she was here on permit number A-27-618-460). But both Nattie and Mario had lived for years in the United States without obtaining citizenship. They remained green card A-12-985-863 and green card number A-11-348-443. They had the upper hand in this event, though, since their alien status was permanent and Alejandra's was temporary.

A custody assessment explores all aspects of a person's character and circumstances. There is actually an official County of San Diego document that lists the items in Alejandra's rented studio apartment. It reads with mundane officialness: "Her furnishings include an adult-size table and three adult chairs, a bed, a playpen, two small chairs and one small table, as well as a refrigerator and hot-plate. She is expecting a regular size stove, until that comes, she is cooking in the kitchen of the elderly gentleman neighbor from whom she rented the studio."

Despite the fact that this was a dispute between Mario and Alejandra, William Sheehan's report said very little about Mario himself. No matter that men were increasingly seeking legal affirmation of their parental rights. When it came to the nuts and bolts of parenting (whether in the traditional Mexican home of the Haros or the upscale two-doctorate family of the Sterns in the Baby M case), the dispute was between the mother on one hand and the stepmother on the other.

In making his decision about where to place the child, there were several legal guideposts for Judge Pate. One was the California statute favoring joint custody. Another was the California case law holding that comparative economic advantage was not a permissible basis for a custody award. The previous year, the California Supreme Court had decided an important case. The court chastised the trial judge for abusing his discretion by assigning custody based on wealth. The court said that if "the custodial parent's income is insufficient to provide proper care for the child, the remedy is to award child support, not to take away custody."

On the issue of custody, the judge rejected Marlene's recommendation that primary custody be given to the Haros. "The child was three months old when Muñoz got an attorney, a year by the time it got to court," says Marlene. "The impression I got was that the judge felt the system itself was working against her. The judge felt badly. Here was a mother who really wanted the child. The judge was sensitive to the context. There was a real possibility that she didn't know what she was agreeing to, that she didn't have a chance to make an informed decision. So even though the experts said don't split the child up, the judge favored joint custody."

The judge let it be known to the parties that he was leaning toward joint custody, but that he hoped that they would come to a decision that they could live with themselves. Nattie, Mario, and Alejandra did reach an agreement. There would be a graduated scale of visits for Alejandra, starting with three days a week for two months, then three days plus a weekend day, working up to overnights at six months.

Shortly after the February settlement, Harvey decided to withdraw from any further involvement in the case. Something complex was happening to Harvey, as happens to many lawyers who get involved in a novel legal issue. Harvey was becoming his case. It was a mental puzzle that occupied him constantly—while he was driving, showering, talking with friends. He may not have needed to spend quite as much time on the case as he had, but, like an overwhelming love affair, it made his other legal activities seem dull and unsatisfying by comparison.

When attorneys get into this frame of mind, the parties in the case cease to become people and instead seem like the metal soldiers to be moved about in a war game. "The case was my brainchild," admits Harvey. "The people became instrumentalities. I didn't want them messing with my work product."

In particular, Harvey wanted to orchestrate Alejandra's relationship with Nattie and Mario. "Don't feud with the Haros," he implored, "or you'll lose altogether since they've got primary custody."

Harvey withdrew from the case, after giving Alejandra time to find another attorney. But his predictions about the case were coming true. The tensions between the sides had caused Marlene to reopen the case.

The problem was that the sides were not communicating about the child. "The child was not well because of the tension between them," says Marlene. "Both were taking the child to doctors, getting prescriptions for her, and not telling the other party." Both were enforcing their rights to the detriment of the child. "No matter how the child felt—if she was cranky, ill, or had an ear infection—if she wasn't turned over at the precise time, attorneys would be on the phone to the other side."

Marlene was worried that the child might be in danger, particularly if both sides were giving the child medications without telling the other. Joint custody only works if both parents talk about the child and work out problems together. Says Marlene: "All that was passed back and forth was the body."

On May 20, 1987, Marlene filed a request that the custody arrangement be changed. She stated her belief that "the continuation of the current custody agreement in which the child is subject and cause of hate, animosity and constant battle will result in substantial long term emotional problems for the child." Marlene urged that custody be given either to Mario or to Alejandra with the contact of the other radically limited to short visits on two days a month.

At the subsequent hearing, which occurred months later, the

Haros fought strongly for sole custody of Lydia. The first argument made for curtailing Alejandra's maternal rights was that the child would be harmed by moving from place to place. Alejandra's new attorney, Gregory Marshall of the San Diego chapter of the American Civil Liberties Union, exposed that argument as being without any basis in child psychology studies. The second argument was that an infant needs to have a single, primary parent. Gregory showed that argument was equally threadbare. He noted that "in a world where literally millions of children spend as much time at the day care center as with either parent, where the number of children who frequently spend the night at a grandparent's or aunt's house is countless," one simply could not say that spending some nights with Alejandra and some with Mario would harm Lydia. Gregory also argued that Alejandra's right to a relationship with her child was protected by the U.S. Constitution, under the right to privacy.

Why does the Constitution protect parental rights from government interference? Nobody, let alone the government, knows the best way to raise kids. And even if there were a statutory guide to perfect parenting, courts would not be able to enforce it. The judge could not sit in each time Mario and Alejandra turned over the baby to assure that they did not exchange angry words (in contravention of his order). A court order cannot enter the depths of people's emotions to assure that they have a spirit of cooperation. The court can set moral guidelines, something for the parties to strive for. It can act as a kindly grandfather, in trying to get the parties at least to recognize the effect of their actions on the child (for example, in one motion, the Haros' attorney Merle Schneidewind requested that the court restrain Alejandra from calling the child by any other name than Lydia Haro). But the court can't force people to be better, or different, kinds of parents. It can only strip them of their rights when they begin seriously endangering the child.

In Gregory's brief he cited Stanford law professor Robert Mnookin: "Deciding what is best for a child poses a question no less ultimate than the purposes and values of life itself." Since the evidence did not show that Alejandra had given her informed consent to be a surrogate, there was no valid contract definitively giving the child to the Haros. In deciding where to place the child, Judge Pate's guideposts were the constitutional protection of Alejandra's relationship with her child and the clear statutory guidance for joint custody. The judge again made clear his preference that legal and physical custody be shared, but, as in the February hearing, strongly encouraged the parties to come to their own appraisal of how the child should be divided.

Another escalating scale of contact between Lydia and Alejandra was agreed upon. As of this writing, Alejandra has the baby during the day, while Mario teaches. Alejandra works in the evening, making tortillas for a local fast-food chain. Lydia stays overnight with her mother on Thursdays.

Through all the financial and emotional traumas of her triangle of parents, Lydia, the infant, seems to be healthy and flourishing. Her life circumstances are a social experiment involving medical procedures and legal precedents. The full result of that experiment will be hard to gauge until Lydia and the other surrogate children come forward to tell their own stories.

9

∞

THE BABY EVERYBODY WANTED

THREE MONTHS OLDER than Lydia Haro, Baby M is a placid, cheerful blue-eyed girl. She is too young yet to recognize photos of herself on the front of magazines or to trace the arcs in the lives of two couples that crossed briefly to bring her life, then swung apart, each side trying to tug her along in their wake.

The girl's mother, Mary Beth Whitehead, seemed at first like any other surrogate mother. When she applied to Noel Keane's Infertility Center of New York in early 1984, she was twenty-six years old, had been married to Richard Whitehead for ten years, and had two children, Ryan and Tuesday. She wanted to be a surrogate to give "the most loving gift of happiness to an unfortunate couple." On her application form, she said that her fee would help her subsidize her children's college educations. "I feel giving the gift of a child would be more rewarding than working at a conventional job," she wrote. "I have been blessed with two happy, healthy children and a loving husband. I am content with my life and would not have any emotional problems."

Richard's first reaction to Mary Beth becoming a surrogate was "No way."

127

"I guess it was my pride," he says. "I thought I would feel like less of a man if she carried someone else's child."

Mary Beth argued that it had nothing to do with him, it was her body. Besides, she explained, this was a chance to help a childless couple and help put Ryan and Tuesday through school.

By the time she reached Noel's office, Richard had given in to her wishes, as he had so many times before in their marriage.

There were a few details in Mary Beth's background that might have given an interviewer pause. She had had her own children quite young—when she was seventeen and eighteen. When she was only nineteen, she and Richard made the decision that they would not have any more children. Richard underwent a vasectomy. This may have been too young an age for Mary Beth to irrevocably cut off her chance of enlarging her family.

As part of the application process, psychologist Joan Einwohner interviewed Mary Beth. Joan's report indicated that Mary Beth was sincere in her plan to become a surrogate mother, but expected to have strong feelings about giving up the baby. Joan recommended that, before Mary Beth was allowed into the program, more in-depth screening and counseling be done to determine whether she would be able to relinquish the child in the final analysis. "She may have more needs to have another child than she is admitting," Joan reported.

In May 1984, Mary Beth was matched with a couple. After eight months of unsuccessful inseminations, she and the couple parted company. But it seemed that her luck was changing. Elizabeth and Bill Stern wanted to meet with her to discuss the possibility that she would act as a surrogate mother for them.

Betsy and Bill, married in 1974, had, like many couples of their generation, postponed starting a family while they pursued their education. Bill obtained a Ph.D. in biochemistry and settled into a job as a research scientist. Betsy, after receiving a doctorate in genetics, continued on to medical school. She became an assistant professor in pediatrics at Albert Einstein College of Medicine.

The Sterns' own childbearing plans were shattered when Betsy learned that she was suffering from multiple sclerosis. Carrying a pregnancy could aggravate the condition, potentially causing her to be paralyzed. The Sterns called surrogate-mother centers around the country to find a woman who would be a gestational surrogate, carrying their IVF embryo to term. But IVF surrogacy was not readily available in 1984, so they entered into an agreement with the Infertility Center of New York for Bill's sperm to be used to inseminate a surrogate mother.

In January 1985, Mary Beth and Richard and Betsy and Bill met at a New Brunswick restaurant to discuss a potential surrogate arrangement. Mary Beth seemed to Bill to be the "perfect person" to be a surrogate. She had Betsy's coloring and build, with the same thick brown hair. The baby would probably look like Betsy, even though Betsy would not be the biological mother. And Mary Beth made it clear that she would not appear on the Sterns' doorstep. Her maternal bond to the child would be satisfied by receiving an annual photograph and letter about the baby's progress.

The couples each felt they had found a good match. Mary Beth was anxious to be a surrogate mother and pressed the Sterns for an answer that night. They agreed to enter into an arrangement with her.

At the end of the dinner, Bill and Betsy got into their car and kissed each other. "This is perfect," they said. "This is too good to be true."

To initiate this relationship with the Sterns, Mary Beth signed one of Noel Keane's contracts. It was similar to the one that had marked the agreement between Judy Stiver and Alexander Malahoff. She promised, for a fee of $10,000, to be artificially inseminated with Bill Stern's sperm, bear the child, and turn him or her over to Bill to rear. She promised to put Bill's name on the birth certificate and to let him name the child. She agreed that she would be paid only $1,000 if she miscarried after the fourth month, even if the child was stillborn. She agreed to undergo amniocentesis and, if the test revealed an abnormal fetus, to abort the fetus upon Bill's request. She agreed not to abort otherwise, unless the physician said it was necessary for her physical health. Also like Judy Stiver, Mary Beth handwrote a Declaration of Intent, acknowledging that it was in the best interest of the child for William Stern to have immediate and uncontested custody. Bill agreed to take the child no matter what its physical or mental condition. Neither Mary Beth Whitehead nor the Sterns were informed of the cautions in Joan Einwohner's report.

On the eleventh insemination with Bill Stern's sperm, Mary

Beth finally conceived. Betsy decorated the house with streamers. She and Bill immediately began making plans for the baby to be part of their family. They chose a room they could see from their bedroom, painted it as a nursery, and added wallpaper with teddy bears. They executed new wills naming the unborn child as a beneficiary.

During the pregnancy, Bill and Betsy got to know the Whitehead children. They took Ryan to a baseball game and Tuesday to a Thanksgiving Day parade. They had occasional dinners with Mary Beth and Rick. Betsy asked Mary Beth advice about caring for the baby. Their close relationship became tense, however, when Betsy insisted that Mary Beth undergo amniocentesis.

Mary Beth's previous pregnancies had been easy ones, but this time she gained an inordinate amount of weight—fifty-five pounds—and developed high blood pressure in the last month. She resented Betsy's insisting that she take to the bed for the last weeks of the pregnancy and otherwise controlling her care. "Betsy called up my doctor behind my back and insisted that I lay in bed and scared me and told me that I could die if I didn't lay in bed," recounts Mary Beth.

A month before the baby was born, Mary Beth talked by phone to a social worker at Noel's center. According to the summary of the discussion in the center's file, Mary Beth spoke of her depression and the physical and medical problems of her pregnancy, which were upsetting her husband and children since she couldn't perform her normal activities. She was resentful of the Sterns for not understanding what she was going through physically. She felt she had no one to talk to.

The report details that her husband was threatening to divorce her and was unhappy with her role as a surrogate. "Mary Beth, too, says, she would never do it again," wrote the social worker. "Mary Beth was quick to say, however, that she has no ambivalence about relinquishing the baby after birth. She knows it's not her baby and says she does not want a child right now."

On March 27, 1986, when the baby was born, Mary Beth felt an overwhelming attachment to the girl, who resembled Mary Beth's other daughter, Tuesday. Mary Beth listed her husband Richard on the birth certificate as the father of the child and named the little girl Sara Elizabeth.

Even Richard, who cried during the delivery, was amazed at the depth of his feelings for the child. "I was in the delivery room when Sara was born and when I first looked at her I realized she looked like Tuesday," he later admitted. "It was then that both Mary and I had realized we had made a mistake. Sara is a part of our family."

Richard had begun to have doubts about surrogacy toward the end of Mary Beth's pregnancy. "The thought of taking $10,000 to help Ryan and Tuesday through college by selling their sister was very difficult to live with," he said.

The unsuspecting Sterns arrived at the hospital prepared to welcome a child into their family. On the way to the hospital, they had seen a rainbow, and now they were ready to hold and love the golden-haired girl at the end of it. But because he had not been named on the birth certificate as the father, Bill could not touch his daughter. He could only gaze at her through the nursery window. When Betsy and Bill told Mary Beth that they had decided to name the little girl Melissa Elizabeth, Mary Beth started crying and told them that she might not be able to give up the child.

In the hospital, Bill and Betsy tried their best to comply with Mary Beth's wishes. "As Mary Beth did not want the hospital personnel to know that she was a surrogate," Bill recounted, "Betsy and I did our best to act reserved during our visit with Mary Beth and my daughter. It took all of my self-control to contain my enthusiasm upon catching the first glimpse of my baby girl."

Mary Beth saw it much differently. "I was overjoyed with the baby," she said. "They stood at the nursery window and showed no emotion. They stood there and just looked at her like they were buying her."

The strains that the Sterns and Whiteheads were experiencing in the hospital may have stemmed from the way that Noel conducted his surrogacy program. In normal reproduction, the decision to have a child evolves out of an ongoing relationship. There might be differences in personality or perspective between the mother and father about how the child should be cared for, but those disputes can be worked out over time, and in the context of the relationship. Friends and relatives who know both members of the couple can be called upon for advice.

Some surrogacy programs try to approach technological child-bearing in a similar way. Before they are matched with couples, potential surrogates receive months of counseling to determine their own needs and desires. The backgrounds, interests, and preferences of the couples are probed to determine what type of relationship they want with the surrogate. Members of the staff attempt to fill the roles of friends and relatives. They are present at the initial meeting between the couple and the potential surrogate. They maintain frequent phone contact with each side during the pregnancy to help prevent or iron out any misunderstandings. They attend the birth to provide an extra resource in an overwhelmingly emotional time.

In contrast, in Noel Keane's program, the experiences surrounding bringing a child into the world were compressed and isolated. Mary Beth applied to the program on a Friday, and was accepted the following Monday. A quick, unsupervised meeting at a restaurant resulted in the decision to create a child with her egg and Bill Stern's sperm. In the hospital, that child became real, and the differences between what she felt to be her style of parenting and that of the Sterns loomed enormous. She felt it was wrong for the Sterns not to put the crib in their bedroom. She felt it was wrong for Betsy to want to return to work after eight weeks. She was annoyed that, at dinner with Rick and Tuesday the day after the baby was born, Bill did not talk nonstop about the baby, but instead described the research he was undertaking at work.

In normal parenting, issues like these would be worked out between spouses, over time. In some other surrogate programs, these issues would be addressed before conception and during pregnancy. But Noel's program had not required Mary Beth to face these issues, and now she was in a position of turning over her child to a couple who she felt would not care for her daughter as well as she could.

The usual arrangement is for the surrogate to say good-bye to the baby in the hospital. The baby then goes home with her father. But apparently because the adoption papers had not been processed, the baby was sent home temporarily with Mary Beth. Betsy and Bill's parental debut was delayed. The next day, when they collected Melissa from Mary Beth, friends and neighbors of the Sterns celebrated her homecoming.

When the baby was four days old, Mary Beth arrived on the Sterns' doorstep. She had called the night before, saying that she felt bad and did not know if she could live any more. Mary Beth pleaded to be allowed to take the child home temporarily. "I just want her for a week and then I'll be out of your lives forever," she said. The Sterns suggested that she stay with them for a week, but then relented. Out of concern for Mary Beth's mental state, they agreed to let her take the child for a week in order to properly say good-bye to the child. (Since then Bill says he has apologized to his daughter for letting her go at that time—and putting Mary Beth's needs ahead of concerns for Melissa.)

For the rest of the week, Mary Beth was unreachable to the Sterns' calls. At one point, Rick answered the phone. According to Bill, Rick indicated that he did not want the child. "This whole thing is a mess," he said.

At the end of the week, Mary Beth called Betsy. She needed more time to think about whether she wanted to keep the child. She also said that Richard had threatened to leave her if she did not turn over the baby to the Sterns.

By April 12, Mary Beth had firmly decided to keep the little girl, whom she called Sara. She told the Sterns that if they initiated court action, she would take the baby and leave the country.

For Betsy, the chance to be a mother was again being shattered. For Bill, who had lost most of his family in the Holocaust, another one of his flesh and blood was being taken from him. They could no more give up the baby without a fight than could Mary Beth Whitehead.

On May 5, the Sterns asked a Bergen County Superior Court to enforce the surrogate mother contract. The court agreed that while the matter was under consideration, the child should be cared for by the Sterns. The judge signed an order directing Mary Beth to deliver the child for temporary custody by Betsy and Bill.

Since Mary Beth had threatened to disappear if there was any court involvement, the judge had police accompany the Sterns to the Whitehead residence in order to pick up the child. A fast-thinking Mary Beth passed the baby out a back window to Richard, who fled with the child. Mary Beth also phoned a lawyer. The next day the Whiteheads, and the baby, disappeared.

It was a nightmare for the Sterns, waking up each day for the next two months, not knowing where their daughter was, how she was, and whether they would ever see her again. In July, Mary Beth called Bill at work. "I'd rather see me and her dead before you get her," she cried. "I gave her life. I can take her life away."

The Whiteheads led the lives of fugitives, staying at over twenty hotels, motels, and homes, neglecting to take baby Sara to the doctor's. At the end of July, the baby was located at Mary Beth's parents' home in Florida. Sheriff's officers and a social worker came to the home to recover the baby. Ten-year-old Tuesday Whitehead tried to ward them off with a hairbrush. The Sterns were reunited with Melissa.

By now, the whole Whitehead family had become attached to the baby. Tuesday and Ryan considered her their sister, and Mary Beth's parents, Joseph and Catherine Messer, considered her their grandchild. Joseph handwrote a three-page letter to Judge Sorkow, pleading his daughter's case. "Sir, I feel that Mari (she never works) can give a child more love, kindness, understanding, guidance than (2) working parents can,—who will employ a sitter to provide what is essential to raise a child in these chaotic days," wrote Joseph. "Ryan and his sister, Tuesday, adore their mother and father in a way seldom witnessed in the modern era."

Joseph detailed his education and his service in World War II, and described the backgrounds of his wife, children, and other relatives. "I, myself," he wrote, "do not think that our backgrounds and education cannot in some way help Mari to raise her flesh born daughter." Joseph had himself been brought up by his grandparents.

"I do not uphold my daughter for running," he told the judge, "but with limited funds and assets, it would be comparable to someone like yourself, taking on the President of the United States, one on one."

When their grandchild was seized, Catherine Messer, too, came to her daughter's defense. Without even attempting to contact a lawyer, Catherine called the *St. Petersburg Times* and gave them the story. This launched Mary Beth into a series of print interviews and broadcast appearances that would dominate her life in the next three years. Betsy and Bill turned away all reporters. They were trying desperately not to have Melissa, as they said, turned into a freak.

The judge also wanted to protect the little girl. As in all custody disputes, he closed the courtroom to reporters. He gave the baby a pseudonym on all court documents—Baby M. While the case was awaiting trial, he granted Mary Beth visitation rights, but asked that she not release any photos of the child to the media. Mary Beth was not allowed to breast-feed the baby or take her home; her two-hour, twice-weekly visits would take place under supervision at the Edna B. Conklin Youth Center in Hackensack. The judge also appointed a guardian, former judge Lorraine Abraham, to represent the child in the upcoming litigation.

After having had such close contact with her daughter for the first four months of her life, Mary Beth grieved at the limited contact she had now, taking place under court supervision. She lashed out by repeatedly reporting to the judge that the baby was being cared for poorly by the Sterns. A physician's examination of the child found that she was in good health.

Mary Beth had no real peer group to relate to. The other surrogates interviewed in the news—Carol Pavek and Jan Sutton among them—had been happy with their experiences. Some were enormously angry at her.

In contrast, the birth mothers in traditional adoptions could relate to what Mary Beth was feeling. Many felt that their babies had been taken away from them against their will. Alison Ward, a New Jersey birth mother and former vice president of the activist group Concerned United Birthparents (CUB), contacted Mary Beth's attorney. CUB's political agenda was to help reunite families separated by adoption and to prevent unnecessary adoption. "Mary Beth may be in too much pain to ever think about reaching out for support, but I would once more like to offer my soft shoulder and support to her," wrote Alison. She also offered CUB's own attorney, Harold Cassidy, to work on the case. By the time the case went to trial, Mary Beth had become friends with Alison, fired her attorney, and turned the case over to Harold. Unfortunately, however, many of the legal arguments made by Harold seemed designed less to get Mary Beth's baby back than to spread the message of CUB.

In August 1986, four newspapers appealed the closing of the courtroom. "There is a general presumption in favor of open court proceedings," argued Corinne Mullin, the attorney for a

Bergen County, New Jersey, newspaper, the *Record*. "Because this case has engendered so much public comment and is so important to future legislation and public opinion on this matter, press and public access should be granted."

Judge Sorkow would not open his court to the press, but an appeal to the New Jersey Appellate Division forced him to do so. The appellate judges felt that, since Mary Beth's mother had already released the child's name to the newspapers, using confidentiality to protect the child's welfare was impossible. At the time, the judges did not realize how relentless and continuing the reporters' pursuit of Baby M would be. By opening the courtroom to reporters, the judges put journalists into the position of writing daily reports about the baby and the case.

If Judge Sorkow had been allowed to close the courtroom, there would have been in-depth coverage of the Sterns, the Whiteheads, and their joint infant at the beginning of the trial and at the time the decision came down a few months later. But by granting daily access, the reporters needed to file not two sets of articles, but hundreds. They burrowed into the private moments of the Sterns, the Whiteheads, the parties' attorneys, the judge. Over a hundred reporters had press privileges for the case. They wrote articles about the past and present moves of the parties—from Rick Whitehead's use of drugs in Vietnam to Betsy Stern's purchase of colored plastic blocks at a Toys R Us.

The *Record* had four reporters working full time on the Baby M case. They became frequent visitors to the Whitehead house. One of them, Michael Kelly, went to work with Richard Whitehead, riding a garbage truck with him, to learn more about the man and his view of the case. When the child's first birthday came around, during the litigation, the *Record* was determined to get a photo of the child. The judge ordered the birthday party to take place at a secret spot, but reporters with walkie-talkies parked outside of a number of likely places, a dragnet to snare the child. Success! The party took place at the home of the guardian, Lorraine Abraham. A *Record* reporter hiding in a woodpile got the coveted photo of the baby on her first birthday.

When Baby M becomes Teen M, there will be a potential scrapbook of clips about her with more volumes than the *Encyclopaedia Brittanica*. Who knows what feelings of disgrace, anger, or fear she will experience when she reads what was said about her parents? Who knows how her life will be marred as schoolmates, teachers, and future employers react to her not as a sweet, pleasant, bright girl and woman, but as Baby, Child, Teen, and Ms. M?

That order to admit the press may have been, in the long run, as big a mistake for the development of Melissa/Sara as was Mary Beth's signing of the contract in the first place. Nor will the end of the litigation be the end of the publicity. At a 1988 meeting of journalists at Princeton University, reporters who covered the case said that they were planning follow-up stories—Baby M goes to kindergarten, Baby M goes to the prom, Baby M gets married.

Judge Sorkow's effort to close the courtroom was not his only attempt to protect the privacy of the parties that was overturned by a higher court. In November, he ruled that the medical records disclosing Betsy's multiple sclerosis were confidential. The New Jersey Supreme Court reversed the order, making these personal facts a matter of public knowledge.

As in the Muñoz case, there were two basic questions before Judge Sorkow. Was the surrogate contract valid, thus giving the baby as a matter of law to Bill Stern? If not, should Bill or Mary Beth have custody of the child? The judge ruled in November that, to answer those questions, the trial would be conducted in two parts. He would try the contract issue first. If the contract was valid, the baby would remain with the Sterns and there would be no need for the parties to present the intrusive, personal kinds of evidence that come up in a custody case. The litigation would end right there.

Again, though, the appellate court thought it had a better idea. It reversed the order for a two-part trial and required a trial which would cover all issues at the same time. On January 5, 1987, amid the bursts of flashbulbs and the whir of television cameras, Betsy, Bill, Mary Beth, and Richard entered the Hackensack courthouse. Two years earlier, they had met across a dinner table in a New Jersey restaurant. Now, forty miles further north, they were trying hard not to look at each other across the fifty-seven-seat New Jersey courtroom.

The room itself was decorated with peaceful pictures of country churches and old-fashioned homes with white picket fences.

In these traditional surroundings, the story unfolded of a most untraditional attempt to have a child.

Judge Sorkow viewed the case as a family law matter—with the goal of trying to find the right home for a little girl. He was adamant that surrogate motherhood itself would not be on trial in the case. He refused to hear testimony from witnesses on the benefits or risks of this novel parenting arrangement. During a courtroom debate on expert witnesses for Mary Beth, Judge Sorkow said, "I must state unequivocally that there will be no public policy testimony by any of these experts. This court will not permit itself to be used as a platform to herald one philosophy as against another on the surrogate parenting issue."

ON THE EDGES OF LIFE

EVEN THOUGH JUDGE SORKOW approached the Baby M case as a family law case, ignoring the societal implications of surrogate parenting, the joys and hurts of surrogacy were touching families across the country. Like death and taxes, birth was inevitable. And so, while Judge Sorkow was presiding over a series of witnesses in the New Jersey courtroom, legislators were grappling with the issue of surrogacy, and the fetuses inside Carol Pavek and Lorrie Jones were rapidly making their way toward birth.

Chris Pavek, now nearly nine, would finally be getting the baby brother that he wanted. His mother would be giving birth at home and Chris wanted to be there, to see the baby from its very first seconds on its own. Later, when his little brother grew up, he would be able to explain to him exactly what had happened. Chris had already been around when his mom had given birth to a surrogate baby and he knew the steps by heart. The baby, red and shriveled, would poke out of her body, head first. His mom would ask someone to find her glasses and then she would cut the cord. She would cover the baby in a blanket to keep him from getting cold. Maybe Chris would even get to hold him first.

During the pregnancy, Carol's nurse-practitioner had noticed that the baby's heartbeat was a little fast, but Carol's physician did a sonogram a week before delivery and said that everything looked fine. He noted that the baby would probably be about seven and a half pounds, which he felt would make it an easy birth. The Paveks had already picked a name for the child—Eric.

On January 27, the twenty-second day of the Baby M trial, Carol went into labor. Some friends joined her at the house, including a woman whom Carol had been training as a midwife. As the labor progressed, the pain was more excruciating than during her previous pregnancies. Carol was worried that she was pushing too hard before she was completely dilated. She wanted the advice of an experienced midwife.

Between contractions, Carol called Ann Houghtaling Wylie. In the past, a rift in their friendship had been created by disputes over their joint clinic and disparate views on the handling of their criminal prosecutions for unauthorized practice of medicine. But Carol had vast respect for Ann's abilities.

"You've dilated about right," Ann said shortly after she arrived. She complimented Carol on how slowly and gently she was pushing the baby out.

"You don't understand," said Carol. "Watch me from the waist up, I'm pushing harder than I've ever pushed and still the baby is not coming."

Finally, Carol could feel the baby's head crowning. "Get Chris," she said. It was after his bedtime and he had fallen asleep.

The baby's head began to emerge, but he was stuck from the shoulders down. Carol was glad Ann was there, for Ann was an expert on shoulders. Earlier in her practice, whenever Carol thought she was going to have a shoulder problem, she would bring Ann along to the births to help.

"Get to it," she said to Ann, "get that posterior shoulder."

Ann felt inside Carol. "It's not here," she said.

The baby's shoulder was transversed. Ann reached back into Carol. She touched the baby's body and immediately realized that there was no muscle tone. She started to dislodge the tiny body.

As Carol managed her last push and moved the baby out of her body, she felt the weirdest sensation. The baby is not present in this room, she thought. There is no soul here.

The others also noticed that there was something terribly wrong with the baby. Carol started cardiac massage on her child, and mouth-to-mouth resuscitation. A moment later, Ann took over. For the next eight minutes, they alternated with another woman, switching back and forth, trying to breathe life into the pale body.

Carol wanted to stop. The baby showed no signs of breathing and, even if they had miraculously been able to revive him, the lengthy period without oxygen would have left him seriously disabled.

"I don't think I can raise a brain-damaged child," Carol whispered.

"No, go on," said one of the friends in attendance.

"I'm not going to raise him," Carol said quietly, looking the woman in the eye.

"That's all right, I will," said her friend. "Keep up your CPR. I will."

The friend, who was thought to be infertile, later learned she had been pregnant at the time. She gave birth to a boy. "It's as if my son's soul jumped into her," said Carol.

The further attempts at resuscitation did no good. The baby was obviously dead. They called an ambulance and called Carol's doctor to come over and pronounce the baby dead. "I don't want to get involved," said the doctor.

Everyone was blaming themselves for the baby's death. The woman who had been training to be a midwife worried that she had ruptured the baby's lungs while giving CPR. Ann Wylie was afraid that when she was trying to get the shoulders out she might have broken the baby's neck. Carol thought that the way she was pushing might have harmed the baby. And even young Chris agonized that his longtime wish for a brother might have somehow caused this horrible tragedy.

The ambulance arrived, with a policeman following it. The policeman walked in just as Carol was squatting naked, delivering the placenta. Her friends were terribly offended, and tried to cover her with blankets. "I just need to use your phone," he said. They were all in such a daze from the birth—and death—that they didn't think to ask why he needed a phone instead of his car radio.

The policeman came back. "What happened here?" he asked.

Together, the various women explained.

"That's fine," he said. "Thank you." He continued to look

around and then said, "I'll be out of your way as soon as someone comes to take pictures of the scene."

He wouldn't leave. He wouldn't let Carol get dressed. He said he was planning to release information that Carol had given birth in her living room and that it was dirty.

Carol called her attorney. More police arrived. They searched Carol's home, taking photos everywhere. They took photos of the other women, because they would not give their names. They carted off all of Carol's birthing equipment.

"Nobody should be treated like this," said one of Carol's friends. She asked the policemen to leave. She told them they had no right to be there.

"This is my fucking scene of the crime and I'll be damned if I'll leave this house," replied one of the officers.

It was past midnight, but Chris was still up. He had just watched his little brother die. He turned to the policeman. "Why are you using that language in our house?" he asked.

"It was a nightmare," says Ann Wylie. "We were all in shock. There was no time to deal with it privately. There was no hugging or holding. We had to be tough and deal with the policemen."

Inside, Carol was on the verge of falling apart. She told herself that she had done CPR at least a dozen times on newborns and all those children were alive and healthy. She asked herself, How could I have healthy surrogate babies and when it finally gets to be my turn he dies?

On the outside, though, Carol was trying to stay calm. She reminded herself that she had been through many emergencies and had not fallen apart. And now, she had her eight-year-old son to comfort and think about. One of the policemen viewed that calm as a strike against her, perhaps an indication that she didn't care about the baby. He commented in the report he filed about how "unemotional" she was. By 6:00 A.M., there was a totally unsubstantiated report on the news about how some midwives (Carol and Ann) had been charged with murder.

Luckily, Carol's home was in Randall County, not the county where her midwifery clinic was located, so the matter was not brought before the prosecutor who had challenged her role in home births. The Randall County prosecutor, Randy Sherrod, had a completely different attitude. When informed of the death of Eric, he said, "I'm not here to prosecute women for choosing where to give birth. I'm here to prosecute criminals."

Randy knew that he could curry political favor with doctors by bringing charges based on a home birth, but that would go against his beliefs. "A woman has a right to dictate whether she has an abortion or not, and this is part of the same packet of rights," Randy observes. "My own opinion is that government should be here to help people and not to dictate morality."

The next few days were torturous for Carol. She gave Rick a list of phone numbers of people to call about the baby's death.

Carol was doing a massive soul search, about this pregnancy and about her previous three pregnancies as a surrogate mother. Carol told Rick that she didn't want to take any phone calls, and that she especially did not want to talk to Rhonda, the East Coast woman for whom Carol had been a surrogate. She and Rhonda had talked frequently in the previous months during Carol's pregnancy, and Rhonda had sent clothes for the baby. But Carol couldn't face her just yet.

One day, Carol picked up the phone and Rhonda was on the line. "I wanted to pout," says Carol about her reaction to Rhonda's hello. "I didn't have any mature feelings."

Rhonda was soothing and sensitive, but Carol explained how difficult it was to talk to her. "It's through no desire to take your sons away," explained Carol. "I just think that it's unfair that someone else has two beautiful sons and I didn't get one."

Rhonda still sends presents for Carol and Chris on the holidays, but Carol avoids opening them. "Ever since we lost Eric, the reminders of the healthy babies are too much," she says.

When the autopsy report came back, it was clear that the baby could not have been saved, no matter where or how Carol had given birth. There were numerous serious malformations of the heart. There were no arteries open to the lungs at all. Chris understands all of this. He says the baby had a "scrambled egg heart."

Carol thinks she has traced the defect back to pesticide exposure during her first month of pregnancy. Some neighbors had been spraying their trees with a powerful pesticide, and the hose was just a few feet from Carol's air-conditioner intake. When Rick, Carol, and Chris came home one day, the house was filled with pesticide.

"Our immediate response was to get Chris out," says Carol. "We didn't even think about the effect on the baby."

Once the autopsy report was filed, it was clear that there could be no charges against Carol and the women who attended her birth. Although her baby's death made her rethink her surrogacy experience, Carol says that she has no wish to snatch back any of her three surrogate babies.

Chris worries about asking again for a little brother.

"We survived," Carol tells him. "We had our friends. We had God. We can do it again."

But Carol's friends say the death has hit her harder than she realizes. With the three healthy babies out there, they wonder, could Carol become another Mary Beth Whitehead?

In Lorrie Jones's situation, there was no question that she would give her soon-to-be-born child to Sandra and Hillel. The only question was whether she had irreparably damaged her existing family by doing so.

Her husband, Casey, had been the person to first point out the surrogacy ad to Lorrie. When she decided to enroll in the program, he said that whatever she wanted to do was fine with him. But his feelings seemed to change when he was hit with the reality of the pregnancy.

"He had a real rough time," Lorrie said. "He just didn't want to see me pregnant.

"I'm told by just about everyone that I glow, I come alive, I blossom when I'm pregnant, but Casey decided he didn't like the look of a pregnant woman, that she wasn't sexy, wasn't cute."

While Lorrie was serving as a surrogate, Casey was pursuing his own dreams. Since he was a child, he had been fascinated by minerals, crystals, and mining. At age six, he had started spending free afternoons at a mineral store in Monrovia, California. He decided to go back to his first love—and took a job mining in Colorado.

A pregnant Lorrie went to Colorado, but the move only lasted two days for her. She felt that her relationship with Casey was tense, and they felt the town of four hundred people would never accept the fact that she was a surrogate. Lorrie returned to California alone.

Once the separation took place, though, says Lorrie, "we started growing apart very quickly." She recounts how Casey called to tell her that he didn't want to be married anymore.

"Here I am creating a family for someone else," she thought, "while my own is being destroyed. Where's the fairness in all that? You know, it doesn't seem fair."

Lorrie had depended as a child and teenager on her father, a well-known surgeon, to take care of her. When she married at twenty, she depended on Casey, too, and when the separation began between Casey and her, she felt sadly adrift.

Her first thought was to turn to friends. She lived for a while with one friend after another until she confronted herself with the fact that she was twenty-six years old and it was about time she struck out on her own. She moved in with a family from her church and began to establish order in her life, taking stock of where she was and how she was doing.

Her parents had always accused her of never finishing things she started. "I went to court-reporting school, and quit to get married," she remembered. "I wanted to take gymnastics and then quit. I wanted to take piano and they went so far as to buy me that piano, even though I hadn't asked them. So they were pretty ticked off when I decided not to pursue piano.

"But now I'm actually pregnant," she told herself. "This is something I decided to do and, by God, I'm doing it! It's a decision I made and I did it. And it is probably a lot harder thing to do than learning how to play the piano. I've grown a lot."

Even though at the time Lorrie felt that she was sacrificing her own family to create one for someone else, she now looks back and says, "It's probably the best thing that could have happened. I think the good Lord did it on purpose because Casey did what he needed to do and I did what I wanted to do.

"We both needed to grow," she says. "It sounds corny and clichéd, but we did. I was always a very dependent person, depending on him for almost everything. When I was faced with not having him, I was forced to grow up very fast. And as a result, I'm very independent, I'm my own person. And that's the kind of person Casey's wanted ever since we met."

Other people have noticed it as well. Bill Handel told her that she was one of the gutsiest people he had ever met. "Gosh," replied Lorrie, "you should have seen me just a year ago, Bill, you wouldn't have recognized me. I just let people walk all over me."

"Maybe to someone else it wouldn't have been a compliment," she recounts, "but to me it was. I think that my self-assurance is one of the things that came out of being a surrogate, because it was a real growing experience for me."

At the very end of the pregnancy, Casey became supportive and they decided to try again with their relationship. He confessed to Lorrie that her decision to be a surrogate mother was not the real issue. In his anger about other aspects of their marriage, he had just focused on surrogacy because, he explained later, "I knew that it would hurt you most and make you want to say good-bye."

Part of the problem had been that Lorrie had found her fulfillment through surrogacy, while Casey had still been at loose ends about his own goals. Once he was alone, Casey began to think about what he would most like to do. He thought about the mineral store in California that had mesmerized him as a child. He learned that the same person was still running it, and he decided to go into partnership with the man and take over the store when the man retired.

The day before Lorrie delivered, Casey called from Colorado. He said that he wanted to move back to California and be with her. "I called to let you know that I care," he said. "Go into the hospital knowing that I care and that I love you."

Sandra and Hillel were standing by, waiting to race to the hospital as soon as they received a call from Lorrie about the impending birth. According to psychologist Hilary Hanafin, how the couples act in the hospital gravely influences the surrogate. Certain reactions of the couple in this volatile, charged time make the surrogate more apt to change her mind. For example, couples at the hospital shouldn't show any anxiety or fear that the surrogate will be unable to keep her promise of giving up the baby.

"What a couple needs to do is be warm, appreciative, supportive," advises Hilary. In one case, the biological father demonstrated considerable anxiety that the surrogate would bond to the baby. She picked up on the fact that, after she had worked with him for fourteen months, he still wasn't trusting her to be able to fulfill her commitment. She didn't say anything, but it hurt. In her mind, she had done such an incredibly beautiful job of helping them have a child and felt so good about it, but his attitude put a damper on her joy.

When a couple is insecure about the surrogate's commitment, they sometimes delay going to the hospital, so that they will not be hurt. This may frighten the surrogate into thinking that they don't really want the child. Even a couple that goes through labor and delivery with the surrogate may fail to tell the surrogate they've been there when they subsequently return over the next few days to visit the child. But without the knowledge that the couple has been visiting, the surrogate may feel that the baby has been abandoned.

On February 8, Lorrie went into labor. Sandra came immediately. Lorrie clung to her arm, digging fingertips into the skin as the contractions became stronger. At one point, Lorrie grabbed so hard that she worried she had broken Sandra's arm. "It's great," Sandra replied, "I was so worried I would feel like a fifth wheel. This makes me feel like I am doing something helpful."

Many years earlier, one of Lorrie's teenaged relatives had given birth out of wedlock and given a baby up for adoption. February 11, the date she gave up the baby, was a day Lorrie's mother referred to afterward as Black Tuesday.

"I was praying to God that I would have the baby on the eleventh," says Lorrie. When she went into the hospital, she asked her doctor, "Can I wait three days to have the baby?"

"You could," he said, "but it's Sunday, Sandra and Hillel are here, you might as well have the baby. Why don't I go ahead and induce labor?"

Lorrie talked to her mother. "I want to have the baby on February eleventh," Lorrie said.

"Why would you want to do that?" her mother asked.

"Well, Mom, wouldn't you like to get two black days over with in one day instead of having them a couple of days apart? You know, instead of having a black week, you can have a double black day."

Her mother was touched. "You planned this baby," she said. "You didn't get pregnant from fooling around. I don't think having a surrogate baby is considered a black day."

PARENTING ON TRIAL

W HILE THE EVENTS surrounding the Pavek and Jones births occurred in relative obscurity, one only needed to turn on the nightly news to learn the most intimate details of the creation of Baby M. Even though Judge Sorkow's goal was to concentrate the case on what placement would be in the best interest of the child, the Baby M trial served as an impetus for the rest of society to debate whether surrogacy should be banned or allowed. This was a terrible way for the issues to be aired. While advance legislative consideration of surrogacy would have enabled the development of a policy that considered the pros and cons of surrogate motherhood, pinning the entire societal debate on one particular arrangement was leading to policy suggestions based not on the inherent qualities of the procedure itself, but on the personalities and problems of Mary Beth Whitehead, Richard Whitehead, Bill Stern, and Betsy Stern.

As if ours were a primitive culture that demanded the sacrifice of a young girl to get the gods' attention, it took the sacrifice of Baby M to get legislators to turn their thoughts to the issue of surrogacy.

"I blame the legislatures for the Baby M case," says Bill Pierce of the National Committee for Adoption. "The Baby M case was absolutely predictable. State legislators knew what was going on with surrogacy. People for years had been calling for the state to take responsibility."

From the first moment Bill heard of the Baby M case, he felt that it would provide the impetus for lawmakers to finally ban surrogacy. "This is going to be the end of surrogacy," he told reporters early in the proceedings.

Whether appropriately or not, biomedical policy in the United States does not get made on the basis of cool consideration, but on the basis of tragic cases. "My rule of thumb for changing public policy," Bill would tell interns at the National Committee for Adoption, "is that one vivid case history is worth two inches of research."

George Annas, professor of health law at Boston University, observes that "we need a drama critic to figure out what the law is doing because in the United States, what we've managed to do is to convert almost everything into entertainment. We are asked to judge medical developments like the artificial heart and legal developments like surrogate motherhood not on any strong basis using any moral standards or any value standards but rather to judge them the way we judge melodrama."

In the larger societal courtroom, surrogate motherhood was not getting a fair trial. People's opinions about surrogacy were being influenced unduly by the ups and downs in the testimony of these two couples and by how fairly or unfairly these people were being treated by the court.

Mary Beth Whitehead weighed in with considerable sympathy from the public. It was a horrible vision to imagine policemen showing up at the home of a nursing mother to wrench a baby from her breast. Her anguish was real—it showed through her tears in newspaper photos; it cried out when she ran away with the baby when the Sterns tried to claim the child.

But Bill Stern's love for the child was also strong. On the stand, Bill wept as he described how important his daughter was to him. "She's the most important person in my life," he said, his voice broken. "And I mean no insult to my wife.

"When she grabs my shirt, I feel so special," he continued. "When she smiles, I see her beaming. It makes me feel very happy. It makes me feel worthwhile."

Apparently, the feeling was mutual. An expert witness, Dr. David Brodzinsky, testified about the relationship between Bill and his daughter: "The interactions I observed are a joy to watch. This is a child who responds exceptionally well to her father." According to Brodzinsky, Bill's strong attachment began "during the pregnancy itself when the reality of the child began. I think for him when he got the sonogram report and this child was suddenly real, it wasn't an abstract or hypothetical entity, it was a real living person and he became very emotionally interested in that child from that point on."

Throughout the trial, Mary Beth insisted that she should retain custody simply because she was the mother. That approach might have worked in another generation, but now, the law of custody was gender-blind and fathers had as much right to children as mothers. Custody was based not on biology, but on merit. It was no longer assumed, but achieved.

Harold Cassidy, Mary Beth's lawyer, did her a disservice by not presenting the strongest picture possible of Mary Beth's maternal capabilities—of how well she could raise the child. Instead, he focused too much on how traumatic losing the baby would be for Mary Beth. He evoked a stereotype of women living through their children and being devastated when those children no longer need them. "The bottom line is, above all, that Mary Beth Whitehead is a mother and without that she has nothing in this life," he argued.

Cassidy called Dr. Phyllis Silverman as a witness. She testified that if the infant were put in the custody of the Sterns, Mary Beth's identity would be compromised and she would have difficulty reconstructing her place in the world. Judge Sorkow questioned Silverman about the effect on a *father* of losing a child. "I'm not trying to diminish the man's investment in the possibility of having a child," she replied. In the end, the judge gave little weight to Silverman's testimony, since the goal of a custody determination is not to serve the parents, but to serve the child.

When Mary Beth had called Bill from Florida, Bill's attorney had advised him to tape the calls. To demonstrate Mary Beth's anguish, her attorney requested that the court allow those tapes into evidence. On February 4, the following interchange was heard in the Hackensack courtroom and on the nightly news:

BILL: "I want my daughter back."

MARY BETH: "And I want her, too, so what do we do, cut her in half?"

BILL: "No, no, we don't cut her in half."

MARY BETH: "You want me, you want me to kill myself and the baby?"

BILL: "No, that's why I gave her to you in the first place, because I didn't want you to kill yourself."

MARY BETH: "I didn't anticipate any of this. You know that. I'm telling you from the bottom of my heart. I never anticipated any of it. Bill, please, stop it. Please do something to stop it."

BILL: "What can I do to stop it, Mary Beth?"

MARY BETH: "Bill, I'll let you see her. You can have her on weekends. Please stop this."

BILL: "Oh God. I can live with you visiting. I can live with that, but I can't live with her having a split identity between us. That'll hurt her."

MARY BETH: "What's the difference if I visit or you visit? I've been breast-feeding her for four months. Don't you think she's bonded to me?"

BILL: "I don't know what she's done, Mary Beth."

MARY BETH: "She's bonded to me, Bill. I sleep in the same bed with her. She won't even sleep by herself. What are you going to do when you get this kid that's screaming and carrying on for her mother."

BILL: "I'll be her father. I'll be a father to her. I am her father."

. . .

MARY BETH: "I'd rather see me and her dead before you get her."

BILL: "Don't, Mary Beth, please don't do—"

MARY BETH: "I'm going to do it, Bill."

BILL: "Mar—"

MARY BETH: "I'm going to do it; you've pushed me to it. I gave her life, I can take her life away. If that's what you want, that's what I'll do."

BILL: "No, Mary Beth, no, Mary Beth, wait, wait."

MARY BETH: "That's what I'm going to do, Bill."

BILL: "Please . . ."

MARY BETH: "You've pushed me."

BILL: "Please don't—I want—I don't want to see you hurt. I don't want to see my daughter hurt. I really . . ."

MARY BETH: "My daughter too, why don't you quit doing that, Bill, okay?"

BILL: "Okay, okay, all right . . ."

MARY BETH: "It's our daughter. Why don't you say it, our daughter."

BILL: "All right, our daughter. Okay, Mary Beth, our daughter."

The emotions in the words of both mother and father were so gripping that spectators at the trial, including some reporters, had tears in their eyes. Reliving the conversation was too much for Mary Beth. She rushed out of the courtroom.

In a second tape, Mary Beth was also making threats to get Bill to drop his legal action for the child. She said that if he did not drop the case, she would tell the judge that he had sexually abused Tuesday. In the course of the trial, Mary Beth admitted that this was a total fabrication. This led the judge to question her mothering ability, since she seemed totally oblivious to traumatic effect such a claim would have on Tuesday. In an earlier deposition, Mary Beth had lied and denied ever making such a threat to Bill.

Many of Mary Beth's supporters were lost over the first tape. While they were willing to support Mary Beth to relieve her obvious pain, the tapes riveted their attention on the child herself, on the threat that Mary Beth would literally sacrifice the child to her own needs.

For other listeners, the effect of the tapes was precisely what Harold Cassidy, Mary Beth's attorney, had intended. "I never had closely considered the surrogate motherhood issue before," said Michelle Harrison, a Boston physician specializing in women's health issues. "But the grief in that woman's voice made me feel that I had to do something." Michelle began organizing a group of feminists to protest on Mary Beth's behalf. On February 18, while Mary Beth was being cross-examined on the stand, Michelle spearheaded a demonstration at the courthouse. Twenty-one women called for the return of Baby M to Mary Beth and demanded legislation to protect other women in her position. They denounced surrogacy as abusive to children and exploitative of women.

"I have delivered hundreds of babies, representing hundreds of years of women nurturing them in their bodies," said Michelle, referring to the male contribution as "only sperm."

Michelle's views about the superiority of mothers over fathers may be due to her belief that a woman can readily raise a child by herself. Fifteen years earlier, her marriage had fallen apart while she was pregnant; she raised her daughter Heather alone. When Heather was two and began asking about her daddy, Michelle told Heather to consider her grandfather, Michelle's father, to be her daddy.

The year that the Sterns first visited the Infertility Center of New York to seek a child with Bill's genes, Michelle—still a single parent—had adopted a daughter from Calcutta.

"The surrogacy agreement is not a valid agreement," continued Michelle. "Women's bodies are not a commodity to be used or sold, and babies are not a commodity." She argued that the feminist position ought to be that "all birth mothers get first dibs on their babies."

"Everyone talks about mother's rights," said Bill Stern in front of the courthouse. "What about father's rights? I'm her *father*. Fathers have dreams, too."

Many men could relate to what Bill was saying. Men are getting more involved in parenthood. Unlike previous generations, they are attending birthing classes and joining their wives in the delivery room. With the increase in the number of working wives, men spend more time with their children. Many feel just as capable as mothers at giving and receiving affection. Beginning in the mid-1970s, men began seeking primary custody in divorce cases in exponential numbers. One sociologist dubbed it the "Kramerization of fatherhood" after the movie *Kramer vs. Kramer*.

"It was a cheap shot for people to start referring to Stern as Mr. Sperm," said John, the California man who became a father through surrogacy. "The fact of men having anything to do with child rearing in this country is a new concept. But I consider myself half of the parenting unit. I'm involved, very deeply involved."

John could identify with Bill Stern. "I would have come unglued if that happened to me," he said. "We were already completely emotionally involved during the pregnancy."

A few days later, on February 25, New Jersey housewives calling their group "Mothers with Feelings" joined feminists in a vigil outside the courthouse, marching around an empty crib. One carried a doll—and the sign, "Women are not dogs for breeding purposes."

The women read a letter from Tuesday Whitehead to the baby: "We were meant to be together. This tragedy has reached everyone's heart, and when you grow up you will know what has gone on at this time and what people have gone through. It will soon end and you will be home. Your crib is in our room. I like it there. It keeps me going. It has all your toys and memories, your bears, your dress, your mobile. I can't wait until we could really be sisters, but right now we are separated by law."

When Betsy Stern walked past the protesting women, one taunted her, "How does it feel to take another woman's child?"

Feminist support for Mary Beth swelled as the courtroom action moved from testimony of the parties to testimony of expert witnesses, mainly mental health professionals. The case was unique—not only because it involved a surrogate mother contract, but also because it involved a custody dispute that began at birth. In the four percent of divorce cases that involve a custody dispute, the child is usually older than a newborn. In such instances, the court can consider specific evidence about the interactions of each parent with the child and the psychologists can testify about those relationships. If the child is old enough, his or her own preference about placement can be taken into consideration. But when a dispute begins at birth, neither side has had the chance to have a normal relationship with the infant. Rather than judging the parents on the criteria of how they actually interacted with the child, psychologists and psychiatrists in the Baby M case were given free reign to examine any aspect of the Sterns' and Whiteheads' personalities and past behaviors in order to make conjectures about what kinds of parents they *might* be for Baby M. And since the trial itself was taking place under a microscope, Judge Sorkow seemed reluctant to keep out *any* mental health testimony, no matter how remote it seemed.

The experts themselves, ever aware of the publicity they would get, used the trial as a way to launch their own untested theories about parenting. In endless hours of testimony—preserved in over a thousand pages of transcript—expert after expert set forth his or her own criteria for what made a good parent. The results were rarely helpful, and often bizarre.

Parenting is one of the most subtle, nuanced, difficult, varied, stressful, fulfilling, instinctive activities one can imagine. As the U.S. Supreme Court has recognized, there is not just one way but myriad ways to be a successful parent. Most kids turn out all right. Although there is widespread agreement about what parents should *not* do (they should not abuse or neglect their children), there is no consensus on what parents should do. Yet each expert witness made it appear that he or she held the blueprint for the perfect parent.

There was no evidence that Mary Beth or Bill or their spouses would be unfit parents; none were thought likely to abuse or neglect Baby M. So the experts undertook the psychological equivalent of an electrocardiogram, to determine if there were any blips in their personalities that would make them less worthy to parent Baby M.

The results were terrifying to any parent or potential parent. A psychiatrist, psychologist, and social worker visited the immaculate Whitehead home, where various of baby Sara's possessions— panda bears, a crib—waited forlornly for her return. Under the watchful gazes of the mental health professionals, Mary Beth bathed her daughter, fed her a bottle, played patty-cake with her, let her wander the living room in a walker, and rocked her to sleep. It might have seemed like the picture of maternal-child bonding and bliss. But when the experts rated her mothering, based on these events, they managed to find fault in virtually everything she did.

One of the first expert witnesses called, Dr. Marshall Schechter, criticized Mary Beth for letting the baby play with stuffed animals instead of pots, pans, and spoons. He also faulted her for saying "hooray" instead of "patty-cake" to reinforce the baby when playing patty-cake. Mary Beth was also criticized, by other experts, for her lack of openness to mental health counseling.

The Sterns were subject to a similar visit, a parallel white-glove test of parenting. They scored higher, it seems, because they sat on the floor to play with the baby. But, undoubtedly, in her twelve years of parenting, Mary Beth had similarly joined Ryan and Tuesday on the floor. Perhaps she had been afraid to do so with Drs. Schechter, Brodzinsky, and Greif present because she thought they would find it vulgar, not right for the mother of a child of a biochemist.

The innermost thoughts and feelings of the couples were held up for scrutiny. The results of their IQ tests were reported in the newspapers. Their ability to parent was not judged by how much they loved the baby, or how they planned to care for her, but how they scored on tests such as the Bender Gestalt, the Cattell 16PF, the Rorschach, and the TAT. With the inordinate pressure of knowing their performance would determine if they would be allowed to rear, or even see, their daughter, the four principals in the case were in the demeaning and frightening position of being asked, in one test, to repeat digits backward.

Mary Beth was penalized by one expert for scoring poorly on a test that asked her to name four presidents since Roosevelt and identify who wrote *Faust*. The same expert testified that it was a drawback of the Sterns that they had no other kids.

Under the microscope of the mental health experts, almost any behavior could be interpreted as pathological. Mary Beth was faulted for being "overly enmeshed" with her children, and unaccepting of outside influences. During one of the psychological tests, Bill was shown a picture of a boy alone in a cabin. Bill cried. This is an abnormal reaction, reported the psychologist.

Betsy Stern was criticized for postponing childbearing while pursuing her career. Brodzinsky came to her defense, however. "As part of our societal changes, it's so very common that I run into it virtually every week with professional women putting it off," he countered. "The decision, in my opinion, in no way makes them less desirable as a parent."

Michelle Harrison could relate to the critique of Mary Beth as being overenmeshed with her children. When Heather was born, Michelle had quit her medical practice for a few years to spend all her time with her daughter. People warned Michelle about getting too close to her daughter and making her too dependent.

"There is something threatening to outsiders about a mother and child close to each other," Michelle wrote in her 1982 book, *A Woman in Residence*. "Women are supposed to stay home, but they aren't supposed to be *too* tied to their babies. I was tied to

Heather; I was free to be tied to her because there was no one else in my life who could lay claim to my time or attention. I said, 'I want to be with her until she is bored with me and seeks others because she wants other company.'"

In the Baby M case, the psychiatric labels applied to the parties seemed endless. Mary Beth was described as having a borderline personality disorder, narcissistic personality disorder, histrionic personality disorder, schizotypal personality disorder, and paranoid personality disorder—and that was just by one of the eleven mental health experts.

Richard Whitehead was upset about the criticisms of Mary Beth. "She's the most loving mother in the world," he said. "She devotes her whole life to the kids. It hurts me to see her attacked like this."

Mary Beth was not alone in incurring the experts' wrath. In fact, most of the expert witnesses managed to condemn all four principals. Dr. Allwyn Levine, for example, suggested that Mrs. Whitehead was too impulsive with an exaggerated sense of self-importance, Mr. Whitehead was too passive and deferred to his wife too much, Mr. Stern was introverted, and Mrs. Stern, though a warm and open person, "could be diagnosed as having an adjustment disorder with depressive features."

But Mary Beth had a particular strike against her. In her past, she had ignored experts' advice. When school officials suggested that her son Ryan be classified as in need of special educational help, she went against their recommendations, going so far as to withdraw him from his New Jersey class to send him to live with her parents and be schooled in Florida. She questioned authority (including having the audacity to disobey the initial court order to return the baby to the Sterns). In contrast, Betsy Stern had sought counseling when she learned of her multiple sclerosis, she and Bill had sought counseling to deal with the trauma of the litigation, and they both acknowledged that Melissa might need therapy in the future herself. Such admissions couldn't help but endear the Sterns to the mental health experts.

"The experts were highly approving of the Sterns' utilization of and belief in mental health counseling," Michelle Harrison observed in the journal *Gender and Society*. "Using professionals was considered by the professionals in this case a universally successful answer to emotions, parenting questions, issues of identity, and so on." Harrison described how it was a strike against Mary Beth that she viewed herself as a survivor who relied on her own resources. "To these professionals, handling problems with the help of family and friends or alone, rather than utilizing mental health services, was evidence of mental illness."

Barbara Katz Rothman pointed out the unfairness of the judgments being made about Mary Beth, arguing that it should be a team of mothers, not expert witnesses, who should do the evaluation. She also said that the economic differences between the Sterns and Whiteheads couldn't help but figure in. "It's not just that the Sterns can buy a better stroller for the kid or shop at Bloomingdale's instead of K Mart," said Barbara. "It's that they've been able to buy for themselves more stable lives that make them look like more fit parents."

The absurd standards for parenting that Mary Beth was being forced to meet boosted her circle of feminist supporters. On March 12, the last day of the trial, a letter signed by over one hundred prominent women was released to the press. It said, "By these standards, we are all unfit mothers." Signers included Barbara Katz Rothman, actress Meryl Streep, singer Carly Simon, writers Betty Friedan, Gloria Steinem, Nora Ephron, Lois Gould, Susan Cheever, Sally Quinn, Judith Rossner, Gail Sheehy, Marilyn French, and Margaret Atwood, as well as a host of female academicians, college presidents, and activists. The letter ended with the statement, "We strongly urge legislators and jurists who will deal with these matters to recognize that a mother need not be perfect to deserve her child."

Their opposition to the criteria the experts were using to divine who would be a better parent did not necessarily mean that they felt that the baby should go home with Mary Beth. Nora Ephron, for example, admitted that she was undecided on the issue of custody. Even some of the adamant opponents of surrogacy, such as columnist Ellen Goodman, nonetheless felt that the Sterns would make better parents.

The feminists' response to surrogacy seemed to be based primarily on a reaction to Mary Beth Whitehead. That response might have been different if their introduction to such arrangements had come through surrogates such as Jan Sutton or Carol Pavek, rather than Mary Beth.

The political response of feminists to surrogacy seemed to ignore the fact that the practice—as well as the way it was being addressed in the courtroom—was a natural outgrowth of the women's movement. Feminist gains allowed women to pursue educational and career possibilities once reserved for men (such as Betsy Stern's position as a doctor and medical school professor). But they also meant that more women were postponing childbearing, and suffering the natural decline in fertility that occurs with age. Some of these women found that the chance for a child had slipped by them entirely and needed to turn to a surrogate mother.

On the other hand, feminism made it more likely for other women to feel comfortable being surrogates. Feminism taught that not all women relate to all pregnancies in the same way. A woman could choose to lead a child-free life by not getting pregnant. If she got pregnant, she could choose to abort. Reproduction was a condition of her body over which she, and no one else, should have control. For some women, those developments added up to the freedom to be a surrogate.

An overarching theme of feminism was that biology was not destiny. The equal treatment of the sexes required that decisions about men and women be made on other than biological grounds. Women police officers could be as good as men, despite their lesser strength on average. And men could be as good at being parents as women were.

Yet remarkably, in the context of the Baby M case, all these lessons of feminism seemed to be forgotten. Feminists were literally begging legislators to protect women from their own decisions, to close off a reproductive option, and to consider biology as destiny with respect to Bill Stern, whom some feminists called "Mr. Sperm." His intentions, abilities, and love for the child should not matter in determining whether he should have custody of the child, they said. All that should matter is that his biological contribution to the baby was less than Mary Beth's.

Betty Friedan argued that biology gave men fewer rights to the child. "In the last analysis," she said, "until technology makes it possible for a man to carry for nine months and go through the risk and the pain of giving birth, then finally the risk and the bond belongs to the mother."

Some feminists viciously attacked Betsy, pointing out that it was Betsy, not Mary Beth, who was the surrogate. "We put her into the same category as the terry cloth–covered light bulb that is given to the baby monkey in the psychology laboratories to study the phenomenon of maternal bonding," Kathleen Lahey, a feminist law professor at the University of Windsor, told a reporter.

Gena Corea, author of *The Mother Machine* and feminist opponent of reproductive technologies, declared that surrogate motherhood arrangements should be made criminal. But encouraging legislatures to enter the private realm of reproductive decision making with respect to surrogacy conflicts with the feminist position on other childbearing choices.

Contraception, abortion, pregnancy, surrogacy: a cornerstone of feminist ideology has been the idea that women have a right to reproductive freedom. The legal doctrine upon which feminists have pinned much of their policy has been the constitutional right to privacy, which protects people's childbearing and child-rearing decisions from government interference. Under that doctrine, laws may not be adopted that interfere with private reproductive decisions except to protect against actual, imminent dangers.

One of the greatest feminist contributions to policy debates on reproduction and the family has been an insistence on an examination of the nature and effects of a particular practice or technology in determining how it should be regulated. Feminists have fought legal attempts to cut off reproductive and family choices when those attempts were based on speculated risks or unquestioned traditions.

In the context of surrogate motherhood, however, feminist opponents of the practice have relied on paternalistic theories and speculative information about risks to women and children to justify a ban on the arrangement. In doing so, they are breathing life into regulatory rationales that feminists have rejected in the contexts of abortion, contraception, nontraditional families, and employment, which could severely undercut the gains previously made in these areas.

"What explains why feminists are opposed to surrogacy?" asks

Santa Clara University law professor Carol Sanger. "I am not sure, but I have an idea. Feminists are often labeled as bad mothers. It sort of comes with the turf. Why aren't you home taking care of your children instead of lobbying or marching or giving speeches on surrogacy? Maybe it was nice in this case to side with someone who changed her mind and decided that motherhood is as good and as important as we know it to be. But the comfort in that particular alliance with motherhood is precarious. Feminists ought to be more concerned about the central issue, which is not what choice women make, but that they have the right to decide."

Not all feminists had yet developed a hard-and-fast position on surrogacy. The New Jersey chapter of NOW, the National Organization of Women, held a meeting on the topic, but remained divided.

"The feelings ranged the gamut," chapter head Linda Bowker told the *New York Times*. "We did feel that it should not be made illegal, because we don't want to turn women into criminals. But other than that, what you may feel about the Baby M case may not be what you feel about another.

"We do believe that women ought to control their own bodies, and we don't want to play big brother or big sister and tell them what to do," she continued. "But on the other hand, we don't want to see the day when women are turned into breeding machines."

One issue upon which there was unanimity among feminists, however, was that surrogate contracts should not give the biological fathers control over the surrogates' medical treatment during pregnancy. It was a grave infringement on the surrogate's right to bodily integrity and freedom of choice to allow the biological father to decide whether she should have amniocentesis or not and whether she should have an abortion or not. Even in the more intimate situation of marriage, the courts had recognized that a woman's decision whether or not to abort was strictly her own, with her husband having no legal right to object or intervene.

Although the feminists who had become active in the case were supporting Mary Beth Whitehead, it was Bill Stern's lawyer who was using feminist rhetoric. At the close of the case, Gary Skoloff said, "You prevent women from becoming surrogate mothers and deny them the freedom to decide. . . . You are saying that they do not have the ability to make their own decisions, but you do. It's being unfairly paternalistic and it's an insult to the female population of this nation." According to Gary, the traditional adoption laws weren't meant to apply to the new social arrangement known as surrogacy. The judge would have to break new ground.

In his closing statement, in contrast, Harold Cassidy criticized Betsy Stern for following feminist tenets. "She consciously delayed decisions with respect to conception and willfully accepted all the risks due to her age, including significant risk of infertility," he said. "Knowing this, Mrs. Stern clearly chose a career over her ability to bear a child."

Cassidy maintained that surrogate motherhood was inimical to women and to children. To protect them, he argued, the judge should apply the adoption laws prohibiting payment to birth mothers and prohibiting prebirth agreements to give up a child.

Cassidy railed against surrogate motherhood under any circumstances: "We must never permit a man to have one woman to share his life and another to experience the sacrifice and pain of pregnancy and a lifetime of suffering as a result of the separation of that mother from her child."

In the last days of the trial, the Vatican had released its pronouncement on reproductive technologies, the "Instruction on Respect for Human Life in its Origin and on the Dignity of Procreation: Replies to Certain Questions of the Day," putting its considerable influence on Harold's side of the case.

The Vatican condemned in vitro fertilization, artificial insemination by donor, and surrogate motherhood, expressing its long-held view that the only proper way to create children was through marital intercourse. The religious document said, "The child has the right to be conceived, carried in the womb, brought into the world and brought up within marriage: it is through the secure and recognized relationship to his own parents that the child can discover his own identity and achieve his own proper human development."

While the Vatican had often tried to influence the reproductive decisions of its Roman Catholic followers, this Vatican Instruction contained a much more radical recommendation. It urged legislators of all faiths to support laws that would ban reproductive technologies, including surrogate motherhood.

Some legislators, like Michigan State Senator Connie Binsfeld, were ready to act on that recommendation. Others were awaiting guidance, not from the Pope, but from a modest trial court judge in Hackensack, New Jersey.

The Baby M trial, which had been in session for thirty-two days over a two-month period, ended on March 12. Over a half-million dollars in attorneys' time had been expended on the case. At a press conference after the trial, Mary Beth was asked how she thought the trial court would rule. "I'm not going to predict," she replied. "I tried to predict and that's how I got into all this trouble."

Bill Pierce had his own fantasy about how the judge should rule in the case. Because he felt that Baby M would never be able to lead a normal life in the media glare, he advocated that she be taken away from both the Sterns and the Whiteheads. "My personal feeling is that the child should be placed in foster care and then given to a well-qualified adopting couple," said Bill.

Judge Sorkow spent two weeks weighing the testimony of the thirty-eight witnesses and crafting his opinion. On March 31, 1987, he read the 121-page tome to a packed audience in an auditorium-sized courtroom. Mary Beth had sensed the decision would not be favorable, so she was at home folding laundry when this occurred. Her lawyer was in the courtroom, as well as Betsy and Bill and their counsel.

Bill Handel, Jan Sutton, and a group of surrogates from the National Association of Surrogate Mothers were waiting in a nearby room to express their support for the Sterns. Noel Keane was too nervous to attend the reading. Later, he admitted, "I didn't want to be around to bleed in public" if the decision came out against surrogacy.

At the courthouse, some of the anti-surrogacy demonstrators referred to Bill Handel and Noel Keane as reproductive pimps. "I worry about not being seen as ethical," says Bill. "That's real important to me. It really fries me when people call me a pimp. It's the furthest thing from what I am.

"You know," he continues, "if I were a personal injury whore, they would consider that to be fine. If I were representing sleazeballs on their fifth bank robbery and getting them off, that would be considered wonderful. But I am just trying to help couples out. I am not making as much money as I would in another field of law. Just once in a while I would like to be given credit for doing something decent."

Inside the courtroom, Judge Sorkow began to read his decision. "There can be no solution satisfactory to all in this kind of case," admitted the judge. "Justice, our desired objective, to the child and the mother, to the child and the father, cannot be obtained for both parents. The court will seek to achieve justice for the child."

The judge found no guidance in current statutes, such as the adoption laws, since they were all meant to deal with other issues than surrogacy. "The concept being tried here did not exist or was not considered when those statutes, be they adoption, termination of parental rights or custody, were legislated," he said. "To make a new concept fit into an old statute makes tortured law with equally tortured results."

Because existing statutes did not cover surrogacy, Judge Sorkow pleaded with the legislature to develop legislation to protect participants in surrogacy arrangements, saying the state "could not ban or refuse to enforce such transactions altogether without compelling reason."

Set adrift without legislation, the judge proceeded to weave his opinion out of constitutional principles and common law traditions. The judge emphasized the importance in our society of being able to create children with a biological link to us. The development of reproductive technologies, including surrogacy, he said, "follows from the social and psychological importance people attach to their ideal of having children who are genetically theirs. The desire to reproduce blood lines to connect future generations through one's genes continues to exert a powerful and pervasive influence. Being unable to bear a child excludes women and men from a range of human activity associated with child bearing and rearing."

Judge Sorkow determined that contracting with a surrogate was constitutionally protected as a part of the right to privacy. He said that "it must be reasoned that if one has a right to procreate coitally, then one has the right to reproduce non-coitally. If it is the reproduction that is protected, then the means of reproduction are also to be protected. The value and interests underlying the creation of family are the same by whatever means obtained."

Just as Bill Stern had a constitutional right to enter into the surrogacy contract, so, too, had Mary Beth Whitehead. "Currently, males may sell their sperm," observed the judge. "The 'surrogate father' sperm donor is legally recognized in all states. The surrogate mother is not. If a man may offer the means for procreation then a woman must equally be allowed to do so."

In discussing Mary Beth's constitutional rights, the judge, though, put great weight on her right to bodily integrity. Contrary to what was said in the surrogacy contracts, the surrogate alone—and not the contracting father—has the right to decide whether or not to undergo an abortion.

Judge Sorkow found that Mary Beth had willingly and knowledgeably entered into the surrogacy arrangement. "Mrs. Whitehead was anxious to contract," he noted. "At the New Brunswick meeting, she pressed for a definitive statement by the Sterns. She knew what she was bargaining for. . . . The bargain here was for totally personal service. It was a very scarce service Mrs. Whitehead was providing. Indeed, it might even be said she had the dominant bargaining position for without her Mr. Stern had no other immediate source available. Each party sought each other to fulfill their needs. . . .

"She had been pregnant before and had to be aware of the risks of pregnancy," observed the judge, who then grappled with whether $10,000 was too low a fee to assume those risks. "Perhaps the risk was great for the money to be paid but the risk was what Mrs. Whitehead chose to assume and at the agreed upon fee. And it is assumed she received other intangible benefits and satisfactions from doing what she did. Her original application set forth her highly altruistic purpose. . . . All in this world cannot be equated to money."

Since both sides of the contract seemed to be legally in order, Judge Sorkow could have chosen to give the baby to Bill Stern on the grounds that the pre-conception contract terminating Mary Beth's parental rights was binding. This is the approach taken with sperm donors in traditional artificial insemination by donor, in which the agreement to give up parental rights is made before conception and is binding after birth.

But flat-out enforcement of the contract gave the judge pause. It would seem to send a message that the child was an object of barter. He decided that he would enforce the contract only if it were in the child's best interest.

Such an approach would put the case in a much different symbolic light. Bluntly enforcing the contract would give the message that a surrogate should be held to her agreement to turn over the child to the other parent. Such an approach would set no precedent for the millions of other custody cases in which a surrogate agreement was not at issue. It would not rely on any frivolous criteria about who would be a better parent.

Adding in a best-interests analysis, though, would force the judge to deal with the criteria set forth by the experts. It would allow class differences between the Sterns and Whiteheads to figure into the decision of who took the baby home. It would set the precedent for an untold number of custody cases. It would end up affecting the rights of more women than would have a decision based on the contract alone.

In applying a best-interests analysis, Judge Sorkow had several possible options: joint custody, custody to the Whiteheads, or custody to the Sterns. Even if custody went to one side, he could grant visitation rights to the other. Lorraine Abraham, the court-appointed guardian for the child, favored custody to the Sterns, with Mary Beth being kept from the baby for at least five years, at which time the situation would be reevaluated. Such an approach had been suggested by expert witness Dr. Judith Greif, who advocated giving the child a period of stability and who felt that Mary Beth, in her animosity toward the Sterns, might psychologically batter the child.

But total termination of Mary Beth's rights, said Lorraine, was too "awesome a step."

"People are capable of change," Lorraine asserted. "Time heals."

In his decision, Judge Sorkow specifically rejected the suggestion of one expert witness that joint custody should be awarded after six months of court-ordered therapy. "The hurt to each of these parties as perceived by each of them at the hands of the other is genuine. Therapy is minimally successful when spouses have many years of common experience. That therapy could be successful for these parties is doubted. A prerequisite for the success of therapy is a desire for help. A court order will not create such a desire."

He pointed out that the Sterns and Whiteheads would have great difficulty in rearing their daughter together. "They have different life styles, social values and standards," he said. "The rancor is too great. This court doubts that they can isolate their personal animosity and 'all of a sudden' cooperate for the child's benefit."

Gary Skoloff, the Sterns' attorney, had similar comments outside the courtroom. "These four adults will never like each other again, or even respect each other," he said. "When a judge proposes joint custody, we have a rule in our law firm: Don't close the file. Postjudgment motions never end." Already, there had been evidence of an unwillingness to cooperate in decisions about the child. Even though Bill Stern was Jewish, Mary Beth had, without telling him, baptized the baby as Catholic.

With joint custody set aside, the judge faced the task of determining which couple should be the legal parents of Baby M. To his credit, he ignored the really trivial tests of parenting that some of the experts used—the patty-cake and pots-and-pans tests. He did fall into an improper stereotype of thinking that the Sterns' higher level of education would make them more likely to encourage curiosity and learning on the part of the child. But for the most part, Judge Sorkow was painstakingly careful in comparing the families, trait by trait, to determine which would provide the better home for the child. He reviewed evidence on the parties' abilities to recognize and respond to the child's physical and emotional needs, to help the child cope with her life, and to explain to her the circumstances of her origin with the least confusion and greatest emotional support.

In the course of Judge Sorkow's three-hour reading of his lengthy decision, a tense courtroom audience waited intently for his final word. At 5:00 P.M., it came. At that moment, Judge Sorkow stopped referring to the child as Baby M. He said that he had found "that Melissa's best interests will be served by being placed in her father's sole custody."

Bill Stern's reaction was one of total joy. "I have a tingling feeling in my elbows and my legs are numb," he said. "I'm so happy." He then fell silent in tears, resting his head on his wife's shoulder.

After reading the decision terminating Mary Beth's parental

rights, Judge Sorkow presided over a brief adoption ceremony in which Betsy Stern was recognized as the legal mother of Melissa.

Judge Sorkow may have been taking a leaf from the story of King Solomon. In that Biblical tale, two women claiming to be the mother of the same child came before the King. In the absence of evidence, Solomon decreed that he would split the child in half, giving half to each woman. At that point, one of the women, horrified, immediately relinquished her claim and begged that the child be spared. In this way Solomon learned who was the real mother.

In the Baby M case, Mary Beth had indicated that even if the Sterns won custody, she wanted visitation rights to the child. This presented the possibility of the little girl being torn between the two families, with Mary Beth calling her a different name than her father did and Mary Beth more than likely undermining the Sterns' parenting decisions—as she had while the case was pending—by making baseless claims that they were not adequately caring for her daughter.

On the other hand, Bill and Betsy testified that if Mary Beth won custody, they would not seek visitation. "She's brought a lot of joy to our life," Betsy stated, near tears, on the second day of the trial. "But I think it is best for Melissa to have one mother and one father and to grow up in one family."

When the one family chosen was the Sterns, Jan Sutton and the NASM surrogates cheered, as did many members of the press. "We were elated, ecstatic," says Jan. "We got the decision we had been hoping for. The excitement was incredible. We felt like we were a part of history."

Noel Keane also celebrated the decision. "I've had fingers pointed at me as a baby broker," he said. "Now, I feel pretty much vindicated."

Some people felt otherwise. Outside of Noel's New York office, about sixty feminists demonstrated in opposition to the decision and to surrogacy. Their signs read, "Mary Beth is a real mother," "No wombs for rent," "Babies are not for sale," and "A one-night stand in a dish doesn't make a man a parent." One of the protestors, feminist author and psychologist Phyllis Chesler, said, "We want to create a mass popular uprising to have the judge's decision overturned."

It was unclear where the mass for this anticipated uprising would come from, however, since Judge Sorkow's decision was in line with public opinion polls, which revealed that most people favored upholding surrogacy contracts and giving custody to the biological father and his wife. Even President Reagan, hardly known as a legal innovator, said, "I do think the judge made the right decision in the Baby M case."

From time to time during the Baby M case, Lorrie Jones's two boys would ask her what the judge had decided. They talked about the lady who was having a baby for the mommy whose tummy was broken. "That's not right," her five-year-old had said about Mary Beth trying to keep the baby.

"What did the judge say?" he asked when the television started to talk about the decision in the case.

"He said she had to give the baby to the mommy whose tummy's broken," explained Lorrie, who had recently turned over her surrogate baby to Sandra and Hillel. The boys had seen the baby shortly after his birth—and had subsequently run into Sandra, Hillel, and the child at a Toys R Us.

"I think it's really good because they don't have any babies," her five-year-old said. "Now they'll have one just like me and my brother."

Since Sorkow had put a seal of approval on surrogacy, a growing number of couples felt comfortable about coming forward to participate in such arrangements. In the month after the opinion, more couples signed up for Bill Handel's program than had signed up in the entire previous year.

At the end of his opinion, Judge Sorkow had pleaded that the litigation be stopped there. "Melissa needs stability and peace, so that she can be nurtured in a loving environment free from chaos and sheltered from the public eye."

But neither peace nor privacy were in sight. Two days later, Mary Beth announced that she was appealing the case. "I will fight to the end—she's my child," said Mary Beth. "We will not accept the decision of one judge as the final determination of a whole society that we should be permanently separated. There's just no comparison for the real mother, the real thing."

The following week, the New Jersey Supreme Court agreed to give Mary Beth two-hour-a-week visiting privileges during the period in which the case was being appealed. The guardian for the baby, Lorraine Abraham, had argued that a total separation would be harmful for the child if Mary Beth ultimately won her appeal and gained custody.

12

~~~

THE APPEAL OF BABY M

W HILE THE TRIAL COURT proceedings had aroused national interest and attention, the appeal of the Baby M case provoked action. Across the country, dozens of groups and hundreds of individuals met to develop amicus curiae briefs, literally "friend of the court" briefs, which judges rely on in controversial cases to provide broader information than the parties themselves provide in their legal documents.

Familiar figures in the surrogacy debate were closeted with lawyers to craft their positions—Connie Binsfeld, Barbara Katz Rothman, the National Association of Surrogate Mothers, Bill Pierce of the National Committee for Adoption. Groups new to the surrogacy debate, such as the AFL-CIO and a group of sociobiologists, also wanted to make their voices heard. Other contenders in the race to file amicus briefs included the American Adoption Congress, the Catholic League for Religious and Civil Rights, Concerned United Birthparents, the New Jersey Catholic Conference, and RESOLVE, the national self-help group for infertile people.

Many of the amicus briefs made no mention of the baby, the Sterns, or the Whiteheads. Some described what the group filing the brief felt surrogacy meant for society. Others presented evidence—about, for example, the psychological effects of infertility or the aftereffects of relinquishing a child—that they thought might help the court in crafting its opinion. All felt that they had a receptive, thoughtful, intelligent audience in the New Jersey Supreme Court. The court was generally acknowledged to be one of the premier state courts in the country. It was unmatched in dealing with issues of medical ethics that challenged existing values. Its past caseload included determining the fate of another young woman who couldn't voice her preferences—Karen Ann Quinlan.

When Michigan State Senator Connie Binsfeld introduced a bill banning surrogacy four years earlier, she had told the senate that surrogate motherhood was like slavery. For her amicus brief, she joined with New York Law School professor Cyril Means, the Odyssey Institute International, and others to make that argument for the New Jersey Supreme Court.

Their brief alleged that the Stern/Whitehead surrogacy contract was the sale of a child and thus violated the Thirteenth Amendment prohibition against slavery. "Mary Beth Whitehead is not the 'surrogate mother' of Baby M, but her mother, the only mother Baby M will ever have," said the brief. "Mary Beth Whitehead clearly contracted to make a postnatal sale of her child. Whether the buyer was to be William Stern, or whether he was merely a conduit behind whom stands the true buyer, Elizabeth Stern, that Mary Beth Whitehead was a seller is beyond cavil."

Cyril and Connie's brief also argued that the surrogacy agreement was an unenforceable contract requiring involuntary servitude by Mary Beth Whitehead: "Stern did not merely rent a uterus, as one expert witness in the court below crudely put it. Anyone who has lived with a pregnant woman knows that not only her reproductive tract but the entire woman is involved in the pregnancy. Stern rented an entire woman."

The brief filed by Bill Pierce's National Committee for Adoption also was concerned with the surrogate. "In the field of adoption," it noted, "the common law has always presumed that the child's best interests lie with the mother. . . .

"The subject matter of the surrogacy agreement, a human life, does not lend itself to a traditionally rational analysis of contractual intent," noted the brief. "A mother's feelings toward the child she bears are not to be measured by the same standards as a merchant's intentions in relation to his merchandise."

Pierce's brief painted a bleak picture of surrogacy, but presented no real evidence for its allegations. It said that "surrogacy strains familial relations through its destabilizing effect on both couples; the confusion it causes the mother's other children; and the psychological impact of bonding and separation on the mother, not to mention the surrogate child's potentially enormous assimilation problems once the child discovers its origins."

The brief criticized Judge Sorkow: "What the court did amounted to making up its own law of surrogacy." Pierce opposed validating surrogacy, but said if surrogacy were to be allowed, that decision should be made by the legislature, not a court, so that the public could participate in the debate.

"If such a debate were held," said Pierce in his brief, "the National Committee for Adoption is confident that its view on the improvidence of surrogacy would prevail."

Meanwhile, in California, the former and current surrogates who formed the National Association of Surrogate Mothers were worried that the future of surrogacy would hinge entirely on how the New Jersey Supreme Court reacted to Mary Beth. They asked Bill Handel and Hilary Hanafin to help them file a brief in the case to let the court hear about their own experiences.

NASM met twice in May and once in June to discuss the amicus brief for the Baby M case. Hilary framed the issue: "If you could tell the justices whatever you wanted to tell them, what would it be?" The women responded with a torrent of ideas about how surrogate motherhood had affected them—and what sorts of legal rules should govern the arrangement.

The first draft of the brief read like a legislative manifesto. NASM proposed a series of guidelines that should govern any surrogacy arrangement. They advocated twenty requirements to assure that surrogacy protected all the parties. These ranged from extensive psychological screening and counseling to financial evaluations of the surrogate (rejecting poor women to avoid exploitation) and the couple (to assure they could provide for the child's welfare).

But the brief seemed too much like a submission to a legislature, not a court. It was a blueprint for the future of surrogacy, not a means of deciding the troublesome case before the court. So NASM refocused its efforts, having Wendy Leitman, a lawyer in Bill's office, redraft the brief so that it showed that Mary Beth Whitehead was not typical and explained why they felt that the baby should go to Bill and Elizabeth Stern.

"The National Association of Surrogate Mothers," began the brief, "has been formed because the very concept of surrogate parenting is being threatened by this litigation and it is the opinion of this group that surrogate parenting must remain a viable option for couples who need it.

"Surrogate parenting has been a meaningful, fulfilling, and exhilarating experience for each one of us in NASM. We are not dismissing the potential risks involved in surrogate parenting. Furthermore, we do not believe that surrogate parenting is an alternative for everyone. However, we strongly believe that when all parties are carefully and comprehensively screened, when infertile couples and surrogates act responsibly, and when every legal, psychological and medical safeguard is provided, then these arrangements can be concluded safely, with a minimum of risk and the maximum joy: a new family.

"We are sympathetic to Mary Beth Whitehead's case; however, we feel that she is atypical of the average surrogate mother and she, alone, should not be responsible for the banning of the entire practice of surrogate parenting.

"Her attorneys are trying to win their case by claiming that surrogacy is *inevitably* harmful to the surrogates and the resulting children. Such an assertion is unsupported and inconsistent with our own experiences and our knowledge of how surrogacy operates. The defense attorneys have used flimsy analogies to situations in which children were abandoned or unwanted, in which a parent dies, or in which their parents divorced, in order to make predictions about the potential effects of surrogacy. Nowhere have they focused on surrogacy as it actually operates. As the one organization which has had extensive experience with surrogacy, we seek leave of the court to file this amicus brief to present information about the nature, risks, and benefits of surrogate motherhood."

The crafting of the NASM brief involved a series of phone calls to people like Jan Sutton and Lorrie Jones. Wendy, the lawyer writing the brief, would dash down the hall to Hilary's office each time she wanted more psychological evidence and facts.

The NASM brief pointed out that surrogates are in a much different situation than birth mothers in the traditional adoption situation—since the decision is made before conception and the child will be reared by the biological father and his wife. The brief also disputed that surrogacy would harm the resulting children, particularly in an era of independent adoption, artificial insemination by donor, divorce, and blended families. They stressed that these children were going to be raised in loving families—and that there was certainly no evidence that the children would have been better off not born at all than born via a surrogacy arrangement.

NASM also challenged the notion that surrogacy exploits women. "Surrogacy was not forced upon us," explained the NASM surrogates in their brief. "No one showed up on our doorstep, like sellers of encyclopedias, to coerce us into participating in the procedure. Rather, we sought out surrogacy because of our own conscious choice that surrogacy would enhance our lives. Many of us would not have undertaken surrogacy if we had not been paid, but the fee itself was never sufficient. As mothers ourselves in our families, we understood the joys of having a child and could empathize with the emptiness in the lives of couples who could not do so. . . .

"Surrogacy does present potential psychological and physical risks to the women involved," continued NASM. "But generally our society has allowed people to undertake potentially risky activities so long as they have given voluntary informed consent. Men are allowed to be coal miners, firefighters, race car drivers, and U.S. presidents for compensation even though these occupations involve risk. It would be inconsistent and demeaning to women to deny them the chance to be paid surrogate mothers."

The NASM women saw surrogacy as expanding women's choices and giving them added control over their lives and their bodies. In contrast, sociologist Barbara Katz Rothman viewed surrogacy as diminishing women's control and turning them into no more than reproductive vessels. The amicus brief that she helped write presented a much different view of the surrogacy enterprise. Rather than focusing on how individual surrogates fared, the brief put surrogacy into a larger context of changing conceptions about motherhood and parenting. In Barbara's opinion, reproduction in general was becoming industrialized and commercialized.

In the course of the Baby M trial, Michelle Harrison and Phyllis Chesler had asked Barbara to join in the protests supporting Mary Beth Whitehead. Barbara refused. "I felt I could do more for the cause as a sociologist in a gray suit on the 'MacNeil/Lehrer NewsHour' than I could holding a sign on the courthouse steps," says Barbara.

Barbara has been drawn increasingly into the media debate on surrogacy. "I've spent more time putting my makeup on in the greenroom with Noel Keane than putting makeup on in the bathroom with my husband," she jokes.

"The 'tag' they use to identify me on television—the white line of print that shows up on the screen but which I never get to see in the studio—sometimes reads author, rarely reads sociologist, but most often they seem to use 'feminist.' And so there we are, 'feminist' and 'priest' or 'rabbi' arguing the same, anti-surrogacy side." Barbara is concerned about these strange bedfellows. She has been struggling to find a way to join them on the issue of surrogacy without lending support to their other ideas about the role of women in society.

"It is only on the very surface that I am on the same side as these religious leaders," Barbara explained in a 1987 article in *Conscience*. "We may have landed on the same side of this particular fence, but we've taken very different paths to get there, and we are headed in very different directions."

The religious leaders oppose surrogacy because they consider it "unnatural" and feel that it violates the sanctity of the family. Barbara, though, concludes that "the institution of motherhood as it exists in our society is pretty far from any natural state." Far from believing that only a birth mother can nurture a baby, Barbara's sociological research has shown that "loving people, men as well as women, can provide all the warm, caring loving nurturance a baby needs."

Moreover, Barbara is not impressed by arguments based on the sanctity of the family—which is taken to mean the traditional male-dominated nuclear family. Maintaining the sanctity of the family, notes Barbara, "was the argument offered to allow men to beat their wives and children, the argument used to stop funding day care centers, the argument used most generally to stop women from controlling their own lives and their own bodies."

In contrast to the religious opposition, Barbara's concern about surrogacy is that it devalues women. "Surrogacy defines pregnancy, not as a relationship between a woman and her fetus, but as a service she provides for others, thus viewing the woman herself not as a person, but as the container for another, often more valued, person.

"We are encouraging the development of 'production standards' in pregnancy—standards which will begin with the hired pregnancy, but grow to include all pregnancies."

The drafting of an amicus brief in the Baby M case provided the impetus for Barbara to apply the insights she had gained in her work on women's experiences with childbirth and with new obstetrical technologies such as amniocentesis to women's reproductive decisions about surrogacy. In many ways, Barbara's worst fear about surrogacy was coming true: it was causing surrogates—and the public—to view a pregnant woman and her fetus as separate entities, rather than one unit. She was concerned that if such a dichotomy continued, the fetus would receive all of society's attentions and protections and the woman, and her needs, would be rendered invisible.

Barbara had already seen this happen with obstetrical technologies such as ultrasound and fetal monitoring. Prior to the development of such techniques, the fetus's presence in society was evident only through the visible expansion of its mother's abdomen. The obstetrical technologies, though, gave doctors the ability to make direct diagnoses of the fetus's health status. Doctors began to think of the fetus rather than the pregnant woman as their patient. This led to a professional norm in which doctors treated the needs of the fetus, no matter what the needs or desires of the woman. There had already been cases in which doctors obtained court orders to do Cesarean sections on women against their will, on the grounds that they were necessary to protect the fetus. Although the Cesarean sections were major surgeries that put the women's health at risk, subsequent studies showed that more than half of the court-ordered Cesarean sections had been unnecessary.

To Barbara, that meant that women were increasingly being viewed as vessels, as fetal containers, rather than as persons with rights of their own. In one case, a pregnant California woman with terminal cancer told her doctors that she wanted to be resuscitated first if chemotherapy put her into cardiac arrest. Her doctors instead felt that she should undergo a Cesarean section which, in an attempt to save the child, would have killed her. The Department of Social Services declared that the woman's directive showed that she was an unfit parent, but the court sided with the woman. The judicial tide, though, seemed to be going in the other direction.

The willingness of male doctors and male judges to subject pregnant women to all manner of intervention to benefit their potential children contrasted greatly with the law's treatment of fathers. If a man's child needed a blood transfusion, and the father refused to provide blood, a court would not compel him. A court certainly would not compel a father to give up a kidney to his dying child. Yet pregnant women were being forced to undergo risky operations to protect potential children.

Barbara felt that upholding the Stern/Whitehead contract and giving legal credence to surrogacy would worsen this trend. "We are moving toward viewing babies as products," says Barbara. "Women, rather like South African diamond miners, are the cheap, expendable, not-too-trustworthy labor necessary to produce the product."

That was how Barbara viewed the Baby M case: "A baby was ordered from a worker, but the worker got uppity and refused to turn over the product. So the court was called in to decide who has rights of ownership in the product—the worker or the employer?"

Barbara was also concerned that women's own perceptions of their pregnancies would change if surrogate motherhood were sanctioned. Women might view their reproductive potential as a lucrative resource, their bodies as factories.

Some of the issues that Barbara Katz Rothman was positing were coming true with Lorrie Jones. Lorrie had said she was dying to have another surrogacy pregnancy for Sandra and Hillel, because of the close bond she had established to the couple. But since they were not ready for a second child just yet, Lorrie had signed up to be a stand-in mom for a wealthy South American couple. They wanted a boy, so the sperm was being centrifuged to increase the likelihood of its bearing Y chromosomes. Her fee— $25,000—was more than twice what she had earned in her first surrogate pregnancy.

Lorrie looked forward to having another child for Sandra and Hillel. She thought back on Sandra's excitement in the delivery room. She was holding onto Sandra's arm. "Because of the epidural anesthesia, I couldn't feel the baby's head coming out," relates Lorrie. "But I felt Sandra's legs buckle and I thought she was going to fall. I knew her son had arrived.

"That was the happiest moment of my life," said Lorrie four months later. "I was on cloud nine for a month afterward." The enthusiasm rose in her voice. "I can't *wait* to do it again for them. I couldn't care less about the money. I would do it for nothing for them."

Sandra and Hillel are equally excited. When Alan quickly began to sleep through the night, Sandra was disappointed. She was so thrilled by the infant that she wanted to wake up every two hours to care for him.

Lorrie clearly loves Alan. "I want another baby to be his full-blooded brother or sister. I care about him and I feel he'll be more secure then." She's worried about what he'll think about her being a surrogate for another couple. "I want him to know that I care about him. I don't want him to say in future years, 'You had a baby for every Tom, Dick, and Harry on the face of the planet.'" Because of this concern, she planned to distance herself from her second surrogate baby. "I'll never see him after the birth," she said. The wife will leave her country during the pregnancy, so that all her friends and relatives will think the baby is her natural child.

"We don't need the $25,000," Lorrie explained after contracting with the South American couple, and indeed her financial situation had improved markedly since the tough times when her second child was born. "We could easily afford to buy a home without my being a surrogate again. For me, the attraction is being pregnant. I admit I'm unusual. I don't get morning sickness or stretch marks. I have a short labor. The money's a bonus."

Although Lorrie claimed the money made no difference, one couldn't help but wonder if she had come to view her body in a new way, with her fertility as a valued resource not to be wasted.

Psychologist Hilary Hanafin is concerned about surrogates who enter the program a second time to create a child for yet another couple. "The vast majority of surrogates should only do this one time, except if they are having another child for the same couple," she says. "To be a surrogate mother once and create a child and have a wonderful positive experience can be a very, very positive thing. What I'm concerned about, if a woman wants to do it repeatedly, is to understand what she is trying to get out of it for herself. To use a terrible analogy, is it like a person who keeps buying new clothes or keeps dieting, but she still doesn't feel any better about herself? If a surrogate is going to do it more than once, I take a much harder look." However, since Lorrie is going outside the regular surrogate program for this second pregnancy, and acting as a surrogate for some close personal friends of Bill Handel's, Hilary could not prevent Lorrie from being a surrogate.

"I'll have this baby for the second couple," said Lorrie, "and then another baby for Sandra and Hillel, and then a baby of my own.

"Then," said Lorrie in language that would make Barbara's hair stand on end, "then, I'm going to close down production."

Spearheading the efforts on the brief that Barbara collaborated on were Jeremy Rifkin and Andrew Kimbrell of the Foundation for Economic Trends, based in Washington, D.C. Jeremy, who established and runs the nonprofit public-interest foundation, concentrates most of his efforts on opposing biotechnology. In the past, he has initiated lobbying efforts, lawsuits, and press campaigns to oppose genetic engineering of plants and animals. He worries that surrogacy is the first step in the bioengineering of humans.

"Our whole idea of producing offspring is to have it done by loving people who are intimate," says Jeremy. "If we allow commercial surrogacy, what message does this send to our children?"

Jeremy had long criticized the way that policy gets made in the area of technology. "With technology, you have a sense of de facto legislation," he says. "Only after the technology is well established do state legislative bodies and Congress and the courts try to sort it out. Our strategy is much different than most public interest groups. It is to engage in debate at the conceptual stages, before a technology gets entrenched. We don't accept the idea that if something can be done, it will be done."

Most of the writing of the brief was done in the modest three-room headquarters that Jeremy and Andrew share with up to four other staff members. A poster of a geep—the cross between a goat and sheep that scientists have recently created—hangs on the wall. To the researchers who manufactured it, the geep represents a stunning advance. To Jeremy, it represents a world gone awry—in which man is trying to play God.

The brief made the traditional arguments against surrogacy: "Instead of bearing the child with a view to loving, nurturing, and protecting it and thereby enhancing the family unit, the mother is induced by much-needed financial gain to sever the bond between her and her baby, to both her's and her baby's detriment." The brief also called for giving priority to the biological mother over the biological father in any custody decision.

But the brief went far beyond these standard legal arguments to put surrogate motherhood into a larger context of medical and social developments affecting reproduction. It described in vitro fertilization, embryo transfer, embryo freezing, and the increasing ability to isolate and identify elements of the genetic code. "Given this technological milieu," argued the brief, "the enforcement of this contract and those similar to it will lead to the full-scale commercialization of women's reproductive organs and genetic makeup.

"As the technology develops, the 'surrogate' becomes a kind of reproductive technology laboratory. She is constantly tested and prodded in order to ensure that she is a serviceable 'maternal environment' for the purposes of bearing the 'customer' couple's child. In short, she has been dehumanized and has been reduced to a mere commodity in the 'reproductive' marketplace.

"It was the opinion of the trial court that the revolution in reproductive technologies offers 'awesome possibilities.' One might respectfully disagree with that assessment—and many *amici curiae* do—because the varied pressures imposed on women by these reproductive technologies may actually reduce, rather than enhance their freedoms, opportunities, and status. Thus, likely candidates for surrogacy may come to be viewed more as reproductive vehicles—uteruses for hire—than as individually important persons, with the right to the integrity of their own relationships with husbands and children, and to the privacy and independence of their reproductive capabilities."

When the brief was completed, it was endorsed not only by Barbara, Andrew, and Jeremy, but also by twenty-one other prominent feminists. Many, like Michelle Harrison, Gena Corea, Lois Gould, Phyllis Chesler, Betty Friedan, and Gloria Steinem, had participated in the original protests and letters of support on Mary Beth's behalf.

Andrew, the lawyer who did most of the actual drafting on the brief, tried to get other national organizations, such as the National Organization of Women and the American Civil Liberties Union, to sign the brief as well. None were willing to do so. Surrogacy was such a confounding issue that these groups felt they needed more time to determine what policies they would advocate in the area.

Surrogate attorney Bill Handel, psychologist Hilary Hanafin, and the members of the National Association of Surrogate Mothers were disturbed that so many of the amicus briefs, including the one submitted by Barbara and the Foundation for Economic Trends, disparaged the role of fathers.

"We are supposed to have equality," says Bill. "Feminists talk about equality. But Betty Friedan portrays the father as a guy who jerks off in a Dixie cup. She refuses to recognize his emotional involvement, his desperation, his putting up his life savings."

Hilary was upset about the "condescending remarks about producing sperm in a cup. No credit was being given Mr. Stern for emotional attachment.

"Men are not given credit again for any emotional attachments which is too bad, because I think that produces a society of men who aren't very well rounded," observes Hilary. "Stern has been teased and viewed negatively because he cares that way."

Mary Beth Whitehead's brief criticized William Stern as "narcissistic" for wanting to have a child genetically related to himself. The NASM brief responded that "such a desire is biologically understandable, morally appropriate and constitutionally protected. Indeed, it is a pillar of our society. It is so understandable and appropriate that no one would even consider criticizing the Whiteheads for having their own biological children, Tuesday and Ryan, rather than adopting some needy orphan."

The Whitehead brief also argued that Mary Beth deserved custody of Baby M because she had been pregnant and Bill Stern had not: "Pregnancy, after all, prepares the mother to care for the child in a very special way that neither the father nor even an adoptive mother could ever have the advantage of." Mary Beth's attorney argued that Judge Sorkow should have considered "the actual emotional preparation of pregnancy in making the natural mother a better caretaker of the baby."

In contrast, Dr. Judith Greif, one of the experts called by Baby M's guardian, had testified that "parenting is a social function and there is no research to demonstrate the notion that mothers are inherently better equipped to deal with the various issues and the various developmental stages of their children than are fathers simply by virtue of the fact that mothers are pregnant and fathers are not."

On September 14, 1987, after the parties and the amicus groups had filed their briefs, the New Jersey Supreme Court convened to hear the appeal of the case. There was a glamour about the occasion, as in the opening of a Broadway play. Indeed, when the principals walked in—the Sterns, the Whiteheads—courthouse personnel felt a little awe, as in the presence of movie stars.

Space inside the courtroom was at a premium. By the time the parties, the lawyers, and the amicus representatives had been seated, there were few spots left for reporters and the public. Admission to the drama hinged on possession of a small pink pass (suitable for a case about a baby girl), festooned with a bright blue court seal and the words, "Supreme Court of New Jersey, A-39 IMO Baby M." One of the guards outside the courtroom had one hidden under his hat, and was jokingly offering to sell it.

Inside the courtroom, Bill and Betsy Stern sat on one side of the room, Richard, Mary Beth, and Tuesday Whitehead on the other. Bill's right arm stretched across his body, his hand resting tenderly on Betsy's. In the Whitehead domain, the tenderness ran between mother and daughter. Mary Beth and Tuesday wore identical blue-and-green plaid dresses, with white lace collars. Each wore her hair braided in back, with a black bow. When the Sterns' attorney, Gary

Skoloff, admitted to the court that there had been no evidence that Mary Beth had been an unfit mother to Tuesday or Ryan, mother and daughter looked at each other and smiled.

During the oral argument, Lorraine Abraham, the attorney appointed to represent Baby M, emphasized that the case dealt with the most ancient of relationships, yet needed to be decided with awareness of both technological and social changes. "This case addresses the most fundamental of all human relationships—the need to procreate and to have love and companionship," she told the justices. "But there is a difficulty in fitting the technology into the existing statutes." Moreover, she argued, the justices couldn't just assume that the mother would make the best parent. "That doesn't reflect society now," said Lorraine, whose experience at the bar included the formation of New Jersey's first all-female law firm. "I say that even knowing my client [Baby M] is a woman. Laws are written to be color blind and to have sex not make a difference."

The chief justice of the New Jersey Supreme Court took an activist role at the oral argument. When Mary Beth's attorney, Harold Cassidy, indicated that most surrogates are poor, Chief Justice Robert Wilentz pointedly replied, "Just as offers of adoption usually come from women who are poor." Another Whitehead attorney, Alan Karcher, demeaned the male role in parenting, saying "the male portion is fungible and transient." Chief Justice Wilentz seemed offended: "I follow the transient, not the fungible."

When addressing the attorneys for the rival parents, the justices raised two concerns: Which side would provide better parenting for the child *in this particular case*? And then, on a broader scale, What rules should society adopt to cover surrogate motherhood in general?

Neither side's attorney handled both dimensions adequately. Mary Beth's lawyer, Harold Cassidy, dealt with the societal implications of surrogate motherhood, but presented no solid evidence about why his client would be a good parent for the child. He went so far as to suggest that, even if Baby M would be worse off with her mother than with her father, Mary Beth should get custody just to discourage surrogacy.

Gary Skoloff, on the other hand, fought ably for the rights of his clients, the Sterns, but did not provide adequate answers when Justice Alan Handler asked him what the general societal policy should be on surrogacy and what standards should be required for surrogacy agreements to be valid.

At the close of the arguments, then, it seemed that the justices were going off without all the pieces of the puzzle. In such a situation, the materials in the amicus briefs would clearly be an important resource.

The justices' decision in the Baby M case took twenty weeks to write and render. On February 3, 1988, they announced the result. In a startling reversal of Judge Sorkow's opinion, the New Jersey Supreme Court held that the existing adoption laws *did* apply to surrogate motherhood arrangements. Until the legislature enacted laws specific to surrogacy, the provisions banning payment to a biological mother and invalidating a prebirth surrender of parental rights would govern surrogacy arrangements.

In refusing to enforce the contract, the court put Mary Beth back in the role of the legal mother, and sent the case back to the lower courts to determine what her visitation rights should be. The court was satisfied that custody should remain with the Sterns, however.

The court noted that, under current law, "the claims of the natural father and the natural mother are entitled to equal weight." Custody is determined based on the child's best interest.

The court chided Judge Sorkow for placing too much emphasis in his custody determination on the educational disparity between the parties. The court wrote that "a best-interests test is designed to create not a new member of the intelligentsia but rather a well-integrated person who might reasonably be expected to be happy with life. . . .

"Stability, love, family happiness, tolerance, and ultimately, support of independence—all rank much higher in predicting future happiness than the likelihood of a college education," the court continued. Using those criteria, however, the court judged the Sterns to be the better potential parents.

Any judgment about the proper home for Baby M is an intensely personal one. "Where you stand on this case probably tells more about your emotional makeup than your powers of judgment," observed columnist Russell Baker. It also tells a lot about your concept of motherhood. If one were to psychoanalyze the New Jersey Supreme Court opinion, one would find within it the justices' dream of the perfect mother.

Unlike the trial court's, the supreme court's decision was supportive of Mary Beth's decision to flee with the baby. They wrote that "it is expecting something well beyond normal human capabilities to suggest that this mother should have parted with her newly born infant without a struggle. Other than survival, what stronger force is there?"

But even though the New Jersey Supreme Court justices lauded the fact that Mary Beth loved the child so much that she ran with her, lied to try to keep her, and put her other children at risk, the justices used that love against her in determining custody. They felt that she would love the child so much that she wouldn't allow her sufficient independence.

The court's decision was very much in line with the testimony of Dr. Greif, who had suggested that Mary Beth was so overidentified with the baby that she was unable to separate out her own needs from the needs of the child. Greif also stated that, with respect to her other children, Mary Beth failed to recognize that they had thoughts and feelings separate from her own, and consequently exploited them to meet her own needs.

At the opening of the trial, Harold Cassidy had told Judge Sorkow, "The defendant in this case is motherhood." In the resolution of the case, the New Jersey Supreme Court seemed uncomfortable both with the traditional view of mothering and with surrogacy's new vision. The old seemed *too* caring, the new not caring enough.

The image the court created of the perfect parent is of one who so loves you that she would go to any length to protect you and nurture you when you are young and dependent, but not interfere a whit with your life once you don't need her any more. This might be everybody's dream mother, but is it realistic to expect any parent who loves a child that much not to show concern, offer advice, and, yes, perhaps even meddle when the child gets older?

The justices also pointed out that "certain of the experts noted that Mrs. Whitehead perceived herself as omnipotent and omniscient concerning her children," as knowing better than outsiders what the children wanted. Such an attitude, though, would seem to be a necessary survival mechanism for parents. Being a parent contains elements of being an educator, doctor, drill sergeant, friend, psychotherapist, philosopher, cook, coach, and more. There are no firm rules; different approaches work with different children, even within the same family. It would be an over-whelmingly intimidating task if a parent didn't feel some level of special confidence regarding his or her offspring. With hundreds of decisions to be made about each child each day, you can't go running off to a professional at each juncture. And if you did run off to experts like Dr. Marshall Schechter, you'd be so neurotic perfecting your game of patty-cake you'd have little time for any other aspect of parenting.

As throughout the whole Baby M debate, women got a raw deal in the New Jersey Supreme Court appeal of the case. Elizabeth Stern got her adoptive rights to the child stripped away, even though she had provided the actual parenting for the infant for over a year. Mary Beth, by the court's description a quintessen-tial mother, was punished for not meeting the standards of experts on the subject. And, through the negative language the court used throughout about surrogacy, the New Jersey Supreme Court was sending a clear message: Women need to be protected from their own decisions. Women do not know what is best for their poten-tial children.

There are dangers with allowing courts and legislatures to sub-stitute their judgments about reproductive arrangements for those of women. Not only does such a substitution constitute a viola-tion of the woman's biological and psychological integrity, but also there is no guarantee it will actually benefit the children.

Those dangers are illustrated most chillingly by a Washington, D.C., case—which the justices in the Baby M case referred to fa-vorably in their decision. In that case, a pregnant woman was terminally ill. She refused to allow a Cesarean section to be done on her to remove the fetus prematurely; such an operation would hasten the woman's death. Although her physicians supported her decision, the hospital attorneys went to court to force her to undergo the surgery. The judges decided that they were willing to shorten the woman's life—in order to protect her potential child. The operation was performed against the woman's will, and the woman died. The premature baby they had forcibly re-moved from her died as well.

The New Jersey Supreme Court did indicate that the Baby M opinion was not the final word on the matter of surrogate mother-hood. The issue properly belonged in the state legislatures.

"We do not underestimate the difficulties of legislation on this subject," concluded the court. "In addition to the inevitable con-frontations with the ethical and moral issues involved, there is the question of the wisdom and effectiveness of regulating a matter so private, yet of such public interest. . . . The problem is how to enjoy the benefits of the technology—especially for infertile couples—while at the same time minimizing the risk of abuse. The problem can be addressed only when society decides what its values and objectives are in this troubling, yet promising area."

PART III

MAKING LAW

13

~∞~

MATERNITY POLICE

A NUMBER OF LAWMAKERS were ready to take up the gaunt-
let thrown down by the New Jersey Supreme Court. Within a
few weeks of the decision, legislatures in several states had authorized study commissions to look into the issue of surrogacy.
But New York State Senator Mary Goodhue and Michigan State
Senator Connie Binsfeld had moved much further than that.
Their legislative activities during the course of the Baby M controversy had put them into the position of being able to introduce
specific legislation on the subject.

In Michigan, the surrogacy center of the country due to Noel
Keane's work, five years' worth of bills had not yet resulted in any
legislation on surrogate motherhood. Connie Binsfeld was furious. "Legislators have a responsibility to educate themselves and
establish the public policy—otherwise it is made by judges," she
told her colleagues in the capitol.

Connie decided that the best way to prod lawmakers into action
was to combine the deliberations of a blue-ribbon panel of experts
with the suggestions of a large cross-section of the public. In July
1985, Connie had persuaded the legislature to hire Judianne
Densen-Gerber, who was both a lawyer and psychiatrist, to pre-

pare a background report on reproductive technologies for the legislature, with an eye toward developing a model bill. Judianne's professional background was in the areas of drug abuse, child abuse, incest, and child pornography. Her path had crossed with Connie's on the issue of sexual abuse of children.

Judianne Densen-Gerber had no particular qualifications to perform a study on surrogacy—the résumé she presented to the Michigan legislature mentioned no background or interest in reproductive technologies.

The Connie/Judianne partnership strikes people as strange at first. Although they are both gray-haired older women, slightly on the heavy side, the images they convey differ dramatically. The round-cheeked, spectacled Connie wears sensible shoes, dark conservative suits with white blouses, and a matronly close-cropped bubble haircut. A former Michigan Mother of the Year, Connie was a stay-at-home wife. She did not run for state office until her youngest child entered college.

Judianne sports straight hair that reaches her waist, and wears colorful Indian clothing, sneakers, and large noisy jewelry. She worked and traveled while her children were young. While Connie cooked and cleaned, Judianne left those tasks to a governess-housekeeper and cook-butler. In fact, Judianne once wrote a book claiming that being a stay-at-home wife and mother was destructive, leading to adultery and disturbed and unhappy children.

Judianne had a colorful past. In 1966, she had founded Odyssey House in New York City, a highly structured communal setting for the treatment of drug addicts. In the next decade, she received federal, state, and local funds for Odyssey and developed similar residences in New Jersey, Connecticut, New Hampshire, Michigan, Louisiana, Utah, and Nevada. On various occasions in the mid-1970s Odyssey House was charged with violations of its city contract—financial irregularities and improper admissions practices. Judianne, the head of Odyssey House, resigned. She switched her focus to child protection issues, becoming a psychiatric witness in cases of incest and child abuse and lobbying for legislation in those areas.

The bond between Connie and Judianne, despite their disparate styles, was that they both focused much of their professional

efforts on protecting a particular group of children—the abused. The heartbreaking situation of these children led Connie and Judianne to distrust adults' willingness and ability to protect all children—and consequently caused them each to advocate great leeway for the government in telling people what they should and should not do in the creation and rearing of a family.

In turning their attentions to surrogacy, the tactics of Connie and Judianne were highly interventionist. Rather than trying to devise a statutory scheme to assure that the couples contracting with the surrogates would indeed provide a good home for the children and that women were making informed decisions to be surrogates, Connie and Judianne favored banning surrogacy altogether. In hearing about their approach, Noel Keane pointed out that "it's easy to take a moralistic approach to something that has never affected you."

When Judianne was hired, Michigan legislators thought they would be getting an objective study. She even managed to convince lawmakers in at least nine other states that her report would be so important that they agreed to give it consideration. But as early as the July 1985 press conference at which Connie announced Judianne's hiring, Judianne tipped her hand. Before collecting any information for her study, Judianne condemned reproductive technologies as being like the experiments of Nazi war criminal Josef Mengele.

Judianne's contract with the state required a final product by September 1986, but that date came and went. As the Baby M case caught public attention, Connie became impatient.

"When the Mary Beth Whitehead case broke," says Connie, "I thought this might help move mine along." She immediately called Judianne. "How long is the study going to take?" she asked.

At that point, Judianne had prepared no background materials on surrogacy to help the legislature. She had begun, though, to conduct a fifty-six-question poll, published in magazines, to get people's opinions about reproductive technologies.

The readers who were asked to respond to this poll were told that their answers would be taken into consideration in the drafting of the legislation. The introduction to the magazine poll said, "Remember, this poll is a rare chance for private citizens to guide the course of legislation on one of the most sensitive issues in sci-

ence and society." It also promised that the lawmakers would be listening to them.

When the Baby M case broke, Connie and Judianne made plans to invite experts from around the country to discuss the results of the poll and to draft model legislation on surrogacy and other reproductive technologies. Judianne wanted to hold the meeting in Bellagio, Italy. A more sensible Connie decided on Rochester, Michigan.

"Our original idea was to meet for one week," says Connie, "but we couldn't get sufficient funding. If it had been about labor negotiations we would have gotten the money. Finally, Gloria Smith, head of the Michigan Department of Public Health, came through with the money."

Connie attributes the lack of fiscal and intellectual attention to this issue in the legislature to male lawmakers' lack of real concern for children. "Men like children," says Connie. "They're interested in children, but when it comes to legislation about children, there's not a lot of lobbyists to promote those causes, so male legislators don't give children's issues much attention."

Judianne had a free hand in putting together the committee, but in February 1987 she was having trouble finding a Catholic priest who would agree to participate. Judianne finally came back to Connie and said, "You find a Catholic priest."

A few days later, the Vatican released its "Instruction on Respect for Human Life in Its Origins and on the Dignity of Procreation" criticizing traditional artificial insemination, surrogate motherhood, and in vitro fertilization. "At first no one would agree to participate, and then the Vatican statement came out and all of sudden we had three Catholic priests who wanted to be on the committee," says Connie.

In all, twenty people, including this author, were asked to be part of the committee and to spend three days deliberating at what they were told would be a "Symposium on Evolving Reproductive Technologies." That title was written on the badges and on the glossy red folder that held the agenda. The invitations highlighted the opportunity for the committee to discuss these issues in greater depth than legislators had time for and promised that any dissents would be published as a part of the report in order for all sides of the issue to be heard. The meeting was to take place

over the weekend as the nation stood poised waiting for the trial court decision in the Baby M case, which was due to be released that Monday.

It was an imposing site for such a meeting: a hundred-room mansion known as Meadow Brook Hall, in Rochester, Michigan, about an hour outside of Detroit. Built in the late 1920s by Matilda Dodge, the widow of auto czar John Dodge, and her second husband Alfred Wilson, the eighty-thousand-square-foot mansion had been willed to the state for the creation of Oakland University, which uses it as a conference site.

The family the Wilsons had raised in the house was an eclectic mixture of children from John Dodge's first marriage (Matilda was his third wife), children from the union of Matilda and John, and two children whom Alfred and Matilda had adopted.

As the committee members arrived at Meadow Brook Hall, they noticed that the mansion still retained all the touches of a private home—little knickknacks in the rooms, worn carpeting, no locks on the bedroom doors, bathrooms down the hallway. It was an intimate atmosphere, despite the size of the place, in which twenty people could become close and supportive like a family. Or, also like a family, they could have bitter disagreements and jockey for power.

This committee, which was to make its assessment over a three-day period, included only a few members with any previous background in reproductive technologies, despite the fact that a vast literature on the subject, representing years of study and research, already existed. Each new bit of data, about surrogacy, each psychological study, each expert witness in a case, each piece of investigative journalism raised new questions about how and whether surrogate motherhood fit into society. Connie and Judianne were asking twenty participants, most of them people who had not before explored the issues in depth, to race through a whole course of policy questions and come to conclusions that could profoundly affect thousands of lives.

Content to sit back and see how the discussion developed, Connie turned the meeting over to Judianne.

Perhaps because Judianne is a psychiatrist, this meeting did not begin like most policy meetings on reproductive technologies. Here participants were seated in a circle and asked to reveal intimate facts about their upbringings and backgrounds.

Judianne described her own life. She recounted how she had undergone surgery and had been implanted with a teflon ureter at an early age. Doctors had told her that she should not bear children. She had defied them, giving birth to five children.

Various participants expressed a conservative view of women and of the family. "Women are goddesses," said Michael Meredith, who worried that "women have lost the right to be worshipped by their husbands."

As each committee member described his or her personal and professional background, it became clear that a number of them had previous and close ties to Judianne Densen-Gerber. One was a pediatrician from Tampa who had worked with her on child abuse issues, another was someone Judianne introduced as her "personal lawyer," one was on the board of directors of the Detroit Odyssey House, another had worked on child abuse issues with Judianne in Utah.

A *New York* magazine article described Densen-Gerber as someone who "demanded an extraordinary measure of personal support and loyalty from those around her." The colleagues and friends she appointed to the committee seemed indeed to have an unswerving loyalty to Judianne. Committee member Michael Meredith, her Utah child-abuse connection, called Judianne "God's gift to this world in these troubled times."

Throughout the telling of these personal histories, participants constantly spoke of their excitement over being the first group to tackle these issues. This impression was understandable coming from the newcomers to the issue, but Judianne and Connie should have known otherwise. Many groups— governmental commissions around the world, the American Fertility Society, the Office of Technology Assessment of the U.S. Congress—had gone before them. Bar associations, medical societies, and infertility support groups had sponsored conferences on the subject of reproductive technologies and law schools offered similarly focused courses. Professional journals carried the results of research in the area. The committee ignored these past deliberations.

A certain ceremony set the tenor of the debate. At the introductions, half of the members of the group specifically mentioned that they had been raised as Roman Catholics or educated at some point in Roman Catholic institutions. There were opening and closing prayers the first evening of the meeting, and a special Sunday mass for the group. At the Friday night dinner, when the participants gathered in a circle to begin their first deliberations, Connie stood up and announced, "Since I didn't order the cherries jubilee for dessert and nevertheless it came for all of us, I think that the flame is the presence of the Holy Ghost and that He is watching over our deliberations.

"People will look back on this as a historic event," she said. Connie was putting a lot of stock in this meeting.

Later, committee member Christopher Flores would comment, "The child abuse and religious perspective had a definite impact on the votes and the decision making."

Originally Connie had described the meeting as "an academic meeting, bipartisan," and committee members had been told that all viewpoints would be represented. Noel Keane had been invited, and he carefully scrutinized the list of participants. There were those members that had worked with Judianne on child abuse issues. There was Cyril Means, the New York Law School professor who compared surrogate motherhood to slavery. There was Gena Corea, author of *The Mother Machine*, who called surrogacy "reproductive prostitution" and argued in favor of a criminal ban on surrogacy. There was a physician who offered artificial insemination by donor, but who had refused to inseminate a surrogate.

There *were* two female lawyers with a background in reproductive issues, but one of them had filed a brief in Mary Beth Whitehead's favor in the Baby M case.

In Noel Keane's eyes the deck was clearly stacked. He decided not to participate.

On that late Friday night, Judianne and Connie discussed the mission of the committee. They had stopped referring to the group as the "Symposium on Evolving Reproductive Technologies," now referring to it as a task force about "the New Reproductive Technologies vs. the Best Interests of the Child." This shift of focus wasn't lost on committee member Nadine Taub, the Rutgers University law professor who was directing the Project on Reproductive Laws in the 1990s. In a later critical letter to Judianne and Connie, Nadine pointed out that the new moniker "presupposes that the new reproductive technologies are not consistent with the child's best interest."

It was about 11:00 P.M. when Judianne turned to the first meaty issue about reproductive technologies. It was hard for the group to address it in its sleepy state, having flown in from various parts of the country that very evening after a week of work. Judianne was asking them to come to cloture on the issue of whether the U.S. Constitution protects a couple's decision to use reproductive technologies. She whetted their appetites by flipping the pages of the thick computer printout of responses to her survey.

Most of the survey respondents thought there was a constitutional right to use reproductive technologies—a response which Judianne criticized. The committee at Meadow Brook, too tired to give this constitutional issue its due, voted to postpone discussion until the next morning.

The Michigan meeting was off to a strange start. Most previous deliberations on reproductive technologies had followed a particular approach. First there was a period of data collection, then data analysis, then policy recommendations. For example, when the New York legislature began to consider this issue, the joint committees on the judiciary of the assembly and the senate put staff members to work reading a vast number of articles on the subject, and then asked people who worked in the field of reproductive technology, who had participated in surrogacy, or whose groups (adoptions groups, religious groups) had an interest in the area, to testify at a hearing in New York. From that point the staff went over all materials and drafted a lengthy report on surrogate parenting. The report in turn was given consideration by legislators, who drafted a model bill on the subject. The bill itself was subject to further scrutiny and subsequent hearings.

Similarly, when the National Academy of Sciences appointed an advisory committee to address the issues raised by reproductive technologies, that committee started the meeting with presentations describing the nature of the procedures, the risks and benefits, how many times each particular reproductive technology had been attempted in the past, how many children to date had been created through the techniques, and how those children had fared. Then experts from the animal field presented the results of their research on alternative reproduction in animals to give participants an idea of where human reproductive technologies were going in the future.

The background materials were not sent out in advance to the Michigan panel. Nor did the meeting start with experts or members of the panel describing what was known about medically assisted reproduction or its potential effects.

Instead, after the long first session which ended with a brief discussion of the constitutional issue, boxes of materials such as the Vatican Instruction, a feminist critique on the new reproductive technologies, and a provocative magazine article about male pregnancy, along with hundreds of other pages of articles were put in piles around a table in the carriage house of the Meadow Brook estate. It was nearly midnight when the participants were told to collect a copy from each stack and read the material that night. Breakfast would be at 8:00 A.M.

The next day, the group again addressed the issue of whether the constitutional right to privacy encompassed the right to reproduce using a surrogate mother. W. D. ("Dub") White, a professor who taught courses in English, theology, and medical ethics, put forward the following statement, which the group agreed with in principle: "All human beings have a basic human right to seek to reproduce. The Constitution protects the right against governmental interference, although a compelling state interest might outweigh this right."

Having that high principle to guide them on their way, the committee began to discuss specific issues in greater depth. Dub White again provided a structure by suggesting that the group take two votes on each issue. The first would register whether people were morally opposed to a proposed arrangement—such as artificial insemination of an unmarried women or payment to a surrogate mother. The second vote would indicate whether they felt the law should prohibit a particular arrangement by providing jail sentences for those who engaged in it. Dub himself felt there were many activities that should be discouraged at a personal level—but with which the law itself had no business interfering. There were limits to the government's ability to legislate a particular view of morality.

Rather than attacking the issues and problems already confronting the citizens of Michigan, Judianne steered the discussion first to the most futuristic science-fiction scenarios. She talked about the potential for male pregnancy in which an embryo might be implanted in the abdomen of a man, to be delivered by Cesarean section. She raised questions about whether it should be permissible to merge man and animal in some way—at the genetic level, at the chromosomal level, or at the whole entity level.

The problem with launching into the discussion of genetics and microbiology was that the people at this meeting were even less prepared for those issues than they were for reproductive technologies. Committee members were incredibly confused about the differences between various genetic technologies and what it might mean to create a chimera. They became mired in a lengthy discussion of genetic technology which seemed outside of their directive to look at evolving reproductive technologies. Precious minutes that could have been spent on the central mission were slipping away. Finally the committee decided to skirt the issue altogether by putting a statement in the preface of the final report saying that the recommendations were not intended to have any effect on genetic engineering since that was not within the mandate of the group.

It was midday Sunday before they finally turned to the crucial issue of medically assisted reproduction. Before the votes could begin, however, the committee was derailed by another issue. Three of the panelists had decided not to come to the meeting— Noel Keane, a state legislator, and a New York lawyer. Another panelist, Gloria Smith, was going to have to leave early. Judianne was not prepared to take any votes until the group had somehow pulled together twenty people for the panel. She explained it as follows: she was only willing to take votes if there were twenty people because then she could multiply it easily by five to get one hundred percent. "This way I will be able to easily report our findings to the media," she said.

To get the numbers up to twenty, however, was difficult. The group had been joined Saturday night by Joan Heifetz Hollinger, who was a professor of law at the University of Detroit, who had written a comprehensive article on reproductive technologies, and who held a relatively liberal position in comparison to most of the group.

Even though it seemed to many on the panel that Joan would

be a good candidate to join the group since she knew so much about reproductive technologies, Connie determined that Hollinger should not be allowed to vote because, said Connie, Joan had not been there for the previous day's discussion. Panel member Professor Cyril Means, who opposed surrogacy, nonetheless recognized Joan's background and advocated that she be allowed to vote. Connie demurred, saying that it would undermine the credibility of the group, and suggested instead that two law students who had been hired to take notes for the session should be allowed to vote in the proceedings. It still did not stack up to twenty, however, and someone pointed out that it would more seriously damage the credibility of the panel to include two law students as supposedly expert members while turning away a law professor who was well versed in the area. Finally, the group resoundingly overrode Judianne's mathematical concerns and decided to go forward with only sixteen voting members.

With over half of its total deliberation time already used up, the group was anxious to get on to the actual voting. They began at a frenetic pace, voting on dozens of issues in rapid succession.

Vote after vote was taken with little time for discussion and the whole affair seemed to career out of control. At a number of points, certain members of the committee had to abstain totally from voting because they could not understand what the group was voting on.

"I had thought that the meeting would include in-depth discussions of the issues with people from a variety of backgrounds," says committee member David Rankin, a minister from the Fountain Street Church in Flint, Michigan. "I knew after the first three hours that it had gone awry already. The leaders—Connie and Judianne—had come with an agenda. They were looking for support. They didn't want dialogue."

"The meeting was overwhelming," says committee member Christopher Flores, a longtime friend and associate of Judianne, who had himself experienced infertility. "The process was not sensitive enough to the degree of importance at stake." Christopher is critical of the lack of background information to help people understand what they were voting on. He laments that other infertile people and other physicians were not included at the meeting since they would be the ones most affected by any laws that were developed.

"The meeting was not structured well," Chris continues. "The votes were too quick, just too quick. In some cases, I had to abstain."

David Rankin comments that "some people hardly knew what was going on at all. They had no background in the area and no research was distributed prior to the conference. These people were lost. In voting, all they could give were personal prejudices."

"We had no history of working with each other," says Nadine Taub. "We were not even familiar with each other's work since many had not written in this area. Since the background materials were passed out at the conference, we really didn't have time to read them."

"The combination of being isolated, having no common background, and no common basis," she says, "made it difficult to deal adequately with issues with such a high emotional content."

At one point on Monday one of the members of the committee asked, "Can we write this issue on the board, so we can understand what it is we are voting on?" Judianne told her that they would not be allowed to write it on the board, since that would "just confuse people even more."

The worst point in the confusion was on Monday, when Judianne called for various votes on banning commercialized surrogacy. The problem was that every time she called for a particular vote, she would rephrase the question so that although she insisted she was describing the same issue, she was actually asking people to vote on a slightly different principle.

Those people who came to the meeting hellbent against surrogacy were anxious to vote against anything that had any connection with surrogate motherhood. Other committee members, however, took seriously their responsibilities in drafting a criminal law. If the deliberations of this group were to result in legislation, the committee had to accept responsibility for policies that might send people to jail. It was crucial to understand the meaning of each vote.

Prohibiting the "commercialization" of surrogacy had too many facets to be considered in one vote. It could have a narrow meaning or a broad meaning and thus the committee members who heard the term might not all have the same thing in mind when they cast their votes.

A ban on commercialization could prohibit payment just to third-party intermediaries, such as Noel Keane, who served as matchmakers between surrogates and couples. Or it could prohibit any money from changing hands in any connection with surrogacy. Under the latter approach, if a woman's sister served as her surrogate and the woman later bought her an expensive gift or gave her some money, they could both be sent to jail. Or if a woman discussed surrogacy with her paid psychotherapist and then went on to serve as a surrogate for a couple, the surrogate and psychotherapist could similarly be jailed.

The leaders of the meeting were apparently so anxious to have some sort of policy disfavoring surrogacy adopted that they seemed unwilling to really discuss the concept and its variations in any great detail. At one point they wrote five different proposals about surrogacy on the board at once—provisions banning advertising, against enforcing the contract, and so forth. Nadine Taub raised a legitimate question about whether they could divide those proposals since some people might want to vote in favor of one of the five and not the others. Connie accused her of stalling, a comment she had not made at any point when people sharing her viewpoint talked at length about their particular perspectives.

The meeting leaders, including Lucille Taylor, a staff person for the Michigan legislature, angrily told the group just to vote on concepts and not to worry about language. But of course the key to any policy is language, and subtle variations in language would either criminalize or decriminalize a variety of different behaviors.

As the votes were tallied, the moral/legal distinction proposed by Dub White came to light. In the votes on artificial insemination by donor, a slight majority of the committee felt that donor insemination was morally impermissible; however, less than one-third of the committee voted that it should be prohibited as a matter of law. Instead, the focus of the committee was on a regulatory scheme to make artificial insemination by donor safer for the participants and the resulting child—for example, through infectious and genetic disease screening of donors, a requirement for recordkeeping, and a provision that the child, at age eighteen, be able to learn the identity of the donor.

In contrast, with respect to surrogate motherhood, the majority of the committee rushed to codify their moral views. They voted that surrogate contracts should be unenforceable and that payment to surrogates and center operators such as Noel Keane should be prohibited by law. The surrogate should be considered the legal mother and her husband should be presumed to be the legal father.

Throughout the entire meeting, surrogate motherhood was condemned as being against the best interests of the child. Connie averred that "to use extraordinary means to create a child is to go against his best interest." Lucille Taylor said, "Unless you shore up the values of nuclear families, other values will take hold."

At no point, however, was any actual evidence presented about why surrogacy contravened the child's best interests. Connie, echoing the teachings of the Catholic Church, viewed all reproductive technologies (including artificial insemination by donor in instances of male infertility) as impermissible because they were "unnatural."

Judianne condemned surrogacy as "narcissistic." She said it was a question of "I want what I want regardless of the consequences."

Since Judianne disapproved of surrogacy, wanting a child created with the help of a surrogate was narcissistic, but since Judianne approved of artificial insemination of unmarried women, wanting to create a child in that fashion was not narcissistic.

What explanation did Judianne give for this distinction? She said about men and women, "We are equal but separate." Similarly, Connie argued, "Feminists have said men and women are equal, but we can't try to imitate men. We don't want to give up these differences."

Judianne went further, implying that men did not deserve to have children because, in her words, "men left their sperm everywhere." Even if that were an adequate portrait of men, would we really want to reinforce such attitudes by allowing donor insemination where men can spill their seed with no responsibility for the child, yet forbidding a man to take a nurturing and caring role by prohibiting him from rearing a child created by the use of his sperm in a surrogate mother?

At every turn, the group seemed to violate the principle upon which it started—that, as Dub had expressed it, parental autonomy should be unfettered unless there was a compelling state interest to justify a restrictive law. No solid evidence was presented about what exactly the risks were to children of these new techniques.

Some committee members overlooked even the broad evidence of recent history and of their own pasts that might have shed light on appropriate policy. A majority of the committee felt that it would be overwhelmingly damaging to children to be raised in anything other than the traditional family—with two married heterosexual parents rearing their own biological children. This majority voted for banning paid surrogate motherhood and also for prohibiting the use of donor insemination by unmarried women.

The requirement of a traditional nuclear family overlooked both the blended family experience of the owners of Meadow Brook Hall and the current social reality that most families in America do not fit the traditional model. About half of the children born today will spend time in a single-parent household by the time they are eighteen. Yet study after study testifies to their resilience. Children in single-parent homes have cognitive abilities and a level of self-esteem that is at least equal to that of children in two-parent families. The children of surrogate motherhood, who for the most part are going into the idealized household of married heterosexuals—the biological father and his wife—could be expected to do at least as well.

The belief that children would be ruined unless they were part of a two-biological-parent family was not borne out in committee members' own lives. At the Friday session, Michael Meredith related how his mother had died when he was a child and his father had remarried a woman from the neighborhood. Connie herself told how her mother had died when she was a very young child and how she had been raised by her father. They were living testimony that people could flourish even if their families were not right out of "Leave It to Beaver."

This commitment to tradition also overlooked the fact that the two-biological-parent family was not a guarantee of the child's happiness. Judianne had spent her childhood in a traditional nuclear family—with such added benefits as servants and riding lessons—and nevertheless she had felt "alone" and "inadequate" as a child. "I experienced a sterile, isolated childhood with anger and misunderstanding being the major dynamics among the three of us—my parents and me," wrote Judianne in her 1976 book *Walk in My Shoes: An Odyssey into Womanlife.*

As dissenting committee member Nadine Taub pointed out, "There was a commitment to an extremely traditional view of the family, without any questioning of whether it existed, whether it was good, and whether it should be fostered and foisted upon people."

In using "the best interests of children" as their touchstone without giving the term any specific content, committee members failed to realize that they were advocating wholesale governmental intervention into reproductive decisions that could provide the basis for denying even those present the right to bear children. Judianne spoke with pride about how she had defied doctors' advice and gotten pregnant—even though they had advised her that pregnancy might harm or even kill her. Under the kinds of policies Judianne was advocating, the state might legitimately have stepped in to forbid her to bear a child since it wouldn't be in a child's best interest to have a very ill mother. Or if she did have one child, the state could stop her from having the next on the grounds that it would not be in the interest of the first child for her mother to risk her life out of a narcissistic desire to have a second child.

There was no good evidence to indicate why Connie's and Judianne's personal concepts of the best interests of the child should serve as the appropriate basis for law. Judianne herself had been quick to reject criticisms that her own lifestyle might not be in her children's best interests. While she pursued her career, her children were left with "surrogate parents," the servants who took care of them. When a family court judge at a meeting Judianne had previously attended suggested that it was in the best interests of children for mothers to stay at home rather than to work, Judianne had grabbed the microphone from him in a rage and demanded an apology.

Judianne's was a history of urging her own values on society. Some years earlier a book written by her and her daughter called

Drugs, Sex, Parents, and You had been criticized in the *New York Times Book Review* for its moralistic tone and its urging the reader that "the best thing the poor addict can do is accept the values of Dr. Densen-Gerber and her family."

On Saturday evening, when the group took a charter bus to a nearby restaurant, a dissenting committee member sneaked away to a country-and-western bar and restaurant, the Silver Spur. She didn't find out until later that the bus had gotten lost, made some wrong turns, and ended up on a dirt path, at which point it could not turn around. Was this a metaphor for the policymaking journey of the group?

The lone committee member ate a hot dog and listened to local bands. Various items were being auctioned off on stage, such as humorous posters and used toys. The beneficiaries of the money would be disabled children. As she looked around the room—at young men and women out for a good time, at older couples whose closeness and dance styles indicated decades of marriage, at the auctioneer who was trying to squeeze the highest price for charity out of a used red wagon—she thought, "I'd much rather have the future of surrogacy in these people's hands than in the hands of our committee."

The opinion of the public, however, was not to figure into the committee's deliberations. On the weekend of the meeting, the reams of computer printouts making up the answers to the magazine poll questions sat in the middle of the discussion table, a magic talisman to guide the work of the participants. However, since the responses did not agree with Connie's or Judianne's philosophy, *the actual results of the poll were never disclosed*, even when the poll had asked people point-blank a question upon which the group was now being asked to rule.

Two months after the Michigan meeting, in June, Dr. Densen-Gerber's report of the committee deliberations was sent to Michigan legislators. The committee members received it at the same time. Even though the committee members had been promised that they would have a chance to review the report for its accuracy before it was distributed to lawmakers, Judianne and Connie felt that time considerations precluded it.

The "Report of the Michigan Task Force Assigned to Inquire into the New Reproductive Technologies vs. the Best Interests of the Child" contained twenty-nine pages of narrative, a tally of votes, and hundreds of pages of such undigested appendices as the Vatican "Instruction" on reproductive technologies and Cyril Means's Baby M brief claiming that surrogacy was slavery. Buried among these appendices were the position papers of the dissenting committee members.

The first third of the narrative was a recounting of Judianne's personal experiences—such as her being consulted in a case of sexual abuse of a three-week-old, her drafting legislation against female circumcision, and her taking a trip to Australia with her son, during which she met a social worker involved in an in vitro fertilization program.

Her subsequent discussion of reproductive technologies began as had deliberations at the meeting, with the bizarre—the possibility of male pregnancies and interspecies fertilization. When the report finally got around to describing in vitro fertilization, artificial insemination, and surrogate motherhood, Dr. Densen-Gerber did not bother to explain the nature of the procedures. Her notions about the effects of the technologies were unsupported— often based on anecdotal discussions with doctors ("my medical colleagues informed me that thousands and thousands of men were standing in line demanding to know the swimming power of their ejaculate"). And her occasional statements about current law were often erroneous. Nowhere in the document was there a "state-wide and national survey of all legislation in the area," which she had promised to provide in her contract with the state.

In describing the votes of the committee, Judianne ignored completely the first critical vote that provided the context for the subsequent deliberations. Nowhere did she mention the committee endorsement of the principle: "All human beings have a basic human right to seek to reproduce. The Constitution protects the right against governmental interference, although a compelling state interest might outweigh this right."

When the legislators got the final report of the committee deliberations, a copy of the computer printout of the magazine poll results was included in the jumble of appendices. But the printout was only a mass of innocent figures, numbers divorced from the questions they answered. The poll itself was contained elsewhere in the report. It seems unlikely that the legislators (whom Connie points out have a short attention span) each took the time necessary to piece the survey together again.

If they had, they would have found that the majority of people (66 percent) favored surrogate motherhood, with only 21 percent opposing it. An even greater number—70 percent—favored IVF surrogacy, with only 18 percent opposed.

The public felt that the surrogate's parental rights should be cut off; only 6 percent felt that the surrogate should maintain parental rights, such as partial custody of the child. Slightly under 20 percent felt that the surrogate should have the right to change her mind. Sixty-five percent felt that the surrogate should not even have the right to visit the child. Just as the respondents felt that the surrogate's parental rights should be cut off, they were in favor of extinguishing her parental responsibilities. Only 5 percent would have required the surrogate to provide child support.

They overwhelmingly felt that surrogates should be paid, with 66 percent in favor, and only 15 percent opposed. This was much greater than the number of people (42 percent) who felt that sperm donors or egg donors should be paid. If the surrogate miscarried, most people felt she should be able to receive her fee. About half would have allowed the surrogate to abort if she wished, with another 10 percent neutral on the subject.

The majority of survey respondents did not even feel it necessary for surrogates to go through adoption agencies or other centers. Fifty-two percent felt that the surrogate should be able to offer her services independently; 39 percent disagreed.

The majority were in favor of stringent recordkeeping. They heartily (69 percent) favored letting the child, once grown, gain medical information about the surrogate and they leaned toward letting the child learn the surrogate's identity.

The findings were in keeping with similar polls in *Newsweek*, *Glamour*, and *Parents*, which found that the majority of people approve of surrogacy. They may not choose to enter into a surrogacy arrangement themselves, but they do believe it should be available to others.

In the *Parents* poll, 58 percent of people approved of surrogacy, while 32 percent opposed it. There was very little support for Connie's legislative approach. Only 22 percent of the respondents favored laws that prohibited surrogate motherhood.

More—39 percent—favored laws that would permit surrogacy with appropriate regulation, while 35 percent opposed any sort of legislation on the grounds that this is a personal matter in which the government should not become involved.

All in all, the respondents to Judianne's poll came up with the blueprint for some sensible legislation on surrogacy. Perhaps embarrassingly for Connie, the type of legislation it suggested was almost identical to that which her political rival, Representative Richard Fitzpatrick, had proposed years earlier. As much flaunted as Judianne's poll was at its inception, the results remained undisclosed at the Meadow Brook Hall meeting, and unintelligible in their presentation to other Michigan lawmakers.

Connie introduced a bill into the Michigan legislature which would make paid surrogate motherhood a criminal offense, with the couple and the surrogate facing up to a year in jail and a $10,000 fine. The lawyers, doctors, and psychologists who fostered surrogacy arrangements could be sent to prison for five years and fined $50,000.

"Under such a law," says Bill Handel, "a doctor who inseminates a surrogate is as much a criminal as if he held up a Seven-Eleven with a sawed-off shotgun."

14

SURROGACY AND
THE ISSUE OF CHOICE

LAWMAKERS IN NEW YORK chose a different route to surrogacy regulation than that traveled by Connie Binsfeld. They had begun to tackle the issue long before the New Jersey Supreme Court ruled on the fate of Baby M. After the October 1986 legislative hearing on surrogate motherhood in New York City, State Senator Mary Goodhue felt that it would be possible to fashion—and enact—appropriate legislation. She had a healthy track record. She had managed to get thirty-two of her bills passed in the previous session.

This surrogate mother bill took the entire fall to write. Staff Counsel Mike Balboni and Gil Abrahamson—both experts in legislative drafting—took the lead. Their mission, said Gil, Mary's chief counsel, "was to give guidance to judges, attorneys, and the parties, in a legal vacuum in a high-risk area." They read carefully the U.S. Supreme Court decisions on reproductive choice and family autonomy to find guidelines for the regulation of surrogacy. They scoured the hearing transcript and sorted through articles, lobbyists' reports, and notes from telephone con-

211

versations. Despite the enormous preparation they had, says Gil, "it was intimidating to sit down with that blank sheet of paper."

Their initial draft went through five major sets of changes, the result of frequent meetings with Mary, Senator John Dunne, and many members of the joint staffs. "We tried to imagine how the proposed statute would impact on areas of law that we hadn't even thought of," says Gil. They explored three basic approaches: prohibition, free market, and regulation. "We tried to think like social scientists, asking, What are the possible outcomes of each approach? What would be the effect of prohibition? Will we just drive people to other states where they won't be protected by New York law?"

Both prohibition and the free market approach left people unprotected. Each of those approaches would generate more cases like the Baby M case. "That's not a good outcome for anyone," says Gil, "that kind of litigation, that kind of living in a fishbowl."

So they devoted most of their energies to playing out the regulatory model. According to Gil, surrogacy presented "a volatile matrix of conflicting values. But we decided to err on the side of people exercising sound judgment on their own behalf and put faith in people doing what's best for themselves."

Much of the refining and redrafting focused on two major questions: Should the surrogate get paid? and Should she have a right to change her mind?

At one meeting, it seemed that John Dunne was leaning toward prohibiting payment. A staff member reports that there was silence in the room and then Mary said, "If a woman wants to get paid for it, why shouldn't she?" She looked John in the eye. "If you ban payment, I'm taking my name off the bill."

"I don't understand this business that, if you pay a woman, you are exploiting her," Mary explained later. "For years, housewives have been saying, 'If I don't get paid, I'm exploited.'

"Nor do I think it is the sale of a child. Who could it be the sale of a child to? It's the father who is paying the bills, the father who is signing the contract. You are getting money to give up your parental rights in favor of the other parent.

"The way we crafted the bill, you cannot say that the couple is paying for the baby, since they must pay even if the baby is stillborn," asserts Mary. "The couple are just buying the woman's time. They are renting a womb, but not without full consent of the landlady."

Mary was equally against giving the surrogate a chance to change her mind. "If you allow the surrogate to change her mind, it defeats the whole thing," says Mary. "I don't think that the father should take that risk. You don't want to go around fathering children that go to someone else and that you still have to support.

"The most troublesome thing is making up your mind that you do not want the child before the child is born," notes Mary. The solution, says Mary, is not to give the surrogate a chance to change her mind, but to make sure she has carefully thought through her decision before she enters into the agreement in the first place.

"I favor a woman's control over her own body," says Mary. "I have some concerns about surrogacy, but they are not moral ones, they are practical problems. It is hard to predict what the effect on the child will be."

Mike, Gil, and their respective senators debated what it would take for the surrogate to give truly informed consent to the arrangement. Should she be of a particular age? Should she have had children before so that she knew what she was getting into? Should her decision be evaluated by some independent body, such as a psychologist or a judge?

To help answer these questions, Mary called upon the aid of her constituents, just as they had called upon her aid in the past. As she struggled with the surrogacy issue, Mary wrote to the sixty thousand people in her district. "Do you think the state courts should regulate surrogate motherhood?" she asked. Seventy-six percent said yes, eighteen percent said no, and six percent were undecided.

The final draft of the bill advocated an intricate series of protections for everyone involved in surrogacy. To enter such an arrangement, the couple would have to show that they were infertile or that pregnancy would pose a serious risk to the wife or the child. There would be psychological screening of all the parties, and the potential biological father and the potential surrogate would undergo medical tests. The surrogate would have separate legal representation and the couple would pay for health and life insurance for her. The contract would be subject to the scrutiny of a court—before the insemination took place. The judge would assure that the surrogate was giving a voluntary, informed consent, and would assess whether the fees being paid were "just and reasonable." If the surrogate arrangement was approved, the surrogate would have the power to make medical decisions during her pregnancy, including the right to abort. After the child was born, though, the couple would be the legal parents of the child, and the surrogate would not be able to change her mind.

The bill was seven pages long, and each line was backed up by hundreds of pages of research and testimony. The naked bill seemed to invite so many questions about why each particular provision was chosen that John and Mary felt compelled to issue a long report with the bill itself. The report reviewed the medical, psychological, and legal implications of surrogacy. It flatly stated that a ban on surrogacy would be unconstitutional. The remaining choices were to take a laissez-faire approach or, as the proposed bill did, allow surrogacy under careful regulations.

On February 3, 1987, in the Baby M courtroom, Elizabeth Stern was describing how the diagnosis of multiple sclerosis had prompted her to seek a surrogate mother. She described the child of that contract as "a bright shining star" in her marriage.

"I feel I am Melissa's mother," said Mrs. Stern. "I've been responsible for her. I bathe her. I play with her. I care for her. Psychologically, I am her mother."

Mrs. Stern also argued that "it is best for Melissa to have one mother and one father and to grow up in one family."

That same day, Mary Goodhue and John Dunne unveiled their surrogacy bill—which would legally assure that the Elizabeth Sterns of the world were considered mothers.

Immediately, the New York State Catholic Conference released a statement opposing the bill and calling surrogacy a "moral disaster."

"If you pass legislation, even in an attempt to regulate it, you condone it," criticized Rev. Kenneth Doyle, the conference spokesman.

Mary Goodhue responded, "Whether or not we approve of surrogate parenting, it's going on. Without laws to control it, there is going to be exploitation. And that is the point of the statute we are presenting today. To protect the surrogate mother as well as the child, the natural father, and the wife of the natural father."

Mary said that the provision to make the surrogate give up the child was "necessarily harsh."

"But that's the only way to prevent another Baby M situation," she continued. "I don't think it exploits women or in any way downgrades motherhood. I would deeply resent that."

John Dunne pointed out that clarifying who the legal parents are in a surrogacy arrangement would "ensure that the child is adequately cared and provided for.

"We based our legislation on the concept of 'informed consent,'" John said, "meaning that if all the parties know and understand the consequences of their actions, then it should be permitted."

Mary and John both said they viewed the draft bill as a starting point for dialogue on the subject. "We don't see that we have a holy writ," said John. "The bill isn't written in stone."

The start of the dialogue came in two public hearings on April 10 and May 8.

Mary opened the April 10 hearing by remarking that the intensity of the debate over surrogate motherhood should not surprise us. "We stand on the threshold of new birth technologies that are mind-spinning," she remarked, "forcing us to confront fundamental questions of morality, ethics, tradition, legal precedent, and that most basic of human emotions, parental love."

She emphasized that she was open to revisions in the bill, then explained why she had taken the particular approach she had.

"We, as legislators, have three choices. First, we could ignore the practice of surrogate parenting and let the courts and the marketplace decide the issue on an ad hoc basis. However, the courts have *already* spoken and have asked for statutory assistance. Uncertain legal rights for adults and children resulting in many Baby M cases is an unacceptable status quo.

"Our second option would be to prohibit surrogate parenting entirely. This would merely drive the practice underground and would make illegal the attempt to have a family—the right of those more biologically fortunate. Additionally, there is a bona-fide question as to whether prohibiting surrogate parenting would also violate the constitutionally protected right to procreate.

"Our third and final option is to reasonably regulate the practice by calling for the informed consent of all parties before they enter into a surrogate parenting agreement," which is the approach the proposed bill takes.

Mary continued, "We sought to achieve three general goals in this bill: protection of the rights of all parties to surrogate agreements, with special emphasis on providing a well-defined secure status for the child-to-be. Secondly, we wanted to ensure that all the parties would be sufficiently informed so they can understand and, in good conscience, live up to the terms of the agreement. Thirdly, we wanted to establish fair and understandable rules to manage a process that is now part of our reality."

A review of the witness list showed that this hearing was to be much different than the one Lorrie Jones had attended the previous October. The people called to testify were not distanced from the subject. This time surrogate mothers would get their say, as well as the infertile women who were their unacknowledged partners in the creation of the child.

In contrast to the solemnity and formal atmosphere of the October hearing in Manhattan, the April 1987 hearing in White Plains took on the aura of a large family gathering. The audience was dressed casually, with grandmothers watching surrogate children, trying to keep them from crawling into the snaking television equipment cords. Not all the visitors were pleased with the idea of surrogacy, though. One woman in the audience sat holding a doll and displaying a sign, "Don't take this baby away from me."

The testimony began. "I'm sure you will have many experts in the fields of law, sociology, theology, and ethics, who will speak today for and against surrogate parenting," said Terry, the first witness. "I am not an expert in any of those things. I am simply a mother, or perhaps not so simply, since I am the adoptive mother of a child carried and borne by one of the most wonderful, caring women I have ever had the privilege to know."

Terry explained how she and her husband had pursued the elusive dream of having their own child, then turned to adoption, only to be told that, in their late thirties, they were too old. Their next hope was with surrogacy. "Is it so unnatural," asked Terry, "for any woman who wants and loves children but cannot bear them, to want and love the child of the man she loves?

"For those of you who have not experienced infertility and surrogate parenting," Terry continued, "it must be difficult to understand how emotionally connected we felt to our child from the moment we knew he was to be. We may not have been able to feel him kicking at night, but there wasn't a day that went by that we didn't talk about him, plan for him, or dream about him.

"I had a baby shower. I bought baby clothes. I'm sure that Elizabeth and Bill Stern had the same deep emotional commitment to their Melissa as we did for Scott, right from the beginning.

"It angered me when people talked only about Mary Beth Whitehead's rights as the biological mother. What about Elizabeth Stern's rights?

"The assertion that the birth mother is always the best mother is a slap in the face to all adoptive mothers whose children, as the poem says, 'grew not under their heart, but in it.'

"And what about the father's rights? I think I must have misunderstood what feminism was all about when I embraced its tenets about equality between the sexes, particularly regarding men's and women's roles as parents.

"Then there is the issue of economics and class differences. I doubt that many of the couples who have sought this option are rich. They are more likely like us, a couple who, because we had no children, had the dubious opportunity of being able to work without interruption for many years and thus save some money.

"Every child should have the birthright that our son has, to know that his creation was planned, that he was wanted and loved right from the beginning. Every child should have the benefit of coming into the world to a stable, loving relationship to two people who are united in their desire to start him on a safe, secure journey into life.

"When people ask us what we intend to tell our son about how he came into this world, we respond that we will tell him the truth, as well as he can understand it, as soon as he can understand it.

"People ask us what we will do if he wants to meet Karen. If she is agreeable, we certainly will be, for knowing her can only enrich his life, as she has enriched ours."

Marilyn Johnston, a surrogate mother, picked up the saga by describing the view from her side of the surrogate contract. "With surrogacy," she said, "an excitement usually reserved for two people was shared by four people." When she gave birth to a girl in September 1983, "the anonymous couple that I had started out to help had by that time become an extension of our own family."

The extended family has continued. "Instead of ending our relationship at the time of birth, we allowed ours to continue and grow. Our friendship had become much too precious to all of us just to dispense with it. We all felt that what we had achieved was so unique that we wanted to repeat the experience.

"Three and one-half years later, on February 19, 1987, I delivered a son and a brother for our extended family," continued Marilyn. "The years between the births were filled with numerous visits, phone calls, and letters. Grandparents, aunts, and uncles on both sides have become acquainted and our family continues to grow. These visits were not mandatory or court ordered. They occurred because of the love that exists between two families.

"The decision to become involved was a voluntary decision made by each adult in our case. No, the children were not asked nor did they have a choice in the matter, but what child does get to choose his parents or whether he will be born or not?

"I believe that any emotional damage will be minimal if not nonexistent. These children will know that four people, the surrogate, her husband, and the parents, loved each other enough to create them, a love not of a spouse for a spouse, or of a parent for a child, but a love of two humans for two other humans.

"Theologians and church leaders the world over have denounced surrogacy on the basis of morality. The Bible orders us to do unto others as we would have them do unto us. What compelled me most to become a surrogate was the knowledge that if I were unable to carry my husband's child I would want someone to carry that child for me.

"I am amazed that as a society we can condone placing a child in a day care center amid strangers for ten to twelve hours per day, six days a week after it is born, yet we condemn a couple for allowing another woman to carry a child for nine months before it is born. We say you can let someone care for your child after it is born but not before."

When Marilyn became a surrogate, she was the mother of a nine-year-old daughter and an eighteen-month-old son. Mary Goodhue and John Dunne were concerned about how the experience had affected Marilyn's own family.

"Critics of the practice," said Senator Dunne, "will say in the context of other children, a child might say, 'Gee, if I'm bad, Mommy might sell me as she did Johnny or Mary.' Have you sensed any evidence of that among your own children?"

"None whatsoever," Marilyn replied. "My oldest was only nine when I was involved in the program, and is now fourteen. She was thrilled for the couple and knows the couple and knows where the children are at." As to Marilyn's younger child, she said, "I told him that there was another mommy that wanted a baby such as him, and that there was something wrong with her stomach.

"My children see the other children. We visit back and forth three and four times a year. I think the openness is what helped both families, including our children."

Although positive about the process, Marilyn was angry about the term "surrogate mother." "I abhor the misnomer 'surrogate mother,'" she said. "I was not a surrogate mother to anyone. I was the prebirth mother of two beautiful children. Upon the birth of those children they had a mother waiting for them and my term as mother ended. Neither one of us is less a mother, we are simply prebirth and postbirth mothers."

The experiences of Terry and of Marilyn were typical of surrogacy arrangements, according to a third witness, psychologist Joan Einwohner. As a consultant to Noel Keane's program, she had interviewed seventy-five women who wanted to be surrogates.

"I find myself deeply outraged by the characterization of surrogates in some articles as 'inferior' beings who are 'rented uteruses' for affluent, privileged couples," said Joan. "The young women I have seen are intelligent. They are almost always high-school graduates and often have some years of college. They are attractive, frequently idealistic, and very concerned with the kind of home into which they will be placing a child.

"Some of the difference in income levels between the surrogates and the infertile parents would partly be due to the difference in their ages. Most of the volunteers are significantly younger than the infertile couples, who are in their late thirties or older.

"The economic circumstances of the volunteers are sufficient to live at a level that is generally average for their age. They are employed and their husbands are also. There have been only two or three that were on welfare.

"On the other hand," said Joan, "there have been couples who have had to borrow money for the surrogate's fee. There is one who is currently working at three jobs to pay its costs.

"I personally do not understand why certain segments of our society continually expect women to receive no material compensations for their services. It would seem to me a new way of devaluing women's work. It should rank with the unpaid status of homemaker. It is rationalized by saying women must fulfill the role of spiritual guardian of our society. Pregnancy is given a special status that should not be 'debased' by being concretely rewarded.

"It is a reasonable contention that the fee for services cannot be considered 'baby buying' because the father is simply assuming custody of a child who is half his own by agreement with the natural mother. He has chosen this path in order to be able to procreate without having to dissolve his marriage and seek another spouse in the style of Henry VIII. The surrogate arrangement from this point of view contributes to the stability of one of society's most fundamental institutions."

Mary Goodhue agreed with Joan. When, later in the hearing, a judge testified that he was troubled by the surrogate receiving money, Mary said, "I am a bit disturbed by your concerns over the compensation. I quite understand in an adoption proceeding where the woman is already pregnant and then you are disturbed if she says or makes an agreement whereby she will give the child to somebody in receipt for some money.

"Now, I think this is baby selling. I think we would all agree to that. She already had the baby and it was already conceived, and the father is somewhere and it is not the father that she is going to give the baby to.

"I don't have trouble distinguishing surrogate parenting. In this instance the natural father has gotten together with the surrogate mother and they have plans to have this child through artificial insemination, and the natural mother is not going to sell the child to anyone. She doesn't have that right. She is going to give the child to its own father.

"Now, she is going to carry that child for nine months, and she doesn't know this man and she is not particularly interested perhaps in having that cost her anything.

"If it was going to cost her something, if this altruism was going to cost her something in terms of lost jobs or in terms of money, she might not do it. She might well not do it if she could not be compensated for her time." As Mary laid this all out for the judge, he quickly retreated. He said he was willing to support a bill even if the surrogate were paid.

Joan Einwohner related surrogacy policy to society's view of women more generally. "I believe that women are fully capable of entering into agreements in this area and of fulfilling the obligations of a contract," she said. "Women's hormonal changes have been utilized too frequently over the centuries to enable male-dominated society to make decisions for them.

"The Victorian era allowed women no legal rights to enter into contracts. The Victorian era relegated them to the status of dependent children. Victorian ideas are being given renewed life in the conviction of some people that women are so overwhelmed by their feelings at the time of birth that they must be protected from themselves. Some people feel women cannot be trusted to know in advance what they will feel at the time of birth. The ability of ninety-nine out of one hundred surrogates to fulfill their commitments indicates that hormonal changes do not overwhelm the preponderance of women."

After Einwohner's testimony, Mary Goodhue asked, "Have you personally had any experience with a surrogate mother changing her mind, either during or after pregnancy?"

"I have had one instance," replied Joan.

"What happened?" Mary inquired.

"That was the famous one, and it is well known to all, the Baby M case," said Joan.

The irony of the Baby M case was that Mary Beth Whitehead had reservations about whether she could give up the child—before she was even accepted as a surrogate. Joan Einwohner had notified the center of these reservations and had suggested a further interview but, apparently, her report got lost in a change of administrators. Neither Mary Beth nor Bill nor Elizabeth Stern had been informed of the assessment. In fact, Mary Beth later filed suit against Noel Keane's center, alleging malpractice in not sharing the report with her. She received a $36,000 settlement.

Joan's testimony provided support for the Dunne-Goodhue bill. If such a law had been in place, perhaps the tragedy of the Baby M case could have been averted. If a judge had been responsible for approving the contract in advance, the psychological assessment would have come to light and the judge would have required Mary Beth to think long and hard about whether she was an appropriate candidate for surrogacy. The Sterns might have decided to proceed with a different surrogate.

At the April hearing in White Plains, the overwhelming majority of witnesses testified in support of the Dunne-Goodhue bill. One month later at the May hearing in Albany, however, a troubling opposition appeared. Three members of the Michigan task force, including Judianne Densen-Gerber, testified against surrogacy. "We should put it 'Surro-gate' and it joins our Watergate, it joins our Irangate and joins our Contragate as opening our gate to a great deal of difficulty which we cannot deal with," asserted Judianne. "It opens the gate to us creating life and us playing God, a very, very dangerous thing."

But, more significantly, two prominent women's groups came out against the proposed statute. The New York chapter of NOW took the position that payment to surrogate mothers should not be allowed and that surrogates should have a right to change their minds after the children are born.

Adria Hillman, testifying for the New York State Coalition on Women's Legislative Issues, similarly came out against paid surrogacy. "To use and pay a woman as a breeder is the ultimate in dehumanization," she said. "Poor women and third-world women could be exploited by the wealthy, and surrogacy could become a new form of prostitution."

The testimony of the women's organizations was surprising to Mary, John, and their staffs. They had thought that women's groups would criticize the bill as unduly intruding into women's decisions, since it required a double check by a court on a contract made by a woman (the surrogate mother) to assure that she gave voluntary, informed consent—and did not require oversight of contracts made by men. But the testimony was just the opposite. Adria Hillman was virtually begging legislators to protect women against themselves, against their own decisions. She criticized the bill as empowering the court to assess whether a surrogacy agreement protects the health and welfare of the potential child, without specifying that the judge should look into the agreement's potential effect on the natural mother.

"I was surprised at the opposition of the women's movement to surrogate motherhood," says Mary. "Feminists have always had the conviction that women should have control over their bodies, so their feeling that women should not be allowed to be paid surrogates is very peculiar."

Mary's staff assistant Robin Bergstrom was equally puzzled. "I truly can't understand the feminists who are now arguing against women's rights," says Robin. "This is the ultimate control of the woman's body.

"Women's rights have been cut back in the past based on male perceptions that women are incompetent to make decisions, but this time women will be putting it on themselves."

Staff counsel Mike Balboni was quick to point out the paradoxes of the women's groups' position. "In New York, two people can have children naturally and the state has nothing to say about when to have them, how to have them, and how many," he observed. "If the man is infertile, they can use donor insemination and the state again has nothing to say about when to have them, how to have them, or how many. In fact, the state facilitates this by the artificial insemination statute.

"Suddenly," continued Mike, "the woman is infertile, and now you're having a court hearing to qualify as parents. From that standpoint alone, if you're really talking equality from a feminist perspective, it is one area in which the feminists should be yelling and screaming about parity. It doesn't mean that there aren't differences between artificial insemination and carrying a child. Of course there are, but do those differences mean complete abandonment of individual choice in the decision-making process or does it mean we should enact guidelines and safeguards?"

A few days before the May hearing, in Manhattan, the feminist Project on Reproductive Laws in the 1990s had held a conference reporting on its two years of work developing model policy statements on prenatal diagnosis, third-trimester abortions, forced medical intervention on pregnant women, and reproductive technologies.

In the first three areas there was consensus about the policies that would best further the needs and goals of women. The project recommended that women have the right to refuse prenatal diagnosis and abortion of disabled fetuses and raised concerns that the availability of those procedures was leading to the withdrawal of societal support for disabled children.

At the same time, the project supported the current constitutional case law holding that, even in the third trimester, a woman should be allowed to abort if such an abortion was necessary to her physical or mental health. The project also came out against court orders forcing women to undergo Cesarean sections and advocated that a woman's right to bodily integrity be recognized throughout her pregnancy, with the pregnant woman—not a doctor or judge—having the ultimate say on which medical interventions could be undertaken on her.

The project's consensus fell away when it came to the issue of reproductive technologies. Some committee members felt that the existence of the technologies was a boon to women, others felt that it was a risk. Barbara Katz Rothman presented her concerns that surrogate motherhood would cause women to be regarded as vessels. In a paper she coauthored for the conference, she advocated applying traditional adoption laws to surrogacy, which would allow a surrogate to change her mind after the child was born and keep the child.

"In the shadow of Baby M, we express grave concerns about threats posed to diverse women's interests in pregnancies by the new reproductive arrangements," wrote Barbara and coauthors Wendy Chavkin and Rayna Rapp. "Pregnant women are people first, and reproducers secondarily and episodically. Our pregnancies grow out of our biological capacities, but are not reducible to them. Any woman who agrees to carry a pregnancy to term enters into a growing social relationship with her fetus. Like any social relationship, it is fraught with intended and unintended consequences, and its outcome cannot be completely predicted from its beginning. In the struggle to find a new legal form (that is, a social fiction) to handle the transfer of a newborn baby, we cannot ignore the agency of women, or the social nature of the relations which grow throughout a pregnancy. Only a 'vessel' can be rented, or used for a 'service' without the right to express or change her mind."

Peggy Davis, a New York University law professor, had a different view. She brought to the discussion the insights of someone trained in psychology, as well as four years' experience as a family court judge. She cautioned against approaching surrogacy based solely on a reaction to the Baby M case.

"These issues are so difficult that we ought not respond to them in the way that lawyers usually respond to them, that is by looking at the particular facts of a particular case, and making law that is based, in part, on generalized principles but also in large part, upon the sympathies that the particular litigants arouse," she recommended.

"For me," said Davis, "the issue is not whether people who dislike surrogacy are morally right. It is not whether it is better to adopt children, or to attempt, by extraordinary means, to have one's own biological children. The issue is whether that moral and personal, indeed intimate, decision should be made by individuals or the state.

"I submit to you that if surrogacy becomes outlawed, there are extraordinarily clever people in my position, who will persuade you that abortion is an easier case. The fundamental issue then, in my judgment, is what is the locus of choice? Should these intimate, personal decisions about sexuality, about sexual behavior, and about the rearing of children be made by individuals, or be made by the state?"

Davis warned that some of the concerns women had about surrogacy had to do with the mythology of motherhood. She posed a provocative question: "Why is it so disturbing to us that a person can bear a child and turn that child over to others for rearing without discomfort? Doesn't it say something about a mythology that surrounds motherhood—a mythology that has been limiting for all of us who are women?

"Is there anything so wrong that we ought to think of criminalization of surrogate motherhood?" she continued. "Or does it not simply challenge or call into question a comfort that we as women have been allowed to have? And that is that the one thing we do well is nurture. The one thing we do uniquely well is mother our young. Isn't it time that we understood that there are a great number of things that we do well? And isn't it time that we accepted a bit of demystification of that perfectly wonderful, but by no means exclusive, gift of women?"

When some feminists, such as Barbara Katz Rothman, came out against paid surrogacy, Mary Goodhue did some soul-searching about the morality of surrogate motherhood. She decided to continue to push her proposed surrogacy bill when she realized, "I wouldn't hesitate to be a surrogate mother."

After the bill had been through two public hearings, Al Vann, the chairman of the Child Care Committee in the assembly, posed the question, "What if, during the pregnancy, the father goes to jail, becomes a drug addict, or his infertile wife dies?" Mary amended her bill to provide that if there is a change that adversely affects the future of the child, the custody issue would go before the judge.

"This does not allow a surrogate to seek custody if she simply changes her mind," says Mary firmly.

As part of a continuing dialogue on the bill, John Dunne wrote to all family court judges in the state, asking for their opinions about the regulation of surrogacy. Some worried that the mechanism for prior judicial review of surrogate contracts would drastically increase their workload; a few even asked for extra funds to perform this new task. Most, though, favored the bill as an appropriate compromise to the many conflicting concerns that had been raised about surrogate motherhood.

At the same time that the Dunne-Goodhue bill was being considered, three other bills were on the legislative table in New York. Assemblyman Patrick Halpin proposed a law that would ban payment to surrogates and give them up to twenty days after the birth in which to change their minds. A bill proposed by Senator John Marchi would make paid surrogacy contracts unenforceable. One proposed by Assemblywoman Elizabeth Connelly would criminalize surrogacy for the next five years to give the legislature a chance to study the issue.

Although the Dunne-Goodhue bill seemed to be receiving the widest support of the surrogacy bills proposed in New York, by late April 1987 it appeared that, if the bill passed, it would be vetoed by Governor Mario Cuomo, who stated that more time was needed to study the issue. One Goodhue staffer was more cynical, suspecting that Cuomo would come out against surrogacy "in order to placate the Roman Catholics on an issue that doesn't affect a whole bunch of people."

By January 1988, Dunne staffer Greg Serio was reporting that "the sentiment in the capital is markedly negative. It is based on the perception that most people oppose surrogacy, even though that perception may be wrong, inaccurate. There's no question that the safest political thing to do would be prohibiting surrogacy or voiding the contract."

"Mary Beth Whitehead really gave surrogacy a black eye," said Kyle, a surrogate in the Maryland program. "I'm middle-class, I didn't do it for the money. Yet all surrogates are now lumped together. It will be hard to change people's opinions."

Mary Goodhue, too, felt that the negative perceptions about surrogacy were based on the specifics of the Baby M case. "A lot of the opposition to surrogate motherhood is really a reaction to Mary Beth Whitehead and the thought that she was being kicked around," she said.

Another source of the controversy about the bill, according to Mary, is that surrogate motherhood "is an unusual situation and lots of people are terrified of the unusual. All new areas are shrouded in darkness. Who ever thought of going to the clinic and picking out the mother of your child, without marrying her or even laying a finger on her? It certainly is not the preferred way to create a child, but for some couples it is the only way."

Mary worried about the future of the bill. Governor Cuomo had stopped legislative debate in its tracks by asking his Task Force on Life and the Law to come up with their own position on surrogacy. But the task force, made up of specialists in law, medicine, and ethics appointed by the governor, was distanced from the realities of surrogacy. It had no mechanism for taking the testimony of the people involved in surrogacy. The task force had produced a useful earlier report, on withdrawal of life-sustaining treatment, but that was an area where the legislature itself was failing to make progress. With respect to surrogacy, Mary Goodhue and John Dunne had already brought together, in their hearings, a wide range of specialists with expertise more directly applicable to the issue.

The wait for the task force report added another delay to the process of enacting valid surrogacy legislation. Moreover, it postponed further debate until the spring and fall of 1988.

"That will put us smack into the middle of an election year," said Mary, when it is unlikely that New York lawmakers will take on as volatile an issue as surrogate motherhood.

Meanwhile, the birth toll was rising. More women were signing up to be surrogates; more children were being born. The Baby M case had been addressed, but Babies N, O, and P were just around the corner.

15

≈≈≈

THE LIMITS OF LAW

NEW YORK AND MICHIGAN were not the only states grappling with surrogate-mother laws. In the wake of the Baby M case, seventy-six separate bills had been introduced in twenty-seven different states. Many of these bills were prefaced with statements about how lawmakers "wanted to avoid a Baby M case in *this* state." There was universal agreement that litigation surrounding surrogacy was detrimental to everyone—the surrogate's family, the biological father's family, and especially to the child torn between.

Throughout 1987 and much of 1988, surrogacy legislation was in a holding pattern. Ten states set up commissions to study the issue; four others—Indiana, Kentucky, Louisiana, and Nebraska—adopted statutes that seemed merely to codify existing law by saying that surrogacy contracts were unenforceable. Lawmakers seemed to be biding time, avoiding the hard decision about the merits of surrogate motherhood itself, avoiding the choice between enacting legislation which would ban the practice and constructing a law that would allow it under careful regulation.

While courts must decide the cases before them—no matter

what the subject matter—legislatures can postpone indefinitely the consideration of controversial issues. This provides little comfort or protection, though, for those people affected by biomedical developments such as reproductive technologies.

The most perplexing—and emotion-laden—question for legislators was what to do if the surrogate changed her mind. It was unrealistic to think that all surrogates would remain forever happy with their decisions. The possibility for regret is an infinitely human capacity. And reproductive decisions, often because of their finality, are particularly laced with the potential for regret, for wishing things had gone another way.

A man has a one-night stand with a woman and, nine months later, she has his child. He is a father, with all the attendant responsibilities and rights, no matter how much he regrets bedding the woman and seeding a life. A woman has an abortion because she thinks it best at the time; she cannot bring that child back, no matter what her regrets, no matter what her needs.

Reproductive decisions are protected by the U.S. Constitution because the decision to be—or not to be—a parent holds such enormous personal consequences. The biological and social experiences parenting entails are central to our very identities. As our life circumstances change, our view of past reproductive decisions may change. The kaleidoscope of our emotions may have tilted a few degrees, changing the color of the original decisions.

In the case of voluntary sterilization, 1 percent of people later regret their decisions, usually because of a changed circumstance, such as the death of an existing child or the decision to remarry. Dr. Sherman Silber, a microsurgery specialist, recounts the case of a diplomat who underwent a vasectomy on one of his rare trips home to the United States. The next day, his wife was killed in an automobile accident and one child was in critical condition. "He knew just one day after his vasectomy that it had been a terrible mistake," observes Silber.

With respect to abortion, 1 percent of women in second-trimester abortion facilities change their minds on the spot and leave. Who knows how many more regret their decisions later?

In surrogate motherhood, 1 percent of women similarly have a change of heart. But what does this tell us about the broader social policies that should be developed to handle reproductive decisions? It is not enough reason to ban sterilization, ban abortion, or ban surrogate motherhood that some people may later view their decisions in a different light.

In any surrogacy arrangement, there is an uncertainty about how the surrogate will feel after giving birth to the child. Casey, the husband of surrogate Lorrie Jones, has seen her through the birth of four children—two of theirs, and two as a surrogate. He describes how each experience was different. "It's like saying every baby's the same," he notes. "Each pregnancy is never the same."

There are many instances in which the surrogate feels much closer to the child after the birth than she ever anticipated. In July 1988, Lorrie Jones gave birth to the baby she had agreed to bear for a South American couple. She had distanced herself from the baby during pregnancy, not even keeping a diary of her experience as she had done with her own children and her first surrogate child.

"All the way up through labor, I was pretty unemotional about the baby," says Lorrie. "But after he was born and I began to feed him, my maternal instincts clicked in. It was so unexpected. I never thought I would get that attached. I did not even feel this maternal with my own kids. Even now I wish I were holding him in my arms."

On the way to the hospital, Casey had said, "Let's get this kid out so we can get on with our lives." But in the hospital he cut the cord and found that he, too, was bonding with the baby. "It was hard to let him go, because he was so cute," says Casey. "I could see how you could get attached without being the baby's father."

Uncertainty about the future colors most of our important decisions. People cannot totally predict how they will feel about having an abortion, getting married, undergoing an operation, or joining the army. The law nevertheless allows adults to make those decisions privately.

A woman considering surrogacy needs to ask herself, "Do I want to be a surrogate knowing that there is a risk I will bond to the child?" Though both Lorrie and Casey still speak longingly of the boy she bore, describing him in the same breathless tone that other proud parents use, they did not feel that their attachment to the child justified an attempt to keep him from his intended parents.

The potential for regret is a natural human component of any relationship—and surrogacy is, after all, the creation of a relationship. Some women will regret giving up the children they created through surrogacy. Other women, who have reproduced in the old-fashioned way, will regret staying at home for twenty years to raise their children. No relationship can be totally risk-free. The question is how much risk we are willing to bear—and what we will do to help avert that risk.

In developing policy in the wake of Baby M, lawmakers had two choices. They could follow Connie Binsfeld's approach and not allow potential surrogates to take any risks; that is, they could ban the procedure entirely. Or they could follow the approach of Mary Goodhue and John Dunne and try to assure that potential surrogates understood the risks in advance.

In their deliberations about surrogacy, lawmakers heard from a unique lobbying source. A group of surrogate mothers who opposed surrogacy and a group of surrogate mothers who supported surrogacy were the loudest voices in the legislative debate. From opposite ends of the continent, the National Coalition Against Surrogacy and the National Association of Surrogate Mothers were crisscrossing the country to make appearances before state legislatures.

The National Coalition Against Surrogacy was the brainchild of Jeremy Rifkin and Andrew Kimbrell of the Foundation for Economic Trends in Washington, D.C. The Coalition's core group were the feminists who had joined together in the amicus brief for the Baby M case. But after seeing the publicity being given to the positive surrogacy experiences of the members of the National Association of Surrogate Mothers, Andrew invited Mary Beth Whitehead, Alejandra Muñoz, and three other surrogates who had changed their minds to be part of the Coalition. Andrew also organized a network of lawyers around the country in case there were any other surrogates who wanted to challenge the contracts and keep the children they had agreed to bear.

On July 31, 1987, the Coalition was launched at a press conference. Mary Beth Whitehead made her first major public appearance since the adverse trial court decision exactly three months earlier. "The only crime we committed was loving our babies too much," said Mary Beth. "I think it's about time everybody in this country put an end to this. I can't do it by myself. I need every-body's help."

The press conference was filled with tenderness and tears. Patricia Foster had been pregnant as a surrogate at the time of the Baby M trial, and had felt her own feelings about the child change as the story of Mary Beth's plight unfolded. Patricia had turned over the baby, but now wanted him back.

"At the time, it seemed like a good idea," Patricia sobbed, holding on to Mary Beth's hand for strength. "I thought I could do it. But after being in my shoes, you find out this is not the greatest thing. You leave the hospital with empty arms and feel so cheated."

Jeremy Rifkin made his own attack on surrogacy: "The loving bond between mother and child is being replaced by the calcula-tions of lawyers," making children "indistinguishable from other manufactured goods." He vowed that the Coalition would try to keep women from entering surrogate parenting contracts.

Michigan State Senator Connie Binsfeld was also present at the press conference. At first there had been some concern among the feminists who were part of the Coalition about whether or not she should be invited. Although she shared their view on surrogacy, she was not in their corner on other women's issues. A round robin of phone calls among Coalition members finally re-sulted in an invitation to the senator.

"After the press conference, we sat down and said, 'Do we need federal legislation against surrogacy?'" says Connie. "I agreed we did because of the potential for the participants to move from state to state. So Jeremy and Andrew went to work on [U.S. Congress-man Tom] Luken."

Andrew energetically lobbied congressmen and senators to sup-port a federal law criminalizing surrogate motherhood. He prod-ded Tom Luken of Ohio to introduce a federal bill banning paid surrogacy. According to a Luken staff member, Andrew put to-gether the witness list for the hearing on the bill. There were no members of the National Association of Surrogate Mothers, but virtually every surrogate mother in the Coalition was given the opportunity to testify—Mary Beth Whitehead, Alejandra Muñoz, Laurie Yates, Patricia Foster, and a surrogate using the pseudonym Elizabeth Kane. These women opened the hearing, explaining in a touching and compelling way how surrogacy had been wrong for them.

"I came here today to stand in solidarity with other mothers who have lost their children and to join with them in urging a ban on surrogacy," said Mary Beth Whitehead. "I'll tell you how this started for me. I saw a classified ad for surrogates. I thought this was a nice way of helping someone out. I didn't want to work a job and leave the kids. I sent an application in and was chosen immediately. When I told a friend of mine that I'd been selected so quickly, she said to me, 'You're prime meat.' That's how I came to feel.

"I never foresaw that the baby would be *my* baby," continued Mary Beth. "I thought it would come out looking like the Sterns. But she came out looking like my daughter. I looked at her and said, 'This is my child.'"

The following witnesses were legal, medical, and ethical experts who were supposed to put the experiences of surrogates into perspective. However, rather than focusing on facts about the potential effects of surrogate motherhood on the biological mother, the biological father, their spouses, the child, and society, the "expert" participants resorted to pejorative language and emotional pleas. Surrogate motherhood was called reproductive prostitution, reproductive slavery, the renting of a womb, incubatory servitude, and the buying and selling of children. The women who served as surrogates were labeled paid breeders, reproductive meat, interchangeable parts in the birth machinery, breeder stock, manufacturing plants, reproductive technology laboratories, and human incubators. The children conceived pursuant to a surrogacy contract were labeled chattel or merchandise to be expected in perfect condition.

Robert Arenstein, an opponent of surrogacy who had served as Mary Beth's attorney, also appeared. "The hearing was a rout," he said gleefully. "It was like the Inquisition."

Some of the congressmen who attended the hearing, though, wondered whether a federal law was the appropriate mechanism to handle surrogacy. "I think it's going to be very difficult for Congress to legislate morality, and that's what we're trying to do here," said Congressman Sonny Callahan of Florida.

Congressman Bob Whittaker of Kansas expressed concern

about banning a practice that may offer infertile couples "the last chance to have a child." He also pointed out that surrogacy legislation should be the responsibility of the state legislatures, not the federal Congress. In making that point, he was not just passing the buck. Family law and medical law matters are traditionally regulated at the state level. Laws on artificial insemination, adoption, paternity, and custody are all state laws.

Influencing state laws was going to be much more complicated for the Washington-based Coalition than influencing a federal law, but Andrew was willing to try. He brought pressure to bear on state attorneys general to investigate surrogacy clinics and charge them with baby selling. With money from the Foundation for Economic Trends, he flew disgruntled surrogates into state capitals for press conferences with local lawmakers who were considering introducing anti-surrogacy bills.

While members of the Coalition were urging lawmakers to listen to their experiences as surrogates, the women in the National Association of Surrogate Mothers were telling their side of the story. Although NASM had far more surrogates as members than did the Coalition, it had far fewer resources.

To the surrogates and former surrogates in NASM, the experiences of the Coalition surrogates were not typical. What was worse, they never had to happen. They pointed to a defect not in the women themselves, nor in the concept of surrogacy, but in the way certain surrogacy programs were operated.

The NASM surrogates, led by Jan Sutton, started out with the obvious: that no woman should be a surrogate unless she understood what she was getting into. This would have clearly ruled out Alejandra Muñoz, who said she had volunteered for embryo transfer only to be told later that she would have to be a surrogate. Further, they agreed that no woman should be allowed to be a surrogate when she still wanted children of her own. This would have ruled out Laurie Yates, who only volunteered as a surrogate in order to obtain money to undergo donor insemination to bear a child to raise with her infertile husband, and should have ruled out Mary Beth Whitehead as well, since she had indicated in an initial psychological interview that "she may have more needs to have another child than she is admitting."

The NASM surrogates made a list of what they wanted in a law governing surrogacy. They knew they wanted psychological screening of the surrogate and her husband to determine that they were emotionally and intellectually capable of making an informed decision and of relinquishing the child. They strongly advocated mandatory group counseling for the surrogate from the time of the contract until at least six weeks after the birth of the child. They favored extensive medical screening and independent legal counseling of all parties. They would limit surrogacy to women who had already given birth. The surrogate would have to show that she was financially stable to ensure that she was not being exploited. The biological father would have to prove his financial stability to assure that the child would be provided for adequately. If all these conditions were met, the surrogate's consent would be irrevocable. The biological father and his wife would be the legal parents no matter what the condition of the child. No adoption would be required.

Although members of the National Association of Surrogate Mothers had created guidelines for surrogacy based on their experience with the process, they had virtually no resources for getting the word out to state legislators. They were funded by their membership dues, which were ten dollars a year. So their voices were generally heard only when legislatures could afford to pay the expenses for a NASM member to attend hearings.

One such occasion was a legislative hearing in Pittsburgh. Jan Sutton testified before a committee that was considering two bills. One, like Connie Binsfeld's bill, would have banned surrogacy altogether. The other paralleled the Dunne-Goodhue bill, with one major departure. It would allow the surrogate twenty days after the birth of the child to change her mind.

The prime movers in the surrogacy debate were present in Pennsylvania. Noel Keane was there, as well as Bill Handel. Gena Corea was there representing the Coalition. Bill Pierce was there from the National Committee for Adoption.

State Representative Joseph Markosek, the author of the bill banning surrogacy, discussed the need for legislation. "The issue of surrogate parenting has achieved national attention since the Whitehead/Stern court proceedings," he pointed out. "It is my opinion that one of the greatest discoveries to emerge from those proceedings is the importance to each state government of having a policy on the books concerning surrogate parenting.

"If we don't," he continued, "then the judiciary through their decisions will in effect be creating public policy, and that, ladies and gentlemen, is not what our judges are supposed to do."

The first speaker at the Pennsylvania hearing was Bill Pierce of the National Committee for Adoption. "Desperation to achieve a good end such as parenting," he testified, "does not translate into social or legal endorsement for whatever means to that end may be required, whether those means include the supposedly high-tech intervention of surrogacy or the decidedly low-tech alternative of stealing someone else's child from a supermarket basket."

Bill Pierce testified that surrogate motherhood should be banned. Instead of encouraging surrogacy, he said, the legislature should make statutory changes to facilitate traditional adoption.

In his media appearances and legislative testimony, Bill Pierce continued to take a hard line against surrogacy, reiterating his opinion that paying the surrogate $10,000 was baby buying. At the same time he was telling Pennsylvania lawmakers to change the law so that couples *could pay more money to adoption agencies*—to cover the woman's room, board, counseling, and transportation costs, which themselves might total more than $10,000. In Pierce's moral universe, apparently, such a payment was wrong when given to the woman directly, but perfectly ethical when fed into one of his agencies.

In federal testimony, at the New York legislative hearings, and in Pennsylvania, Bill Pierce pressed for lawmakers' aid in encouraging young pregnant women to carry a pregnancy to term, rather than to abort. At the latter hearing, he pointed out that in Pennsylvania there was one adoption for every sixty-four abortions. He dismissed the notion of unwanted pregnancies, saying "every child is wanted by someone." He also pointed to the drain on public funds by unwed pregnant women who decide to keep their babies. Apparently Pierce would prevent surrogates from having babies for infertile couples who wanted them, prevent mothers from aborting unwanted pregnancies, and push unwed women who might want to keep their children into giving them away.

"Before the legislature legalizes surrogacy as a solution to infertility, reasonable efforts should be made to promote the adoption choice for the babies who are conceived in a regular, old-fashioned way," Bill testified. "Otherwise, it seems as foolish as it would be to create a factory to make artificial coal when Pennsylvania has rather ample supplies." Bill criticized surrogacy proponents for causing babies to be viewed as products, yet his own arguments about normal reproduction fostered a view of baby-as-commodity.

Lynne Gold-Bickin, a Pennsylvania lawyer who serves as a liaison to the National Legal Resource Center for Child Advocacy and Protection, responded curtly to Bill's suggestions in her own testimony and took issue with the Coalition's idea that surrogacy turned women into reproductive vessels. Lynne felt that the real danger of becoming reproductive vessels would occur if legislatures banned surrogacy or otherwise denied women control over their own bodies.

"I for one do not feel that we have to tell women who get pregnant that they have to be baby machines to enable us to produce children for Mr. Pierce's adoption center," Lynne told the legislators. "I don't think that is an appropriate view of women either."

Bill Handel resented Pierce's cavalier attitude that the adoption of a child with no biological tie to the couple was an adequate substitute for creating a related child through surrogate motherhood. "Even our most vehement detractors will say that no one enters a surrogate motherhood arrangement lightly," said Bill Handel. "They come virtually as their last chance of having a child. I am speaking on behalf of these people. Why should they not be given the opportunity of having children in a controlled, systematic approach? We're asking for a lot of controls. We're asking, let's go in front of a court to have the arrangement approved in advance. Have as many judicial controls as you want. Legal controls, medical controls, psychological controls. Let people have children. They have a right to have children like everyone else does."

Bill Handel's commitment to surrogacy was by now well settled. The real estate market in California was booming, and his brother had tried to tempt him back into the construction business full time, in a position in which Bill would earn more than he does through his agency. Bill wouldn't even consider it.

The proposal of statutes to ban surrogate motherhood altogether sobered up Bill Handel more than Ralph Fagen had ever been able to. Bill began to feel that he had a responsibility to couples to help secure for them the option of surrogacy. His legislative and television appearances began to take a new, serious turn. He started being more scholarly, less flamboyant. "I realized that if surrogacy is banned, I'm going to do fine in some other field," says Bill. "But what are these poor people going to do?"

At the hearing, Noel Keane made a similar point. "If I didn't make a living at surrogate parenting, I would do it another way in the law. . . .

"I have two books here of photographs I will show you," Noel told the legislators, pointing to a pair of volumes documenting the histories of his clients. "They are real people with real problems, with real babies, that are very, very happy. Because of that and because of the support I have had within my own family, I believe in what I am doing. I must, to put up with the criticism and comments that have gone on for thirteen years. I can honestly tell you that I believe that there are probably more people that support what I do than don't. Unfortunately, the people that we represent, the infertile, are not organized. They are not willing to come forth and expose themselves to whatever criticism might come from their testimony."

In a later interview, John, the biological father of one of Jan Sutton's surrogate children, explained why he does not testify before legislatures about the issue. "I tend not to be a particularly shy person," he said, "but I didn't want my name used, didn't want my picture used, didn't want to be involved with the issue of surrogacy. I asked myself why. Is it that I'm ashamed because my wife couldn't have a baby? Is it because I don't want people to misinterpret my involvement with this other woman? Is it because I didn't want it affecting my business? I'm proud of what I did. It's just that I don't want to deal with and I don't want my child to have to deal with the religious bigots and other people who are responding to surrogacy on an emotional level."

John said the main opponents of surrogacy within the legislatures have a traditional view of the family and of women's roles. "The zealots that want to ban surrogacy are the same people that, if they could, would dictate that everybody have the same moral code as their own," said John. "They have the same feelings about in vitro fertilization—that it should be banned. I think psychologically and ultimately it is the fact that they want to put women right back where they were in traditional roles. The reality is that anytime you get away from the traditional, they can't handle it. 'This isn't the way my parents did it. This isn't the way I was brought up. Therefore, you can't do it.'"

At the hearing, Noel responded to the concern that surrogate motherhood was unnatural. "You have to realize that if these couples could produce their child in the natural way, in the confines of their homes, they would love to do it," he said. "They don't enjoy going into my office, doctors' offices, courtrooms for paternity, and courthouses for adoption."

The chairman of the legislative committee, State Representative William DeWeese, was concerned that approving of surrogacy might lead ultimately to eugenics. He asked Bill Handel how surrogate motherhood could be allowed without giving rise to genetic engineering. "You simply say no to genetic engineering," testified Bill. "You have to understand, personally speaking, I am Jewish and my parents are Holocaust victims. My entire family on my father's side was wiped out during World War II on behalf of the master race concept. I am the last person in the world to argue for genetic engineering. I think moving genes to make people bigger, taller, stronger is reprehensible. All we're doing is what nature failed to do. We're simply filling in the gap. If there is a uterus available, let us use one. If we don't have sperm available, let's use sperm donors. That's where it stops and that's where it goes."

At the hearing, Jan Sutton was particularly concerned that the bill banning surrogacy not be adopted. She tried to explain the positive aspects of surrogacy for both the child and the surrogate, the two parties that lawmakers most wanted to protect.

"The child born of this process is not 'bought,' 'rejected,' 'abandoned,' or 'sold,' but it is 'planned,' 'desired,' 'loved,' 'given' and 'nurtured' by the adults involved," she explained.

Jan called comparisons between surrogate mothers and biological mothers giving up babies for adoption "inappropriate and unjust" since the surrogate "makes her decision in advance of the conception at a time when she can become fully informed in an emotionally unpressured environment." She detailed how "surrogate mothers most typically leave the experience with feelings of satisfaction and self-confidence. . . .

"The bonding, attachment and separation issues raised in connection with a surrogate mother and the child suggest that when a woman gets pregnant and gives birth, she absolutely bonds with the child," continued Jan. "Opponents of surrogate parenting have used this argument since the beginning of the surrogate controversy without having studied women who have gone through the surrogate parenting experience with a positive outcome. I am telling you, and I speak for all the women in NASM, that these issues are significantly different in a surrogate parenting situation.

"The surrogate mother does have feelings for the infant before and after birth," explained Jan. "There is a fondness, concern, and curiosity about how he or she will grow up. However, this attachment *is* different than the attachment we feel for our own children. It is more like the attachment we have for a niece, nephew, or best friend's child.

"We think of the child as the couple's child from the very beginning and truly believe that the child was conceived and brought into the world *only* because we, as surrogates, and the parents together wanted the prospective parents to have a child," stressed Jan. "You may have a hard time comprehending this concept, but despite all the unsupported statements you have heard about the bonding process, I am telling you, as a surrogate mother, than when the process is carefully executed and only appropriate surrogate mothers are allowed to participate, *this* is how we feel. . . .

"Finally, in response to the feminists who have spoken out against surrogate parenting, we, in the NASM, are appalled," emphasized Jan. "We view ourselves as progressive and wonder why these women think they have the right to tell us what we can do with our own bodies. We are disappointed in the assumption that we cannot make voluntary and intelligent choices about pregnancy. We thought feminism was about breaking *down* the barriers between the sexes, not about creating another presumption that only the woman who produces a child can have its presumed interest at heart. Fathers and adoptive mothers have rights too.

"We must be free to be the arbiters of our own best interests," she continued, "and part of freedom is the obligation to act responsibly when things turn out badly.

"It is your responsibility to listen to the voices of those you are trying to protect," Jan urged the legislators. "We are telling you we want certain protections, but you must also afford us the dignity of participating in an alternative form of reproduction, if it is properly regulated, if we see fit to do so."

"Jan was wonderful," Lynne Gold-Bickin recalls. "These legislators were so naive. They thought that all surrogates were like Mary Beth Whitehead. They had no concept that many women do this willingly. Jan said, 'I'm a nurse, I make $45,000, I didn't do it for the money. I did it joyfully.'"

Gena Corea ignored Jan's testimony entirely. Gena, a founding member of the National Coalition Against Surrogacy, was not a surrogate mother herself. But she had been long involved with the issue. She had written *The Mother Machine*, a comprehensive critique of reproductive technologies. She had intervened on Alejandra Muñoz's behalf in the San Diego case, joined in the amicus brief of the Foundation for Economic Trends in the Baby M case, testified against surrogacy in the congressional hearings, and served on the Michigan Task Force on Reproductive Technologies vs. the Best Interests of the Child.

Gena, like Barbara Katz Rothman, was concerned that the existence of surrogacy would change society's perceptions of motherhood and of women. "The rise of the surrogate industry does not take place in isolation," she said. "It's part of the industrialization of reproduction. It's part of the opening up of the reproductive supermarket."

Gena talked about surrogacy arrangements that she felt typified the industrialization of reproduction. She noted that Mary Beth Whitehead had been required to undergo amniocentesis. She described other surrogates who had been given fertility drugs or had carried the couple's in vitro embryo. She criticized all surrogacy arrangements as exploiting the surrogate.

"The new reproductive technologies such as amniocentesis, in vitro fertilization, sex predetermination, embryo flushing, have already been used in conjunction with surrogacy and will be to an ever-increasing degree unless there are public policy decisions stopping this," said Gena.

State Representative Robert Reber, Jr., who had introduced the bill to allow surrogacy under strict regulation, took issue with Gena's view that the reproductive technologies she listed were necessarily harmful. He said that his wife had undergone amniocentesis when pregnant with their son and they had viewed it as a positive experience. "We went out with flowers and dinner and everything else," said Reber. "I don't think there is any indignity involved in [undergoing amniocentesis]."

Reber also pointed out that the problem cases Gena had testified about, such as the Muñoz case, could have been avoided if his legislation was in place to require screening and judicial preapproval of surrogacy arrangements and to give the surrogate a brief period in which to change her mind after the birth. "I think every member of this particular committee empathizes with those people that have in fact been exploited," said Reber. But, he continued, surrogacy itself need not lead to exploitation.

"I don't believe that the issue or the concern or the practice has exploited these people," he said. "I think it was the frailty of a few human beings who took advantage of the situation just like situations are taken advantage of every day in practices that go on statewide."

The appropriate legislative response, according to Reber, was not to ban surrogacy, but to regulate it. "That concern of exploiting lower-income people," he explained, "that's a concern that can be counteracted by the impartial tribunal reviewing the situation, making sure that that type of exploitation is not in fact taking place."

"In thinking about all this," countered Gena, "an image that keeps coming to mind is that of a shell game played at carnivals. The barker quickly shuffles the shells around, and you choose under which one the pea lies. The public thinks the pea, that is, the heart of the matter in the issue of new reproductive technologies, lies under the shell marked 'personalities of the people involved' or 'new hope for the infertile' or 'prevention of genetic disease.' But the barker-huckster is using sleight of hand to keep an eye focused on the wrong shell. The pea is really under the shell cumbersomely marked 'Reproductive slavery. Industrialization of reproduction. Reduction of women to raw material, to interchangeable parts in the birth machinery. Eugenics. Control over human evolution. . . .'

"We do not have to accept using women as breeders and selling women in this new way," argued Gena. "That is not inevitable. We can stop it. There is now a large national coalition built around the attempt to stop it."

Committee chairman DeWeese interrupted her. "What about the one out of six that cannot have children of their own?" he asked. "The simultaneous scarcity of white children for adoption. Are there no sympathetic bones in your body for some of the women who have undergone this process and given of themselves willingly and participated as surrogate mothers, like Ms. Sutton, who is sitting in back of you, who, as you have, favorably impressed this committee?"

DeWeese was clearly torn between the two visions of surrogacy that NASM and the Coalition represented. "I speak for myself," he continued, "but I am very perplexed about this whole issue. I gave her a great deal of credit in my own heart and mind. I give you credit in my heart and mind."

As the legislators approached the issue of surrogacy, their task was similar to that of the writers of science fiction. They were asking themselves, What would society look like if one policy or another were selected? The conflicting testimony of NASM and the Coalition on that issue prevented either of the Pennsylvania bills from being adopted. Legislators tabled the issue while they ruminated further.

Standoffs between NASM and the Coalition were repeated in other legislatures around the country. In California, State Senator Diane Watson chaired a hearing on surrogacy. Jan Sutton again testified that, if handled correctly, surrogacy could be beneficial to all parties.

An attorney representing the Coalition, Sharon Huddle DeAngelo, countered, "Let's assume we have a happy case—the mother is happy, the baby is happy, the couple is happy—and nobody is disagreeing. The broker is happy, everybody got their money, everybody is happy. What we as a society have said is that it's okay to breed women, just like you breed animals. Now, to use a woman's body for reproductive purposes has to be the most—the highest insult to a woman."

Senator Watson probed further. "Well," said Watson, "that might be true if it's against her own will. We had people testify here who said they enjoyed it, they loved it, and they'd do it again. And they saw it as a gift of love."

Nevertheless, Watson admitted, "we always have to deal with perceptions when we write the law." NASM and the Coalition had set forth different perceptions about whether the practice of surrogacy was baby selling and about whether it exploited and demeaned women. So in California, too, the issue was referred for further study.

With the deadlock on surrogacy, it looked as if it would take another Stiver/Malahoff or Baby M case to provoke lawmakers into action. And it seemed, for a time, that such a case was starting to unfold in Maryland.

While legislative debate was continuing around the country, Cynthia Custer, eight months pregnant, was reassessing her own surrogate pregnancy. When Cynthia had entered Harriet Blankfeld's surrogacy program, she agreed not to try to meet or learn the identity of the couple whose child she was carrying. Harriet told her that she and the couple could write letters back and forth through the agency.

Cynthia had gotten interested in surrogacy because a close friend, a navy wife like herself, was infertile. She spent a lot of time with this woman while their husbands were away on an eight-month stint at sea. They happened to watch a "Nova" TV show together and were introduced to the concept of surrogacy.

"We decided I would be a surrogate for her," says Cynthia. "But then her husband came home and nixed it. It wasn't right for him."

When Cynthia's husband was transferred to Maryland, she hooked up with Harriet Blankfeld's agency. If she couldn't be a surrogate for a friend, she thought, she would help some other infertile woman.

The day she got her positive pregnancy test, she wrote a lengthy letter to the couple and asked the agency to forward it. According to Cynthia, the letter was rejected for forwarding by the agency because it was too long and it revealed too much about her identity.

As Cynthia's pregnant belly grew, so did her questions about the couple. What was their religious background? she wondered.

Would they raise the child in the city or the country? Had they gone to college?

Cynthia wanted to know what type of home she would be sending the child to. She had a letter with ten questions and she said she would be satisfied if she just got those ten answered.

Her request was refused.

Cynthia began to feel troubled about giving the child over to Harriet without knowing anything about the father. In March 1988, she decided to tell her story to the *Washington Post* to encourage him to come forward. Because she was no longer willing just to turn the baby over to Harriet, she wrote to the agency, "We revoke any parental consents we have given to you regarding paternity."

When the newspaper article appeared, says Cynthia, she received calls from some of the attorneys and the surrogates associated with the National Coalition Against Surrogacy. "They were all very supportive, but they know how to hit your vulnerable spots," she says. Cynthia wanted to give the child to its father. Coalition members put pressure on her to keep the child herself. She says that Sharon Huddle DeAngelo of the Coalition called her and said, "This baby wouldn't want to be given up. He doesn't have a choice. Please, mommy, don't give up your baby."

"Two days before I'm supposed to deliver, they had all these women calling me," says Cynthia. "They would call me and tell me all their sad stories. Finally I just told them, 'You've made your mistake and I would appreciate it if you would just let me make mine.'

"I never, ever misrepresented myself with the Coalition," says Cynthia. "I said, I believe in commercialized surrogacy. I know that it can be done right."

When she said that she thought it best for the child to go to its father, she says, Coalition members "started telling me that I could be prosecuted for accepting money."

At the end of her eighth month, when the father still had not come forward, Cynthia was giving serious thought to giving the baby up for adoption. She had heard of Bill Handel and she got in touch with him to help her find a good home for the baby.

"I can credit Hilary Hanafin for straightening the whole situation out in the end," she says. Hilary got on a conference call with the couple and their attorney. Hilary told the couple, "She's not an animal. She just wants to meet you." After Hilary described in detail the kind of loving, caring person Cynthia was, the couple agreed.

"When we met, they answered every question without hesitation," says Cynthia. "We could not have handpicked a better pair. It was all a real waste because of the anonymity."

Cynthia says the current legal environment creates "an emotional abyss" which harms the relationship between the surrogate, her husband, the biological father, and his wife. "It's a real scary frontier," she says. "With no legislation, it's terrible for the surrogates and the couples. You don't know how the woman is going to feel when she gets pregnant. So, obviously, you are always going to be frightened to death that she's going to keep your baby.

"Ours was basically a storybook case where everything turned out and everyone lives happily ever after," observes Cynthia, "but it doesn't always happen that way. It is very dangerous that legislators don't think surrogacy is important enough to tackle the subject. I would like to see more guidelines to go by. I would like to see legislation to make sure that the couple will get their child."

In Michigan, however, Connie Binsfeld had just the opposite sort of legislation in mind. She had introduced a bill which took three tacks toward eliminating paid surrogacy. It made the arrangement a crime. It held the contracts unenforceable. And for the couples who wanted children badly enough to break the law, Connie added an extra penalty: if the surrogate changed her mind, she and her husband would get to keep the child. The biological father and his wife would not even be allowed to sue for custody.

Fellow lawmakers were uncomfortable with the third provision. Was it really in the best interests of the child? How would the surrogate's husband feel about raising a child who was not his?

When Mary Beth Whitehead broke down after giving the baby to the Sterns and kept saying, "God, what have I done?" Richard told her, "Go and get our baby."

Later, Richard testified, "I felt like it was my child." He admitted, though, that there were times when he felt "pulled both ways" since he was not the biological father.

Rick Pavek, in contrast, did not have any fatherly feelings toward the three boys that Carol had borne as a surrogate. Rick explains that he put a lot of effort into the pregnancies, but he does not feel that the surrogate children should be considered his children. "I don't think about the kids," he says. "I don't think about the good times we could have had with them. I do think about the good times we could have had with Eric, because he was our son."

Even those lawmakers who were comfortable that the surrogate's husband would be a good father nonetheless had qualms about disenfranchising the Bill Sterns of the world. The time had passed when mothers were automatically given custody of young infants. Now fathers had rights, too. So Connie's bill was amended so that it would not automatically give custody to the surrogate. The bill still prohibited paid surrogacy, but provided that in a dispute, custody would be determined according to the best interests of the child.

Connie's 1988 bill banning paid surrogacy echoed the bill she had introduced in 1983 at the time of the Stiver/Malahoff case. Yet, in a speech to other lawmakers, she made it seem that the 1988 bill had been drafted as a result of an eighteen-month legislative study. "We contracted for a national study to find out what people in medical ethics and people who were sociologists and so forth thought about surrogacy," explained Connie, referring to the hiring of Judianne Densen-Gerber, but failing to mention that this part of Densen-Gerber's study had never materialized. "And then at the end of that year-and-a-half study we convened a committee of twenty from across the country—constitutional lawyers, clergy, feminists, legislators, doctors, the head of the public health department, and so forth. The twenty of us spent a three-day weekend arguing with one another, sharing our resources and information that we had gathered and out of that I wrote the law which prohibits surrogacy for compensation."

Connie was offering old wine in a new bottle, but this time she had a new marketing technique. By now she had picked up the rhetoric of the feminists to strengthen her political position, talking more in terms of the "exploitation of women."

At the National Forum for Women State Legislators, Connie was distributing anti-surrogacy literature written by feminists. Instead of passing out the brief that she filed in the Baby M appeal (which likened surrogacy to slavery), she distributed the feminist brief filed by the Foundation for Economic Trends.

Despite her conversion to feminist speech, there is no evidence that Connie's underlying philosophies are now feminist. Certainly her voting record is not. A May 1988 report by Public Sector Consultants, a non-partisan think tank, ranked Michigan lawmakers on a scale from 0 (very conservative) to 100 (very liberal). Michigan Senator Lana Pollack, a recognized booster of women's causes, got 89 points. Connie Binsfeld got 8.

Connie's approach to surrogates is a maternal one. When surrogate Laurie Yates gave birth to twins (after filing suit to keep the babies), Connie was on a Labor Day boat trip. Her staff called and left the message, "You're a grandmother."

Connie is possessive about the surrogates, particularly the ones who have had problems. "Did you hear that one of our women died?" she asked when the death of a Texas surrogate mother was reported. Each surrogate tragedy is treated like a tragedy of her own family. Each time a surrogate arrangement is successful, it is ignored, discounted, or resented. Connie, for example, complains about a Michigan woman who has twice served as a surrogate and who writes letters to editors explaining her positive experiences whenever Connie makes an appearance in the paper to blast surrogacy.

Connie's intense feelings about surrogacy have led her not only to try to choreograph the law through the process of legislative activity, but to attempt to orchestrate judicial and executive activity and influence the personal decisions of the surrogates as well.

Connie admits to putting pressure on surrogate Laurie Yates to file a custody suit during her pregnancy, rather than after her twins were born. And when Laurie had difficulty finding a lawyer, Connie called an attorney and asked him to represent Laurie.

That attorney, Robert McAlpine, prefers other types of litigation to custody cases, but didn't feel it would be politic to turn down the case. "It can't hurt to have the second most powerful senator in Michigan in your debt," he says.

Connie pushed hard for judges and executive-branch officials to validate her anti-surrogacy position. She was the only legislator to file an amicus brief in the Baby M case. ("I didn't discuss it with my staff," she says. "I just had a gut feeling that I should file.")

And she wrote to the attorney general of Michigan, Frank Kelley, asking him to begin a criminal investigation of Noel Keane's surrogacy arrangements.

In April 1988, a new surrogacy case broke that furthered Connie's cause. A Michigan surrogate, Patty Nowakowski, gave birth to twins—a boy and a girl. When it came time for the father to pick up his children, he said that he only wanted the girl. The boy was left with Patty and Aaron Nowakowski who, because they had not intended to raise him, put him in foster care.

"I just kept thinking 'That poor child,'" said Patty. She and her husband took the child back to rear as their own. They named him Aaron, Jr. Once he joined their family, though, they felt sad about his separation from his twin. They retrieved the girl from her father and are now the parents of two children they had never expected to raise.

"I have thought through many different scenarios," observed Connie Binsfeld. "But I never thought of this. I was shocked."

For once, Connie and Noel Keane were in agreement. "Nauseating is what it is," Noel told reporters. "This is probably one of the most upsetting cases I have ever heard of."

Further fuel for Connie's cause was arriving from New York. In May 1988, one year after Mary Goodhue's public hearings on surrogacy there, Governor Mario Cuomo's Task Force on Life and the Law issued its report on surrogate motherhood. The task force report emphasized the importance of developing policies on surrogacy: "At stake in the debate is nothing less than the psychological, social and legal content of the terms 'mother,' 'father,' and 'parent.' The psychological and social content of the terms may be shaped by new practices, including the possibility that children will have two biological mothers."

In assessing how surrogacy should be regulated, the report relied heavily upon the Baby M brief that Barbara Katz Rothman had helped prepare with the Foundation for Economic Trends, raising concerns about how children will fare if parenting is split into its genetic, gestational, and rearing components and expressing fears about the creation of a "breeder class" of women.

In fashioning its report, the task force ignored most of the witnesses who had appeared at the three New York hearings—even though many of them had provided information about how surrogacy was actually being carried out in the state. From the wealth of witnesses, the report cited only the testimony of surrogacy opponents—a Catholic priest and representatives from two women's groups that had come out against surrogacy. Nowhere in the report were there interviews with infertile couples or surrogate mothers.

The report concluded by denouncing surrogacy: "The practice places children at risk and is not in their best interests or those of society at large. It has the potential of undermining the dignity of women, children and human reproduction by commercializing childbearing." Backed by the report, Cuomo offered a bill challenging the Dunne-Goodhue proposal. The Cuomo bill would codify the task force's recommendations. It would make paid surrogacy a crime, hold the contracts unenforceable, and—except in rare instances when the surrogate was unfit—would give the child to the surrogate in the case of a dispute.

Also in May, ABC aired a two-part television movie based on the Baby M case. The drama that had originally provoked lawmakers into contemplating surrogacy legislation was now being relived before them on the small screen. As a tie-in to the movie, Mary Beth Whitehead and other members of the National Coalition against Surrogacy appeared on numerous television news and talk shows, urging that surrogate motherhood be banned. Some years earlier, the media had spurned surrogate motherhood by giving so much airtime to Noel Keane and his happy surrogates. Now the media was helping to close the doors on it.

"It's the children who are the victims of parents who will use any means to fulfill their desires," Connie told reporters. She said that her surrogacy bill was designed to put Noel Keane out of business.

On June 9, 1988, the Michigan legislature considered Connie's bill. The vote was 90 to 10 in the House and 28 to 3 in the Senate—in favor. Three weeks later, despite his reservations, Michigan's pro-choice governor, James Blanchard, signed the measure into law. Surrogate motherhood became a crime. Noel's actions became a felony.

"What we're hearing," said a pleased Andrew Kimbrell, "is the death knell of surrogacy."

16

≈

LADY MADONNA

IN SURROGATE MOTHERHOOD, a woman intentionally conceives, carries, and bears a child to be raised by someone else. It is an action that, for many, is difficult to fathom.

When women first began to volunteer as surrogate mothers a decade ago, scholars like Hilary Hanafin tried to understand their behavior, asking the question, What lies behind these women's attraction to surrogacy? Now other scholars, including Lisa Newton, Carol Sanger, and Margaret Somerville, are asking another question: What lies behind the growing movement to ban surrogacy?

"In the context of a virtually untested practice, with no time to observe long-term effects, the volume of immediate opposition to surrogacy suggests that it must touch nerves unused to insult," Lisa Newton, director of the Program of Applied Ethics at Fairfield University, told a conference of fellow philosophers in April 1988. In the eighteen months since she had testified at the first New York legislative hearing on surrogacy, Lisa had been trying to unravel the emotional tangle, the apparent taboos that are touched by the issue of surrogate motherhood.

Surrogate motherhood, says Lisa, "invokes frightening scenarios buried sufficiently deeply within us that we are probably unaware of them. Teaching ourselves to bypass these scenarios and evaluate surrogacy on the basis of common sense alone may be very difficult."

Surrogate motherhood violates a number of taboos, challenging deeply held emotional beliefs about the proper relationship between mothers and children and the customary roles of men and women in society. But the problem with creating public policy on the basis of emotion, rather than reason, is that the rationales given for the policy may come back to haunt us in other areas.

Once women are held incompetent to make surrogacy contracts, they may be denied the right to make other contracts. Once policymakers deny women the reproductive choice of surrogacy in order to protect the potential children against putative harm, they may deny women other prenatal choices—to undergo amniocentesis or not, to rule out Cesareans, to abort—on those same grounds.

The raw nerves that surrogacy seems to have hit are the individual and societal instincts about motherhood. Traditionally, in our culture, a mother's bond to her child was considered absolute. We could all have the assurance that our first love, our mother's love, was an undying, all-encompassing one. But now that a group of women have decided to be mothers without mothering, to conceive children for the sole purpose of giving them up, mother love has somehow been called into question. A fire has been lit under our secret fear that our mothers didn't want us.

"I think policies against surrogacy in a quite uncontrollable way relate to the fear of separation from parent, particularly mom," says Santa Clara University law professor Carol Sanger. "We don't particularly care whether men give away fatherhood before they masturbate away their heirs. Why not? In part, because the bonding has not occurred, but also because we have different expectations of fathers and their children than we do for mothers and their children."

Surrogate motherhood is also unsettling from a larger perspective. According to Lisa Newton, the fear of separating infants from their mothers runs deeply through the societal subconscious. It raises animal-like images of mothers abandoning their young which, if widespread, could cause the species to die out.

"That doesn't mean it is *wrong* for a mother to give up her child," Lisa explains. "But it does mean that any attempts to institute a practice that allows mothers freely to 'lose' their young is going to run into every obstacle that human fear can erect in its way—obstacles from law, from religion, and from every form of dramatic representation, for it raises terrors for the fate of the species that go well back beyond our ability to calm them with ratiocination."

The emotional wellspring is also responsible for the assumption that a surrogate who, with premeditation, gives up a child is uncaring and unloving—a stereotype that Lisa Newton disputes. "The evidence is that the surrogates love the children dearly and derive their highest joy from seeing the child in the arms of *its mother*, the wife of the father, the woman for whom the child was borne," says Lisa. "Love is the motive, not something that is set aside."

Margaret Somerville warns that the symbolism of surrogacy should not be underestimated. Director of Canada's McGill Center for Health Sciences, Ethics, and Law, she holds professorships at both the law and medical schools at McGill. "If you look into the myths of our society and phrases that talk about young men sowing their wild oats, leaving a young girl pregnant, going away—'poor girl, lucky man' is usually the type of phrase that you will hear," says Margaret.

"Why do we insist that that girl should be bonded to that child?" she asks. "I think she does bond, but there's a societal insistence on it apart from the reality of it. Could it be, for example, that we need in our society to have an automatic and necessary bonding to children, and that we've chosen women to carry that symbolism and allowed men not to carry it, and that's why surrogate motherhood so upsets society when artificial insemination by donor doesn't?"

The law, says Lisa, approaches family matters according to the scenario that Margaret described. Men are seen as playboys who get women pregnant and abandon them. In all states, for example, the paternity laws allow unwed pregnant women to sue a man for child support. At the time these laws were passed, no consideration was given to the possibility that a man might wish to sue for custody or visitation to a child created outside of marriage. Even with the recent emphasis on fatherhood, only half the states amended their laws to allow men to bring paternity actions to gain access to their children.

"The common law," says Lisa, "has simply bought a picture of human life and family which is not necessarily true, but which tugs at the heart in certain persuasive ways."

When Judge Sorkow in the Baby M case went against that legal tradition—and gave custody of the baby to her father—he stirred up a surprisingly angry response. His personality and ethics were attacked by reporters. And he was chastised by the New Jersey Supreme Court for not following existing laws, even though those laws were meant to deal with a situation that was morally and biologically different from a surrogate mother arrangement.

For charting the future of surrogacy, though, courts have turned the policy decisions back over to the legislatures. The existing laws are not designed to deal with surrogate motherhood: a Kentucky court likened it to "trying to fit a square peg in a round hole."

In the legislative debate about surrogate motherhood, the emotional taboos—which Lisa Newton calls "scenarios of the heart"—influence people's positions on surrogacy. The fact that the opposition to surrogacy has brought together unlikely allies—the Catholic Church, conservative politicians like U.S. Congressman Henry Hyde and Connie Binsfeld, and a group of feminists—shows how deeply these taboos run.

The feminist opposition to surrogate motherhood seems particularly ironic. "For women to argue that this choice of surrogacy is so qualitatively different from its closest neighbors on a continuum of reproductive decisions is logically unpersuasive," says Carol Sanger.

The "scenario of the heart" against separating mothers and their children, the thought that it is *unnatural* for a mother not to rear her own children, has led surrogacy opponents to presume that a woman is not exercising true choice if she decides to bear a child for someone else. The thought that she would voluntarily part with her offspring may simply be too frightening to credit. At some level she must have been tricked into it, or coerced. These opponents argue that the surrogate is incapable of giving valid consent because of her domination by men or her susceptibility to economic exploitation. They also argue that the surrogate mother is being a "bad" mother since, in their minds, the children created through surrogacy, and the surrogate's own children, will invariably be emotionally scarred by the arrangement.

As intuitively satisfying as these arguments are, they do not stand up to the facts. When looked at closely, says Lisa Newton, "they are bad arguments, devoid of sense. The fact that very good people, among the best scholars in the field, can take them seriously suggests that there are mechanisms at work in this issue that will not partake of reason."

"The delegation of parental rights has been long accepted as the practice among families and in family law," explains Carol Sanger. "Adoption, foster care, extended families, guardianships are all examples where children are transferred to others to raise by choice. I think that the practice takes new titles but not new shapes in surrogacy."

The law allows this transfer of children so long as the parents have consented. But surrogacy opponents call women's consent into question. In *The Mother Machine*, Gena Corea, speaking about other forms of reproductive technology, asks, "What is the real meaning of a woman's 'consent' . . . in a society in which men as a social group control not just the choices open to women but also women's motivation to choose?"

It is a dangerous step backward for women to argue that their decisions are not fully their responsibility. Clearly, everyone's choices are motivated by a range of conscious, unconscious and societal influences—economic, social, religious. The fact that a woman's decisions could be influenced by the individual men in her life or by male-dominated society does not by itself provide adequate reason to strip her of her right to make such decisions.

"I choose to believe that although masculine influence in our society is profound, one can attain logical clarity," says Carol Sanger. "Women are capable of rational choice in the surrogacy arena, and if society chooses to prohibit surrogacy, it must be for other reasons than protection of the mother in her inability to make a decision."

Rather than being weak and overpowered, most surrogates seem to be articulate and strong women who have sought surrogacy out, often going to great lengths to track down an agency and to convince their husbands, parents, and friends that surrogacy is an appropriate choice for them. In the Baby M case, Judge Sorkow commented on Mary Beth Whitehead's strength, saying, "This court has a sense that Mrs. Whitehead would be a very difficult person to unduly influence once her mind is made up." Likewise, experts in the Baby M case noted that Elizabeth Stern was stronger than her husband.

"I have read volumes in defense of Mary Beth, her courage in taking on a lonely battle against the upper classes, the exploited wife of a sanitationman versus the wife of a biochemist, a woman with a 10th-grade education versus a pediatrician," wrote *Washington Post* reporter Jane Leavy during the course of the Baby M case. "It all strikes me as a bit patronizing. Since when do we assume that a 29-year-old mother is incapable of making an adult decision and accepting the consequences of it?"

At the New York hearings, surrogate mother Donna Regan testified that she found it "extremely insulting that there are people saying that, as a woman, I cannot make an informed choice about a pregnancy that I carry," she said, pointing out that she, like everyone, makes other difficult choices in her life. Lisa Newton agrees, saying that this is another instance of women being protected by "Daddy Legislature."

"I find that whole point of view very objectionable," she says. "The Michigan law banning surrogate motherhood establishes one more precedent that we didn't need, that male-dominated legislatures have got to make decisions on what a woman should do in order to protect herself from exploitation. It's awful. It says she is a criminal if she tries to make decisions about her own body.

"If they are going to deny women the right to sign contracts for their own services, I don't know where we've gotten with the feminist movement."

Nonetheless, the potential for the exploitation of poor women troubles many people about surrogacy, including John, who contracted with surrogate mother Jan Sutton.

"We were lucky that when we decided to enter a surrogacy arrangement, the pool of people was rich enough that we could pick someone who would not be financially or psychologically exploited," says John. "We would not have gone ahead otherwise. I can't speak for other people, though. The human animal being what *he* is—and I use the term *he* deliberately—there might be an attempt to get a street urchin pregnant. This is the Pandora's box of surrogacy. . . .

"If it became rent-a-womb, I would feel a lot less inclined to take as strong a pro-surrogacy stand as I do. Just as fifteen-year-old runaways are induced to be prostitutes, they could be turned into surrogate mothers."

For both Jan and John, though, this potential is not a sufficient reason to ban all surrogacy arrangements. Jan supports a legal approach, like that of Mary Goodhue and John Dunne, that would require a separate attorney to represent the surrogate and would mandate judicial approval of any surrogacy arrangement before the insemination ever takes place. "People who need the money for day-to-day living should be excluded from the program," Jan says. "This may cut out some good surrogates, but it's important to protect couples."

Other surrogates, Carol Pavek included, believe that allowing a court to second-guess a woman demeans her decision-making ability. Carol feels that we are guilty of hypocrisy if we deny poor women a means of making money that they might feel is a good one for them, without offering them other viable options.

Moreover, Carol does not feel that poor women will be attracted to surrogacy for purely financial reasons. "Rick and I figured it out on a calculator and learned the $10,000 was $1.57 an hour for full-time child care," says Carol.

Jan concurs that it is unlikely that poor women will be attracted to surrogacy once they understand the actual financial arrangements. "This is not a way to earn much money," she stresses. "The $10,000 fee is paid for almost two years of counseling, medical and legal appointments, group sessions, and so forth. In addition to the work of being pregnant and delivering the child, there are over two hundred hours of meetings. There are numerous out-of-pocket expenses."

Surrogate mother Kyle points out that she actually received less as a surrogate (turning the child over to the father) than she could have if she had given the child up through a private adoption (turning the child over to a stranger).

"I paid $3,000 in taxes, thus reducing my fee to $7,000," she says. "I would have been better off if I had been paid expenses, so much a month for food, clothing, and so forth as in an adoption.

"It's okay for a teen who gets into trouble to give a child up for adoption," continues Kyle. "Even though she is paid a sum for her expenses, that is applauded. But when I took money as a surrogate, people looked down on me and said, 'How could you do it?'"

In 1988, Florida passed a law prohibiting surrogate mothers from receiving a fee, but allowing them to have their expenses paid in the same amounts as is permissible in adoption. Rather than discourage surrogacy, it has encouraged it. Under the law, surrogates can legitimately be paid the usual $10,000 or more—as long as it is justified as expenses.

For some policymakers, the financial aspects are the most troublesome elements of surrogate motherhood. The Michigan anti-surrogacy law, the New Jersey Supreme Court decision in the Baby M case, and Cuomo's Task Force on Life and the Law all oppose paid surrogacy, but would allow unpaid surrogacy. This prompted one surrogate to ask, "Why am I exploited if I am paid, but not if I am not paid?" By criminalizing payment to surrogates, this approach may lead infertile couples to put great pressure on emotionally vulnerable friends or relatives to serve as unpaid surrogates.

Lisa Newton feels that the charge of financial exploitation has been overused. "Disparity in income," she says, "does not mean poverty, let alone poverty and desperation. In point of fact, the women who volunteer for surrogate motherhood, including Mary Beth Whitehead, are hardly the penniless type.

"Sanitationmen, I believe, make less than biochemists, but not that much less," she continues. "William Stern commented to the press at one point that the Stern family income amounted to about $10,000 more per annum that the Whitehead family income. That disparity is hardly sufficient these days to define a different 'socioeconomic class.' Even the New Jersey Supreme Court in the Baby M decision stated that 'the Sterns were not rich and the Whiteheads not poor.'"

Stern was not from a privileged family, nor was Whitehead from a lower-class one. Mary Beth's father had a master's degree, and taught school. Bill's father worked as a short-order cook. Yet the Baby M case is generally described as a battle between the classes. Rather than acknowledge that a woman might become a surrogate willingly, enthusiastically, it is necessary to construct a fable about a desperate woman needing money.

As Lisa Newton observes, on an emotional level the Baby M case "simply plunges us into the scenario: Mary Beth Whitehead is Mother, and Cruel Lord Stern is trying to take her baby away from her. The characters in the drama are already in place, from time immemorial: the Cruel Lord is wealthy beyond measure, his selfish wife, the Lady, thinks it would be fun to have a baby to play with but abhors the inconveniences associated with pregnancy and childbirth, the Mother is desperately poor, and the Lord confronts her with the unendurably cruel choice of starving (along with her baby) or handing the baby over to him in exchange for an enormous sum of money! Can she sell her own baby for money? In her condition, can she afford *not* to?"

In testimony before the California legislature, Sharon Huddle DeAngelo, a member of the National Coalition Against Surrogacy, declared that there were other victims in this scenario: the surrogate's other children—the baby's brothers and sisters.

Traditionally, except in cases of clear abuse, parents have been held to be the best decision makers regarding their children's interests. Not only are parents thought best able to judge their child's needs, but parents can profoundly influence the effects of surrogacy on the child. Children take their cues about things from the people around them, as was the case with the Jones and Sutton children. If the children are told from the beginning that this is the couple's baby—not a part of their own family—they will realize that they themselves are not in danger of being relinquished.

Surrogate Donna Regan told her child that "the reason we did this was because they [the contracting couple] wanted a child to love as much as we love him." Donna contrasted the Whitehead case: "In the Mary Beth Whitehead case, the child did not see this as something her mother was doing for someone else, so, of course, the attitude she got from that was that something was being taken away rather than something being given."

Jan Sutton explains how her children have been benefited by her being a surrogate. "Kris and Jeff were very involved in the whole process," she says. "They had to forgo certain things as I went to the doctors' appointments and as I got more tired at the end of my pregnancy. In the end, they have seen what an incredible difference this has made to a family. They have seen that a little bit of sacrifice can bring a lot of joy."

Although parents can strongly influence their children's attitudes, the possibility of negative reactions from intolerant outsiders is a matter largely beyond their control. Is this a sufficient reason to ban surrogacy? Bill Pierce seems to think so, testifying in federal hearings that the children of surrogates "are being made fun of. Their lives are going to be ruined."

Pierce's hyperbole aside, it would seem odd to let societal intolerance guide what relationships are permissible. Along those lines, a judge in a lesbian custody case replied to the argument that the children could be harmed by stigma by stating, "It is just as reasonable to expect that they will emerge better equipped to search out their own standards of right and wrong, better able to perceive that the majority is not always correct in its moral judgments, and better able to understand the importance of conforming their beliefs to the requirements of reason and tested knowledge, not the constraints of currently popular sentiment or prejudice."

Then there is concern for the baby in question. "The ultimate victims of surrogacy are the babies," Sharon DeAngelo testified. "Their very existence was prenegotiated, predesigned, and contracted for just like any other commercial transaction. The child is a product with his or her status indistinguishable from other manufactured goods." Others have expressed concern that parents will expect more of a surrogate child because of the money they have spent on his or her creation. Washington, D.C., Councilman John Ray, who introduced a bill banning paid surrogacy, testified in the federal hearings that "it would be a rare couple who would be eager to write out that check for $10,000 if the merchandise didn't turn out to be in perfect condition."

But many couples spend more than that amount on other types of infertility treatments, such as in vitro fertilization, and without evidence that they expect more of the child. A Cesarean section costs twice as much as natural childbirth, yet the parents don't expect twice as much of the children. Certainly, the money paid to the surrogate is a modest amount compared to what parents will spend on their child over his or her lifespan. It is also no more than is spent on many private adoptions.

"It's kind of funny when you hear psychologists talk about how damaged these children are going to be," says Carol Pavek. "I can't conceive of the children having a problem if the adults don't. If society tells these children that they have problems, then they will get problems. But society could say, 'Gosh no, you were loved more than anyone. There were two families that loved you in order to create you, rather than just one family.'

"If society accepts the children, then the children will accept themselves," Carol continues. "We underestimate children. We get our prejudices from the life we've led. It's like a three-year-old watching a home birth. He doesn't know yet that blood is a bad thing. He doesn't think it's yucky."

John, whose daughter Anna was born to surrogate Jan Sutton, is angered by Connie Binsfeld's claims that surrogacy is against the best interests of children. "What kind of evidence does she have to prove that?" he demands. "She's responding to it emotionally—from her own value system. There's no data to base that on."

What about a concern that the child will be confused by the split between biological and social parentage? "Oh come on," says John. "Most of this country is raised by split families anyway. The predominant family unit in this country is biological kids of one parent and biological kids of another parent being raised in a mutual household. So what's the difference? From a pragmatic standpoint there is no difference. You can't say normality is a tragedy.

"Look at my daughter," says John. "She's healthy and happy and having a wonderful time. To me that refutes any argument that surrogacy is against the child's best interest."

Governor Cuomo's Task Force on Life and the Law suggested that paid surrogacy harms the resulting children because they may be the subject of a legal dispute. But Lisa Newton points out that such a dispute could be avoided by clear legislation stipulating who the legal parents are. Genetically the baby is the child of both the surrogate and the man providing the sperm. Biologically it may well be seen as the child of the surrogate since she has put in the nine months of pregnancy. But, in ethical terms, to whom does that baby belong? From the outset the creation of the relationship, the commitment, the trust, are expressly toward the creation of a child for the father and his wife to raise.

Bill Stern himself made that point: "She came on to this earth because of a dream that Betsy and I had. Without that dream there would have been no contract with Mary Beth—and no Melissa." When a reporter asked Bill why he didn't just go have another child with another surrogate, Bill replied, "That's like telling someone who's had a miscarriage that they can always go out and have another child. That's a cruel thing to say."

In deciding what should happen when a surrogate changes her mind, people are swayed both by the general taboo against separating mother from child and, in many cases, by their specific identification with Mary Beth Whitehead in her attempts to keep her child.

"If you have children of your own, think of how you would feel if someone tried to steal them," suggests Lisa Newton. "Would you not turn over heaven and earth? Would not everything else lose importance beside getting the child back? And that is apparently exactly the way Mary Beth Whitehead reacted and exactly the way I would react if it was my own kid.

"But there is a big difference between us," says Lisa. "Mary Beth Whitehead signed a contract which said it was not her child, it was his child."

There are two potential models for determining legal parenthood, explains Lisa. One is to consider the baby the legal child of the biological father and surrogate mother. The second is to consider the baby the child of the infertile couple from conception.

"The trouble with the first model is that if the terms of the agreement become a matter of dispute, it is the child itself that is put in play," says Lisa. "If both 'natural parents' want the child, as in the Baby M case, they must attack each other with all the bitterness, slander, and unbearably painful accusations of 'unfitness' for parenthood that accompany custody fights in cases of divorce, none of which can be good for the child, who within a very few years will be reading the transcript of those proceedings.

"If neither parent wants the child, as in the case of a child born severely handicapped, the ceremonies of faultfinding and rejection will rival the Baby M proceedings for displays of human cruelty," continues Lisa. "On the second model, at least we know where the child goes: he or she goes to the father and his wife, who initiated the contract for surrogacy."

As a policy matter, whenever there is a legal situation in which parental rights are transferred, the law requires that at a certain point in time the decision be final. Some states in their adoption laws suggest that six months after the birth the adoption is final. It's easy to imagine a situation in which a mother seven months after the birth or seven years after the birth may want that child back. Such a mother may present as compelling a picture as Mary Beth Whitehead did in her love for the child. Nevertheless, we do not reopen adoptions once the deadline has passed.

With surrogacy, Lisa Newton argues that the point at which the decision is final should be before the birth, not after the birth. The reason we give an already pregnant woman a chance to change her mind after the child is born is to insure that she has a chance to make an informed, unpressured decision. A surrogate is not faced with the *fait accompli* of an existing pregnancy about which she must make a difficult choice. She has a range of choices and alternatives available to her *before* she conceives. That she must go to some trouble to become pregnant in this arrangement is further evidence of her determination.

When a surrogate changes her mind it creates a different situation than when a mother changes her mind about giving her child up to strangers for adoption. The would-be parents in the adoption situation have no legal link to the child, so the child immediately becomes part of the biological mother's family, with no period of insecurity. In surrogacy, the man wishing to rear the child is the biological father, who himself has a claim to the child. The surrogate's change of mind thrusts the infant into legal uncertainty, requiring the parties to go to court to determine custody. In order to avoid that possibility and to protect the child, argues Lisa, it is important to uphold the pre-conception agreement of the parties to determine who the legal parents are.

The legal recognition that the contracted-for child is the couple's child comports with most surrogates' own feelings about the arrangement. But what message does it convey about mothers and children? Some people argue that giving the father and his wife a legal right to the child fosters the notion that the child is the property of the father. They say that the baby should belong to its mother. But this argument does not mitigate the concept of property; it merely shifts ownership. In fact, many of Mary Beth's statements about Baby M—"She's mine," "She belongs to me," and especially "I gave her life and I can take it away"— seem pretty clearly premised on an ownership notion of parenthood.

Surrogacy does not create the idea of children as property. It merely forces us to confront the fact that parental rights over children, no matter how those children have come into the world, resemble in some ways the rights people have over property. Children do "belong" to their parents, in some of the same ways cars and houses belong to their owners, although laws against child abuse and neglect circumscribe how parents treat their children. Surrogacy adds nothing new to this equation.

"We cringe to think of children as the property of their parents," explained Carol Sanger at a 1988 meeting of professors. "But I think that the right of parents over their children is indeed a form of property. Parents have tremendous legal power and authority over their children. As a parent you can make your kid wear braces, be a Catholic, etc. As a parent, you can also transfer your child to another person for caretaking, whether it is a day-care center or a grandmother. You can transfer your child to this person for an eight-hour work day, five days a week, or for several years. As a parent you may decide that you do not wish to raise your child at all. . . . The transfer of children by the biological mother to the substitute parent of her own choice, whether we call it a sale or not, seems to me neither novel nor immoral."

But does a policy recognizing the biological father and his wife as the legal parents give rise to an image of the surrogate as a reproductive vessel? Barbara Katz Rothman is concerned that, if the fetus is considered the child of the couple, the surrogate will be forced to accede to the couple's wishes during pregnancy— undergoing amniocentesis or a Cesarean section based on the whim of the couple.

In recent years, there has been a growing willingness on the part of courts to force women who have become pregnant in the normal manner to undergo certain procedures (such as Cesarean sections) for the supposed benefit of their fetuses. But there are legal grounds to block such interventions, whether or not the child-to-be is viewed as the offspring of the couple. There are many legal precedents that put a high value on bodily integrity. In one case, for example, a man dying of leukemia needed a bone marrow transplant to survive. He went to court to get his cousin to donate marrow. The judge refused to require the cousin to provide the bone marrow. Even though the judge felt that the cousin had a moral obligation to help his dying relative, he held that the law's protection of bodily integrity prevented him from turning this moral obligation into a legal one. Other cases have similarly held that one has no legal duty to consent to bodily interventions to help another person. Applying these precedents, courts should refrain from ordering interventions on the surrogate's body, even though the fetus she is carrying will soon be someone else's child.

This right to refuse bodily interventions is also grounded in contract law. If an opera singer reneges on her contract, she can be sued for damages, but a court will not force her to sing. If a man agrees to donate a kidney, and then changes his mind, he cannot be forced to undergo the surgery and donation. In legal parlance, you can't force people to perform "personal services."

Using those precedents, a couple couldn't force a surrogate to be artificially inseminated if she changed her mind between signing a contract and achieving a conception. They couldn't force the surrogate to continue a pregnancy if she wanted to abort—or to have a Cesarean section if she wanted a vaginal delivery.

The issue of control of a woman's behavior during pregnancy is much different from the issue of who should be recognized as the legal parents once the child is born. After the birth, the child is a separate person. Placing the child in the home of the couple requires no personal services on the part of the surrogate. Her bodily integrity is in no way violated by the fact that the child is being raised by someone else.

The seemingly compelling critique that surrogacy is akin to baby selling doesn't hold up under scrutiny, either. If the child is viewed as the couple's child from the start, the payment made by the child's natural father to the surrogate is no different from other payments for child care. In illegal baby selling, the child is handed over, for a fee, to a stranger—quite possibly an undeserving one—who has no biological tie to the baby.

Payment for parenting strikes some people as unseemly. Yet most people agree that child rearing is a more important component of parenting than childbearing, and society allows all sorts of payment to surrogate child rearers like baby-sitters, nannies, and day care centers.

As Lisa Newton observes, "It seems irrational to forbid this service when it seems that there are those ready and willing to render it, there are certainly those ready and willing to purchase it, and the service is a simple extension, as far as I can see, of baby-sitting and other child-care arrangements which are very widely practiced."

But there's another contention about the issue of surrogacy—not over what it does, but over what it doesn't do. It does not provide homes for minority children and children with special needs who are available for adoption.

Surrogacy has been criticized by some feminists as racist on the grounds that childless couples seek surrogates to get a white baby rather than adopting a minority or Third World child. But couples who seek to have the husband's biological child through surrogacy are merely attempting to have a child as close as possible to the child they would have had if they were fertile. (It is no coincidence that Mary Beth Whitehead resembles Betsy Stern.)

Infertile couples who turn to surrogacy were labeled "selfish" by one of the members of the Michigan Task Force in her testimony on the Dunne-Goodhue bill. Mary Beth Whitehead's brief called Bill Stern "narcissistic" for wanting his own child.

Similarly, a former surrogate who uses the pseudonym Elizabeth Kane testified in Congress that surrogacy has developed "to satisfy the obsessive desires of couples unwilling to adopt or become foster parents." But is it really obsessive to want your own child? Kane has children of her own. Why is it obsessive for a man to want to create a child through a surrogacy arrangement—and not obsessive for a surrogate who has willingly entered into that arrangement (as Kane says she did) to want to keep the child?

Psychiatrist Dr. Robert Gould went so far as to suggest that an infertile couple's desire to pursue surrogacy instead of adoption demonstrates that they would be unfit parents. "One parenting quality that I believe is important is a couple's willingness to adopt a baby," he testified in the New York hearings. "If they do not, I think they lack an important parenting quality."

Isn't it absurd, though, to suggest that infertile couples be forced to adopt children instead of creating a child through surrogacy? It has never been suggested that a couple able to procreate naturally must adopt needy children instead of having their own.

Harvard law professor Martha Field, in her book *Surrogate Motherhood*, agrees that adoption should be encouraged, but says, "It is hypocritical to raise the needs of deprived children against surrogacy when we as a society in other respects follow policies so contrary to their needs. If we provided minimally adequate welfare for poor families with children, . . . poor families would be able to stay together, and there would be many fewer children in need of families. If we provided free prenatal care to those who cannot afford it, there would be many fewer special-needs children. Society does have a responsibility toward existing children in need, and it should exercise that responsibility, but it is unfair for it to meet its obligation simply by transferring the responsibility to couples who need surrogates to reproduce."

Nevertheless, the policy solution proposed by many people to avoid wrenching children from their loving surrogate mothers is to encourage adoption. The adoption of babies of teenagers. The adoption of babies of a different race. The adoption of babies from another country.

Those babies, the babies to be adopted, generally have mothers too, mothers who may love them at least as much as Mary Beth loves the baby that she contracted to bear.

Is it not another form of bigotry—the presumption that minority and Third World children would invariably be better off in the homes of the white American middle class?

In fact, we should be much more concerned about the exploitation of girls and women in the traditional adoption situation than about surrogates who, for the most part, are engaging in arms-length transactions with the opportunity to be represented by counsel, prior to pregnancy.

In his federal testimony, Bill Pierce said, "Research has shown us that adoption works for children because it is a plan made out of love by a pregnant woman in crisis." But, precisely because of that crisis, the consent of biological mothers in the adoption situation is more suspect than consent in the surrogate situation—and the potential for wrenching psychological damage is greater.

In contrast to the surrogate, the mother in the traditional adoption situation generally has gotten pregnant as the result of a relationship. In most cases, she would like—from the beginning—to keep the child, but external forces (such as coercion from parents, teachers, the baby's father, or counselors, or lack of financial ability to rear the child) prevent her from keeping the child.

Biological mothers in the adoption situation are usually younger and less likely to be part of a stable family than potential surrogates, who usually have established lives of their own with children and husbands or significant others. Potential surrogates are likely to be more certain about their futures and generally less vulnerable than girls and women who get pregnant and consider giving their children up for adoption.

Moreover, almost all surrogates have already given birth and are rearing those children while for the biological mother in the adoption situation the child is likely to be her first. For that reason, too, the surrogate is in a better position to make an advance assessment of what her experiences will be and how she will respond to the birth of the child. This difference is attested to by the fact that only 1% of surrogates change their minds about relinquishing the child, while, according to a witness at the New York hearings, 75% of biological mothers considering adoption change their mind at some point in the process.

With all the attention given to the possibility that a surrogate's financial need might cause her to conceive, carry, and relinquish a child for a fee, surrogacy opponents who promote adoption (including some feminists) overlook the fact that mothers giving their children up for adoption are almost invariably more needy than potential surrogates. There seems to be little attention to the fact that, in Third World countries, there is rarely evidence attesting to the quality of the mother's consent to the relinquishment; indeed, we tend to avert our gaze from evidence raising the possibility that the mother was coerced or even that the child was kidnapped.

Despite all this, Bill Pierce argues that the solution to the surrogacy problem is "promoting adoption." He says that in the United States only 5% of teens who give birth choose adoption and that 30% would choose adoption if "counseling and other services are provided properly." He argues that this will not only benefit infertile couples, but will also give the teens the chance to "avoid" a "tragic life script." Here is the other side of the paternalistic coin. If surrogacy opponents feel that it is "natural" for a surrogate to love her child, isn't it natural for a pregnant teen to love hers as well? Does youth invalidate those feelings? Pierce also throws in a coldly financial reason for talking more teens out of their children—if 30% of the teens chose adoption instead of welfare (and here he assumes one excludes the other), it would save taxpayers $71 million per year!

When Pierce tried this approach in front of the New York legislature (with his figures revised to reflect tax savings in New York), he was taken to task by Senator John Dunne, who pointed out that Pierce's approach would be like creating and enforcing a public policy against single parents—"a policy that single parenting is not so desirable as the option for placing a child in a more traditional family setting."

As the New Jersey Supreme Court pointed out in the Baby M case, people have a constitutional right to create their own biological children—even if this requires employing a sperm donor or a surrogate mother. The American Civil Liberties Union has taken the position that the Constitution also protects the right to compensate a surrogate. Just as couples may pay a doctor for helping them effectuate their decision to abort, they should be able to pay a surrogate to help them effectuate their decision to have a child. According to ACLU policy, though, the surrogate's involvement in the creation of the child is so great that she should be allowed a certain time period after the birth of the child to seek custody.

Allowing the surrogate to change her mind has its downside. Women who are unsure about whether they really can give up the child may nonetheless become surrogates since they know they will have a second chance at the child after its birth. There is also the troubling possibility that a surrogate will be able to coerce the couple into paying her more money once the child is born by threatening to seek custody.

"I've gone back and forth in my own mind over the idea of a grace period," says Jan Sutton. "I do think it would be better if the child were legally recognized as the child of the couple. But I could live with a law giving surrogate mothers a grace period, because with the right screening, the women who become surrogates would not change their minds."

After the passage of Connie Binsfeld's statute, the Michigan chapter of the American Civil Liberties Union filed suit to declare the statute unconstitutional. The lawsuit was brought on behalf of three infertile couples and two women who wanted to be surrogate mothers. Two of the infertile couples had tried unsuccessfully to find children to adopt before they each created a child with the help of a surrogate. Now they wanted siblings for their children.

The suit charged that Connie's law violated the couples' right to privacy since it entailed "an unjustified interference with fundamental rights relating to marriage, family, reproduction, children, and intimate association." The suit also pointed out that surrogate fathering—paid sperm donation to help couples in which the husband was infertile—was permissible in Michigan. Equal treatment of men and women required that surrogate mothering be allowed as well.

"In the final analysis," said the ACLU brief, "the ban on surrogate parenting arrangements involving the payment of compensation to surrogate mothers reflects nothing more than the application of an 'archaic and overbroad generalization' about the role of women in American society. It proceeds on the assumption that it is not 'proper' for a woman to use her reproductive capacity to enable another woman to become the mother of a child, and in turn to receive reasonable compensation for her invaluable assistance."

Michigan's attorney general, Frank Kelley, had previously taken the position that paid surrogate motherhood was baby-selling, while ACLU attorney Robert Sedler argued that the compensation of a surrogate was merely the payment for the woman's "valuable services." As the lawsuit progressed, though, they could see that there was a common middle ground. Both could live with an interpretation of the law that allowed payment to surrogate mothers, but gave her time after the baby was born to change her mind and seek custody. At a September 19, 1988, hearing in the Wayne County Circuit Court, attorneys for the state and for the ACLU proposed this interpretation to the judge, and he gave it his seal of approval.

Richard Fitzpatrick points out that the tables have been turned on Connie. "Ironically, commercial surrogacy is now legal here in Michigan with far fewer constraints than I had proposed in the bills I introduced," he says. "There is no screening necessary, no contractual approval by a judge." Noel Keane's practice is now on firmer legal ground than it had ever been in the decade since his first surrogacy arrangement.

At the federal hearing on the Luken bill, Richard Levin, the head of a surrogacy center, tried to put the risks of surrogacy in perspective. "Annually, thousands of contracts fail in business, thousands of marriages end in divorce, and thousands of people are killed in automobile accidents," he said. "Failures go on and on, but society does not outlaw such activities, it merely seeks to improve our abilities to lessen the failures and increase the successes."

"There is nothing wrong with the practice of surrogate motherhood," says Lisa Newton, "no arguments against allowing the practice freely to flourish that reason cannot defeat. At the conclusion of such a transaction, all parties are better off; the infertile couple has the child they could not have got themselves, the surrogate is paid and has the satisfaction of giving others a gift beyond price, the child has the gift of existence, no small item, and an excellent life chance in a fine home."

Surrogate motherhood has just begun to prompt the personal and societal soul-searching that is needed to develop policy in this area. In describing her research to fellow mental health professionals at a psychological convention, Hilary Hanafin said, "We need to reassess the values, beliefs, and assumptions of our culture and of our profession regarding acceptable ways to create families. We may now have to question what is commonly perceived in our society as an absolute attachment that every women feels to every child she carried. Perhaps surrogacy will become another behavior that we will come to understand as not pathological, but as one that broadens the continuum and definition of what humans can think and feel."

EPILOGUE

BRAVE NEW BABIES

IN MAY 1987, Rick Pavek threw a surprise party for Carol for their tenth wedding anniversary. They had been married before a justice of the peace because they couldn't afford a large celebration. "When we had been married for just a couple of years, Carol had said, 'When we have our tenth, I want you to give me the wedding we never had,'" explains Rick. "That was the last she ever mentioned it."

As the anniversary date neared, Rick realized that he still couldn't afford a big wedding. "So I decided to recreate with a little more grandeur what we had originally done," he says. He got the justice of the peace to agree to do a wedding reenactment and arranged for friends to attend.

Rick was planning to squire Carol over to the surprise party by asking her to get dressed up and get some tenth-anniversary pictures taken. But Carol said she didn't want any pictures taken. Eric had died four months earlier and, in her grief, Carol had not lost the extra weight of her pregnancy. She was in no mood to have her current look immortalized.

"Let me tell you," recounts Rick, "we almost got divorced over this. Getting her to get dressed and go out was probably harder than seeing her through her pregnancies."

On the way to the supposed photo session, Rick said he had to drop some papers off at the courthouse. Once they arrived and Carol saw all her friends, she was totally surprised—and thrilled. "I couldn't have gotten her drunk and gotten a more stupefied reaction," says Rick.

The celebration began a new chapter in their life, as they began to plan like newlyweds. There was a computer programming job Rick wanted in Seattle. "Rick had always supported me, so now it was my turn to support him," says Carol. She held a sale of their furniture and belongings and put the money in Rick's pocket.

"The move to Seattle has been very difficult," says Carol, "but it's important to Rick and he has stood behind me for ten years. There are times when he has suffered a little bit, but he always stood behind me."

In many ways, Carol is back to square one. She has no ties to the midwifery or feminist health care communities in Seattle. She and Rick have little money. Their first Christmas in Washington came and went with a sparsity of presents under the tree. Gifts from Rhonda and Jerry remained unopened: Carol still did not want to be reminded of the healthy surrogate babies.

Carol has taken a job, caring for the newborn infant of a businesswoman who works at home. The woman does not know that Carol ever was a surrogate. "She recently said to me, 'I can't understand anyone being a surrogate mother,'" says Carol. "Yet she talks about a friend who is dying of cancer and how much she wishes there was something she could do—bone marrow transplants, or kidney donation. She says she would do *anything*. But she can't imagine doing what I did, even though what I was donating was just a seed, just ovum."

One day in Seattle, Carol was watching television when she heard, "Tune in next week when we will have a surrogate mother, Elizabeth Kane. Call us if you would like to be in the studio audience."

Carol called and asked for tickets, mentioning that she had been a surrogate mother herself. The show's producer asked her to be a guest, and sent her Elizabeth Kane's book. In it, Elizabeth describes her experience, her subsequent regret, and her participation in Coalition efforts to ban surrogacy.

"Rick hated watching me read it," says Carol. "I was getting so angry, underlining in red pencil, turning down corners. Early in the book she says that she wanted to be the first paid surrogate 'at any cost.' Imagine that—*at any cost*. It didn't matter if it hurt her family, hurt her. And then once it went wrong, she blamed everyone else.

"If you read her book," observes Carol, "her depression began

not when she gave up the baby, but when she stopped appearing on talk shows eight months after the birth. When she stopped getting the media attention is when she went into the great depression."

In contrast to the many television shows that encourage controversy, this particular show's producers did not want Elizabeth and Carol locking horns. They kept them in separate rooms before the show and called them on stage at different times. Carol was watching Elizabeth on the television in the greenroom when Elizabeth said, "It's better to have a dead baby than a surrogate baby."

Carol was stunned. "How could she say that?" Carol raged. "Of course it's better to know that your child is alive, healthy and happy, somewhere else, than to suffer the death of a child."

Some policymakers—such as Connie Binsfeld—argue that surrogate motherhood is against the best interests of children. In essence, they are saying that it is better for these children not be born at all than to be born as a result of a surrogacy arrangement.

Carol disagrees. "I don't see how the children could feel anything negative," she says.

"These children will feel special," says Carol. "Mentally got pregnant. No one just had sex with the had fifteen kids and another one came along place for adoption. There were two couples of whether or not to bring a child into the

"In no sense of the word are these throw about the three boys she conceived as a si thing happened and they ran out of rel would still be another family—us— they got the best we could give t

From her earliest contact with that it was not a cold business tra ment, but the creation of a r would only work with a co pregnancy, feel comfortabl involvement, and not f Andy and Nancy, she would not recognize adopt the child, Rick an

Hilary Hanafin stresses the complexity of the relationship in her sessions with couples and surrogates. She turns away couples who want to pretend that the baby "just dropped out of the sky." She emphasizes to couples that "the surrogate will be a part of your life for the next generation."

Lisa Newton points out that both the couples and the surrogates can be hurt if they view surrogate motherhood as a medical process, rather than a social one.

To underscore that fact, Lisa suggests that couples and surrogates meet in their living rooms, instead of in a surrogacy center. In the center, says Lisa, "the contracting couple sees the surrogate mother not as a person, but as a treatment, and the surrogate is overwhelmed with details of hygiene, payment, restriction, ovulation, and insemination until she totally forgets about the real live baby that will appear on the scene in nine months."

If the process is viewed as a medical one, the surrogate may feel more justified in changing her mind. "We do many things in a medical context that are at odds with what we do in the rest of our lives," says Lisa. "There is a certain objectivity in a medical setting. And this mood, this understanding that certain things are permitted in a medical setting (such as taking your clothes off in front of a doctor) that re not okay outside, is a dangerous tendency when you are talking out surrogacy. Because it means that it is acceptable to say, 'Well, I de this agreement in the clinic or the clinical setting, but now that outside, I see that it is totally wrong.'

Removing the whole contractual arrangement to the living s of the women involved may permit much more truthful as- ents of the possibility and desirability of the contemplated ement," says Lisa.

, whose daughter Anna was born to surrogate Jan Sutton, underscores the importance of the human dimension in ing surrogacy. "There is no way we would have done ut having the chance to meet Jan," he says. "When you all the veneer, the Bill Handels and everything else, oral and human agreement between Jan and Elizabeth fact, it may have been more between Jan and he two developed a relationship that transcended the spects, and I did, too."

rrogacy of the close relationship that can develop

between couples and surrogates may foster a dehumanized approach to reproduction. "There should be a lot of feeling, a lot of caring in surrogacy," says Cynthia Custer, the surrogate who became disillusioned with the anonymity of Harriet Blankfeld's program. "A woman has to be a caring person to do this. And there is so much to share during the pregnancy.

"Anonymity when applied to surrogacy is so dehumanizing. It dehumanizes us. It makes it more like a business."

Kyle, another surrogate in the Maryland program, felt alienated by the anonymity as well. "During the whole nine months I had worked on a cross-stitch for the baby," she says. "It was very important to me that the couple get the picture, so I took it with me when I delivered. Since I was never allowed to meet the couple, I had to give it to someone from the agency. I never knew if they even got it."

Not seeing the couple with the child left Kyle with an eerie feeling. One morning when she was back at home, she turned to her husband and said, "Did I really have a baby? I don't believe I did. I feel so bad and so depressed that there's no proof."

Kyle says she wouldn't have any peace at all if it hadn't been for what a nurse at the hospital had told her. The nurse had said, "You may not realize what you have done for these people. That mother has sat and held the baby for the past nineteen hours, the whole time since he was born. She keeps saying to her husband, 'Tell me this isn't a dream.'"

Whether or not the surrogate is in touch with the couple or the child after the birth, the relationship remains an important one for her. "You think it's going to be over and done with once you give up the child," says Kyle, who served as a surrogate two years ago, "but it's never over and done with. There's always something bringing it up—a newspaper article, a friend trying desperately to have a child.

"That child will never be out of my mind," says Kyle. "I loved that child for nine months, but I didn't fool myself into thinking it was mine."

The children created through surrogacy are born into a triangular relationship of two mothers and a father. They may wish to know the circumstances surrounding their creation, and have a chance to meet the surrogate and her family.

"I don't have a right to tell a mother and father what to tell their children," says Bill Handel. "But my feeling is that if a kid finds out that his parents have been lying to him for fifteen years, you're going to have one pissed-off kid, especially on something as fundamental as this."

Carol Pavek's experience as an adoptee has influenced what she feels the surrogate children should be told. "I resented being lied to about it for twenty-five years," she says. She hopes that the couples who contract with surrogates will be honest with their children about their roots.

Rhonda talks about Carol openly with her sons. The older one knows that he has a birth mother from Texas and that is where his little brother came from. He understands that mom's body is not working and so dad's sperm was used to make a baby in another woman. Since that time, Rhonda has been trying further medical treatments, including in vitro fertilization, to combat her infertility. Rhonda was recently talking to her five-year-old son about her own efforts to get pregnant, and some of the side effects. "Why don't you just get the woman from Texas to carry it for us?" he asked.

In Hilary's follow-up research on sixteen couples who had participated in surrogacy arrangements, all the couples said that contact with the surrogate had been beneficial. Fifteen out of the sixteen couples planned to tell the child of its unique origins. Under Bill's contract, the surrogate must keep the center advised of her address changes for the next eighteen years in case Bill has to contact her for medical information needed by the child.

"We've taped all the television shows that were done on Jan [Sutton], and most of the other shows that were done about surrogacy," says John. "As the time comes and the opportunity presents itself, we'll expose Anna to it. We're not going to make a secret of it."

"We still talk to Jan fairly regularly and hope to stay in contact all through Anna's life," says John's wife Elizabeth. "We all went to Yosemite together and then to Disneyland last year. Her children have a tighter bond with Anna than kids who are just friends. They are very close. Right now Anna, who is three, just thinks of Jan as a friend. But later, we plan to tell her all about it."

The Seattle television program served to crystallize Carol

Pavek's view that surrogacy should be protected as a part of reproductive freedom. It also served to put Carol back in touch with Rhonda, who joined the show via telephone.

Carol plans to be available whenever her surrogate children want to contact her. And her son Chris says how much fun it would be to have a reunion with his half-brothers.

The expanded family created by surrogate motherhood has caused some sperm donors in traditional artificial insemination by donor to reassess their roles. One such sperm donor called Mary Beth Whitehead's lawyer, Harold Cassidy, and asked for legal representation in trying to track down any children created with his sperm. Harold, whose loyalties are with birth mothers, turned him down.

A Canadian attorney, Carey Linde, was more sympathetic when a group of Canadian sperm donors approached him. He has agreed to represent them to determine if any children have been created with their sperm and, if so, to learn how those children are faring. "Some donors want to know who their children are in case they discover late in life that they have a genetic disease that could affect those children," says Carey.

The traditional scenario of the medical student donating sperm is not as casual an experience as infertility specialists would have us believe, asserts Los Angeles psychotherapist Annette Baran. "At the time they donate, they are young students with no notion about what it means to be a parent," says Annette. She studied men who had been sperm donors earlier in their lives. "Twenty years later, they had families of their own. They said, 'It really troubles me when I think of how cavalier my attitude was. There are human beings out there whom I fathered and whom I'll never see.'"

After a newspaper article reported Carey Linde's activities, he was contacted by other Canadian donors, as well as recipient couples. They have all joined together in a group, the New Reproductive Alternatives Society, to press for social and legal changes in the way donor insemination is handled. They would like to see a clear recognition that the couple are the legal parents, as is the case under statutes of thirty states in the United States. But their biggest concern is that there be more counseling and greater attention to the complex familial dynamics of letting a third party into the reproductive process.

"Artificial insemination is not a scientific, sterile procedure," says Linde. "It's a human reproductive procedure."

At the heart of that procedure is the creation of a child, who may want to know about his or her unseen parent. At most donor insemination clinics, no record is kept of the donor's identity. One sperm bank, though, highlights the emotional dimensions of artificial insemination. Beginning in 1984, the Sperm Bank of Northern California asked its sperm donors if they would be willing to list their names and addresses so that any resulting children, at age eighteen, could contact them. Seventy-five percent of the donors encourage such contacts. Some of the sperm donors, like surrogate mothers, actually create scrapbooks about themselves and their families to be shown to the child.

It is as if some of the suggestions of Barbara Katz Rothman have been put into play. She had visions of donors and surrogates becoming like uncles and aunts to the children they helped create. "Aunts and uncles have a relationship with the child, but they don't have parental responsibilities," she explains. "Sometimes they have very meaningful relationships, and sometimes not. You have a right to know who your aunt or uncle is, but you can't take them to law to make sure they take you to the circus, nor can they sue for visitation rights."

Bill Handel tells law students that surrogacy is "reestablishing the definitions of human relationships. We're redefining who mom and dad are and that is fairly mind-boggling. The parental relationship is probably one of our basic concepts, if not *the* basic concept of our belief system. Inevitably anybody who has problems, I don't care if they're ninety-five years old, it goes back to their relationship with their mother and father."

"Everyone involved in the child's origins should be available on behalf of the child," says Annette Baran. "If a father and mother conceive the child out of a relationship, that adds another dimension to it. But even a sperm donor is a genetic parent and has a genetic responsibility."

In response to suggestions like Barbara's and Annette's, Bill admits, "To be honest, when I talk about changing parental concepts in surrogate motherhood, I do so in a very conservative manner. I'm still saying in the end there's one mom and one dad who should raise the kid just like my mom and my dad raised me. I think it's complicated enough growing up with just one set of moms and dads. But it's possible the future will bring a relationship with the genetic mom, the gestational mom, and the rearing mom. I'm not saying that it is inherently wrong, it's beyond my notion of understanding. I wish I were more sophisticated and could appreciate some of those more sophisticated arguments in terms of parental relationships. I don't understand parental relationships. I'm still trying to figure out my relationship with my mom. I'm thirty-six years old and haven't figured it out yet."

The way their children will react to the news of their unique beginnings—and the relationships it generates—will be profoundly influenced by what type of legislation there is. "The biggest problem will be what society's reaction will be to the surrogate child," says Elizabeth, whose daughter Anna was born to surrogate Jan Sutton. "I worry about her being labeled, stigmatized by society. Before Anna was born, I did a show with Bill. There was a lot of anti-surrogacy sentiment. People from the right-to-life groups were saying hurtful and damaging things. So that's what I worry about."

"In our own circle of friends, it was not an issue," says her husband, John. "We're both, roughly speaking, highly educated and come from an urban, culturally rich area. But there were people on the periphery of our circle of friends who equated this with prostitution. They responded to it in a very emotional way, much less rationally than I would have wanted. I don't want my child having to deal with those problems."

"I am very concerned about what's going to happen," Elizabeth continues. "Without a favorable law on surrogacy in California, the social identity of these children is in limbo."

"I want to protect my child," explains Sandra, for whom Lorrie Jones served as a surrogate. "I want him to feel good about himself. I'll try to give him that feeling. But when he grows up I want there to be a law approving of surrogacy."

The people who have become parents through surrogacy arrangements worry that laws like the Michigan one criminalizing surrogacy will harm the self-esteem of surrogacy children. "When I was born, I was considered *illegitimate*," says Carol Pavek, whispering the last word to emphasize how horrible that status was considered to be at the time. "Society has legalized children. They are no longer illegitimate, whether or not they were born in wedlock. We got rid of all that. Now we're going back to stigmatizing children with the laws against surrogacy."

Sandra and Hillel have recently asked Lorrie Jones to bear another baby for them. She and Casey are considering the request, but need to explore first their own desire to have a child. As more time passes, though, the chances increase for surrogacy to be made a crime in California.

Lorrie has already contemplated what her choices will be in a future surrogate pregnancy. If there is no law against surrogacy in California when the time comes, Lorrie will once again make her way to the Fertility Center of California. If surrogacy is criminalized, she will buy a drugstore syringe and inject herself with Hillel's sperm.

The manner in which the child is conceived will make little difference to Lorrie. But whether or not he is born in the shadow of the law could make a lifetime of difference to Sandra and Hillel's brave new baby.

INDEX